FROM FIRE TO
FREEDOM

JAIME ALONSO YRASTORZA

FROM FIRE TO

FREEDOM

*Childhood in Colonial Philippines to
a Post-WWII Adulthood in America*

TATE PUBLISHING
AND ENTERPRISES, LLC

Published by Tate Publishing & Enterprises, LLC
127 E. Trade Center Terrace | Mustang, Oklahoma 73064 USA
1.888.361.9473 | www.tatepublishing.com

Tate Publishing is committed to excellence in the publishing industry. The company reflects the philosophy established by the founders, based on Psalm 68:11,
"The Lord gave the word and great was the company of those who published it."

Published in the United States of America

ISBN: 978-1-62854-982-9
1. Biography & Autobiography / Cultural Heritage
2. History / Asia / Southeast Asia
14.06.20

DEDICATION

To my "twins": Hannah, Marie, Luke, Melissa, Grace, Leah, Cole, Gabriela, Jaime, Ellie, Jack, John, Will, and Dylan, whose beliefs and viewpoints reflect the values inculcated by their parents: Teresa and Bassam; David and Wanda; Timothy and Arlin; Laura, Pete, and Kent; and Anne and Jeffrey and by the overall major influence and love of their grandmother, mother, and my wife, Patricia Anne Laverty Yrastorza.

Through each of them the legacy will assuredly endure.

Composing "Surviving the War" refreshed personally evocative sentiments. The whirlwind of emotions and sacrifices that the catastrophe exacted on my parents while sustaining the love and devotion they held for their family and for each other is a valued memory to treasure, beyond words. With moist eyes, I wistfully dedicate the narrative in their memory.

ACKNOWLEDGMENTS

Today, the world continues to face yet again another of the innumerable crises that have come to pass since the intervening decades from that halcyon time so long ago. Our global conundrum, punctuated by nightmarish killing and unimaginable loss of property, once again decries the despicable levels of inhumanity that man can exact on his fellowmen. Pundits and prognosticators are kept busy arguing about the fate of the many who suffer the wrongs of a few, even suggesting mankind's dire future of Armageddon proportions. One is left to wonder of their impact on our modern society, even wont to speculate about implications which prognosticate of a hazy future that might portend for our offspring. These crises are occasions to pause and contemplate about the legacies we leave those others who are a part of the web of interlocking relations with me.

I am resolved to pen profiles of my past, albeit it is an excursion which will necessarily be limited by my own capacity to recall. In this undertaking, I am fortunate to have had the able assistance, collaboration, and anecdotal gifts of many. Prominent among the collaborators, each particularly pleasing to single out are my sisters, Josefina and Adelina, and my brother, Gregorio, Jr., who, by having remained residing in the Philippines at a time when I went abroad, have been a well of historical information; and, an invaluable editor, a most competent critique and friend Carol Irwin, Ph. D.

The probing queries and stimulating commentaries of my friend Art Meyers, himself a published author, helped my efforts to maintain the focus of my writings. For the final fine-tooth comb editorial scrutiny, I am indebted to an erudite friend, Barbara Stimson, M.Ed. From her thorough read, she shared the following observations: "This book spoke to my heart, reminding me that the most important thing to remember, as humans, is our humanity and the human kindness of those around us. You looked at the world with your eyes wide open, rejecting the reproachable concerns, if need be. But mostly, you accepted the responsibility of treating our fellow beings with respect and care. The threads of your love for family, friends, and everyday acquaintances were woven throughout this book.

"It was uplifting and heartfelt. Thank you, Jaime, for openly and honestly sharing your heart with others."

This narrative is arranged in chronologic order, gearing my reminiscences and viewpoints largely as I held them at the time. My commentaries and perspectives are aided by references to publications, without specific attribution. As appended, the list on Recommended Readings provides a source for more detailed information on the various topics I address and I hope readers may be persuaded to peruse them. They are worth reading.

I write this tome remembering those whom I love, those who have made my life personally rewarding and those who have contributed to the making of this one grateful, abundantly blessed individual. I am especially fortunate for having parents who nurtured me with love and provided the foundation of my being; and, for my loving and devoted ally, partner and lifetime companion, a fetching wife, Patricia Anne Laverty. She remains my patient and unwavering supporter. To them all, I extend my fervent *daghan ug maraming salamat*, *muchisimas gracias*, thank you!

CONTENTS

THE DAWNING

Not to know what has been transacted in former times is to be always a child. If no use is made of the labors of past ages, the world must remain always in the infancy of knowledge.

—Marcus Tulius Cicero (Roman philosopher, Statesman...
b106-43 BC)

It is the true office of history to represent the events themselves, together with the counsels, and to leave the observations and conclusions thereupon to the liberty and faculty of every man's judgment.

—Francis Bacon (Philosopher, Scientist... b1561-1626)

We can chart our future, clearly and wisely, only when we know the path which has led us to the present

—a Spanish proverb.

My early beginnings were spent in a rural community with a society having an everyday pace that was tranquil and untroubled. Both my parents were healthcare professionals who ensured my upbringing to be free of wants. I was enfolded with kinfolk and friends, many of whom had, like me, ties with Spanish relatives. World War II scrambled those halcyon times. In the Far East it was a conflict between America and Japan. Of the many battle-fields of the War, one was fought in the Philippines—the country I refer to as *Perla del Mar de Oriente*, an appellation immortalized by the nation's most prominent hero before sacrificing his life in martyrdom in 1896. The war was destructive to people's lives, institutions, and treasure. My family and I were among the millions who came in harm's way.

The colonization and occupation of the country over four centuries by three major imperialist powers exacted consequences to them as it had to the mores, traditions and society of the Filipinos. I am keen to clarify how my upbringing, adolescent experiences and adulthood odyssey bear significance to the historic events of the country of my birth and to those of the adopted country that would become my life-long home, America. This story is knitted as an embroidery of my reminiscences.

THE ISLANDS...A HISTORICAL PERSPECTIVE

The islands are believed to have had their earliest inhabitants around 10,000 B.C. Their present-day descendants are commonly believed to be the Aetas who likely lived as hunter-gatherers. Today, they are found in rural highlands, driven away from coastal regions by Malay people who came from the Asian mainland about 8,000 years later. It is from this latter group that melting and production of iron tools, pottery, and rice cultivation is known to have developed. The communities they formed were plutocratic, known as *barangay*s. Their headman was referred as the *Datu*. He ruled families predominantly bound by kinship. The different tribes were separated from each other by mountain ranges and expansive seas. As a result, they communicated in dissimilar languages and, more often, had disparate relationships among themselves. Their internecine quarrels not only prevented harmonious interactions, they deterred concepts of a united realm and a centralized mode of governance. Nonetheless, distinct maritime-centered harbor principalities did form around the sixth century.

By the tenth century, Muslim traders from nearby Indonesia had ventured to the Sulu archipelago of southern Mindanao. The inhabitants were known to have established the beginnings of trade with merchants of Indonesia and Borneo. Those outside traders brought with them their dominant religion and gained converts that conveniently spread to mainland Mindanao. The religion had thereafter penetrated northward along with the expanding commerce. Profiting from their geographic surroundings, *Maynila* and *Sugbu*, pre-Hispanic names of present day Manila and Cebu subsequently became the active centers of inter-island and region-wide trade. Among the latter merchants were Arabians, Indians, Japanese and mostly, Chinese. Some of the trade items were silk, other fine fabrics and spices.

To the Old World, spices were a salacious, albeit rare and expensive attraction. They came to markets of the West from the Middle East, India, and China by an ancient overland trade path known as the Silk Road. In the thirteenth century, following the same route, Venicean explorer Marco Polo popularized his travels to China between 1260 to 1269. He so animated a curiosity about the Orient such that there followed numbers of travelers and explorers who would further enlighten the West to the civilization of the East and their exotic markets. The era is regarded as the Age of Discovery.

By the fifteenth century the avowed major powers and seekers of unknown places were Portugal and Spain. In their search for a pathway to the East by sea, they agreed to divide the world and its newly discovered lands for exploration, conquest and trade along a north-south line of demarcation. In 1496 both countries, as signatories to the Treaty of Tordesillas, bestowed rights over the eastern segment of the Atlantic Ocean and the African continent to Portugal, the other side of the divide to Spain. Eight years earlier, 1488, the explorer Bartholomew Dias seeking a seaward path that would enable Portuguese enterprises access to East Asian trade centers, led the initial exploration into the Indian Ocean. He accomplished the route by cruising south along the western side of Africa and passing eastward through the Cape of Good Hope. Towards the end of the century, cargo-loaded Spanish ships that sailed the same itinerary, now contrary to the agreed treaty, risked attack and seizure by the Portuguese armadas. The treaty, in effect, had coerced the Spaniards to search for a different route.

During the early years of the 16th century, a Portuguese vagabond adventurer, *Fernao de Magelhaes* -Ferdinand Magellan, gained the attention of Spain's Monarchy. He had been to the Portuguese settlement of Goa, India and the nearby Molucca islands—a group within eastern Indonesia—where he became acquainted with the spice markets. In deference to the Treaty, he envisioned reaching the region by plying westward across the Atlantic Ocean towards the South American continent, which he believed had a channel to traverse across as the threshold to the uncharted sea where the Orient lay. Magellan's vision of a route to reach the area was convincing. So it was that on 10th August 1519 Magellan sailed from Spain in a five-ship convoy, ostensibly organized to reach the fable Spice Islands of the Orient, but it turned out only by trial and error. Before the convoy came to the sea that he named *Mar Pacifico* (Pacific Ocean), the passage across South America they discovered was, instead, through the labyrinthine islands of its southern isthmus now known as the Straits of Magellan.

At their first landfall, the inhabitants were so attracted to the ships, they boarded and took with them fixtures for souvenirs. The fleet promptly departed. They named the island *Isla de Ladrones*, Isle of Thieves, which is present-day Guam. Sailing onward, they sighted a group of islands, as yet unknown to the Old World. They disembarked on one that the natives called *Homanon*; then, following their suggestions, proceeded to the more populated island of *Muktan*, Mactan of today, which is adjacent to the city of Cebu. There, the adventurers were offered the sustaining supplies needed to proceed on the journey; a Malayan named *Enrique* whom Magellan had acquired in his earlier travel to the Moluccas was the effective interpreter. During their stay, they attempted to Christianize the inhabitants and, contrary to their avowed peaceable mission, engaged in a battle by taking sides between warring tribes. On 27th April 1521, when fighting against an overwhelming native force led by Chieftain *Lapu Lapu*, Magellan was killed, felled by spears made of bamboo.

Battle of Mactan, 27th April 1521. A commemorative painting of Ferdinand Magellan felled by Lapu Lapu warriors. Courtesy of <philippinehistory.com>.

The tragic defeat was as much a result of overconfidence in the invincibility of the Spanish armored troops as it was a flawed underestimation of the fighting spirit of their opponents.

The straggling group eventually returned to Spain, after stops in the Moluccas for cargos of spice. Risking discovery by the Portuguese fleet, they cruised the Indian Ocean and passed through the Cape of Good Hope to arrive back on 6th September 1522. Of the 237 men who set out on the five-ship voyage, only 56 returned, in two vessels as the other three were lost to storms. By then, after surviving a number of near-mutiny episodes, shipwrecks, and death by disease and starvation, their leader was Juan Sebastian de Escaño. Magellan and the expedition members would be credited as the first circumnavigators of the Earth.

Three years later, Spain would send the first of many more expeditions. In the ensuing centuries, they eventually led to the vaunted Spanish imperial dominance over major portions of the world and, by conquest, extended the continuing colonization of regions of the Americas and the Orient.

THE COLONIAL EXPERIENCE

The islands continued to be a magnet for Iberian explorers. On 21st November 1564, López de Legazpi led a complement of troops and friars on a voyage that retraced the route Magellan had taken. They landed in Cebu on 13th February 1565. Two years later, a reinforcement of thousands more soldiers enabled the buildup of *Fuerza de San Pedro* (Fort San Pedro). The stronghold provided a harbor for the continued shipping activities from Spain and *Nueva España* (Mexico); it afforded protection from hostile native attacks and became a base for the exploration of other islands. Maynila at the time had a thriving community organized as a sultanate as a result of the Islamist spread northwards to Luzon. The Spaniards, aiming to occupy the settlement, battled and defeated the defenders who were led by Rajah Sulayman on 24th May 1570. Thereafter, Legazpi proclaimed the sovereignty of Spain over the islands and chose Manila (the Hispanized name) the capital. His governance, as the first Governor-General of Spanish East Indies, began the establishment of a centralized administration through which it intended to maintain peace and order, collect taxes, build schools, and other public capital works. Parenthetically, in 1543, the Viceroy of Mexico, on directive of the Spanish Crown, charged Ruy López de Villalobos to venture in search of spices. En route, he tarried in the island of *Kandaya* (Samar of today) and named it Filipinas but without any pretence of establishing a colony. The explorer group departed and, before reaching the Moluccas, soon were captured and retained by the Portuguese. Villalobos never got to return to Mexico; he died in 1546, leaving Legaspi to name the archipelago colony *Las Islas Filipinas*, the Philippine Islands, its Westernized version, after *rey de España Felipe III*. Spain reigned over Las Islas for the next 333 years.

The accompanying friars, intent on a crusade to convert the populace to Christianity, ventured to the many rural areas. They found the inhabitants worshipping the moon, stars, and among some tribes, an all-powerful but mysterious deity. These were beliefs the friars decried as infused with superstition and the occult. The Catholic proselytizer offerings, proposed as learned and reasoned, were made more persuasive by support and advocacy of the domineering colonist governance. To the natives, the compelling argument for conversion to Christianity was its avowed pathway to after-life salvation combined with the threat of eternal damnation to non-believers. Inadvertently, the indigenous population had exchanged nativist beliefs with those whose icons were embodied in likeness to that of the Friars and the overlords. One is led to believe that the colonialists were thereby readily able to create an assenting, compliant populace who subscribed to a social hierarchy of their choosing. It had at its peak the immigrant Spaniards, *peninsulares;* below were the Spaniards born in the Islas, *insulares*. Lower yet were the *mestizos,* those born by a native and a foreigner, most commonly a Spaniard. Those educated natives who would become the first group to refer to themselves as Filipinos were classed as the *ilus-*

trados. At the lowest stratum was the common-man, *indio*. Local chiefs and Datus were designated *principales*, a select group who were extended special privileges in exchange for their fealty. They served as the administrators of tribute collection and organizers of forced laborers. In effect, there developed a racial and societal hierarchy which gave discriminatory privileges to the "us" and subordinating servitude of the "others." The class division would further segregate the indigenous populace and retard their concepts of nationalism.

In 1565, the Manila Galleon Trade was formed. It was an enterprise to bring the wealth of the Orient to Spain by a more direct, if arduous route. It utilized Mexico's ports—Acapulco in the Pacific and Veracruz in the Atlantic—for the land transfer. Manila served as the trans-shipping hub. The journey from Spain was filled with export goods that included gold and silver mined at their South American colonies. The traffic in passengers across the Pacific Ocean to Manila had immigrant Spaniards, many of whom had been born in Mexico; the one-way trip could last up to four months. This highly profitable undertaking did contribute to underscore the importance of the Islas Filipinas to Spain's Empire. It lasted until just before the Mexican Independence in 1821.

In the shuffling of commercial enterprises and re-orientation of trading sources, the Chinese remained active participants. Many had served as middlemen merchants and liaison to traders in China. The Spanish, perhaps envious of their successes, set restrictive and discriminatory policies which included confining their Manila quarters to a ghetto referred as the *Parian*. Many would intermarry with native women to overcome the prejudicial impositions. Notably, their mestizo offspring shortly became, and remains today, a prominent contributor to the economic foundation of the country. During the same period, the ilustrados and many of the Spanish and Chinese mestizos, were broadening their worldview by seeking added education in Spain and Europe. They returned home to share participative opportunities with the penisulares and insulares in the overall concerns of the land.

As early as the late 18th century, the Islas had developed a society with identifiable, lasting Spanish influences. For one, Christianized women had adopted greater modesty and humility. Celibacy outside of and fidelity within marriage was more universally accepted. Polygamy and the easy dissolution of marriage—more common in earlier times—were effectively disallowed. The names of provinces, towns and even dialects used words of Spanish orthography. Roman Catholicism was rooted firmly, albeit in rural areas the blending of traditional beliefs in the supernatural roles of such native icons as mystery-powered amulets and protective medallions—known as *anting-anting*—persisted. Artisan indio*s* and Chinese merchants had become commonplace in the larger settlements, each developing and refining their crafts. Most of the secular and religious officials were the peninsulares and insulares. At the same time, the mestizos and ilustrados were getting participative roles in the colonial administration. In the countryside. however, the population remained linguistically and geographically underdeveloped and segmented.

On 21st November 1849, the *Catalogo Alfabético de Apellidos*, Catalogue of Alphabetical Surnames, was instituted. It compelled indios to select a surname from an approved alphabetically organized list which included names of religious icons, saints, towns and places. It was implemented to facilitate census surveys, taxation records, and eliminate confusion of individual identity. The process would continue over time and eventually all inhabitants had last names.

In 1857 Spain inaugurated public school education for its masses; it was an offshoot of developments in Europe attributed to the Age of Enlightenment. Fortuitously, by edict of Queen Isabella II, the process was extended to Las Islas to include the establishment of schools in the primary, secondary, and tertiary levels with Spanish their language of instruction. At the same time, a rise in patriotism was being fomented by the ever-growing numbers and influential role of the ilustrados, to the disaffection of the colonists.

By the nineteenth century, Spain was decidedly in a spiraling throes of economic hardship, its glorious and heraldic past increasingly tarnished. To the everyday Spaniard, immigration to its many colonial possessions became a common, if necessary decision. As a result, a wave of immigrant Spaniards ventured to Las Islas, seeking their fortunes in communities favorable to promote commerce, interisland trade and agriculture. What may have compounded the wanderlust was the Spanish tradition of assigning the oldest son, without contest, as the sole heir of the family resources and possessions, especially land holdings. The women siblings were expected to marry or, together with the younger brothers, become dependents of the heir. What more likely developed is that the spinster sisters entered the convent while the brothers sought their fortunes in the colonies.

Meanwhile, the church and their friars had become heavily vested in large land holdings. They were so politically powerful that their religious self-interests synchronously represented the colonial goals, chiefly, keeping the indio populace in bondage and uneducated. In the island of Leyte, there was a village named *Ogmuk* by the inhabitants; it was among the communities to where the Jesuit religious and adventurous Spaniards came. By 1834 they had built a chapel named after Sts. Peter & Paul, the *Iglesia de Santos Pedro y Pablo*.

I grew up in this town, now known as Ormoc, as a Catholic. In my youth, the structure had enlarged and if there were other churches, of any denomination, I was unaware of them. The house of worship faced the main plaza of town where stood a statue of the national hero: José Rizal.

*Jose Rizal, martyred by Spanish colonists
on 30th December 1896.*

Rizal was a worthy inspiration to his contemporary compatriots, as he is equally regarded today and will be in the future. As school children, we became well acquainted with the icon, proudly pointing out that he was born on 19th June 1861, the seventh of eleven children of a rich family in the city of Calamba, Laguna. His Chinese father had married a Filipina and changed his original surname to a Spanish equivalent, a common practice of the time. We would learn he was educated in medicine, philosophy, and letters at Manila's *La Real y Pontificia Universidad de Santo Tomás de Aquino,* now known as University of Santo Tomas. The institution was founded on 28th April, 1611, four years before the world-famous Harvard University of Massachusetts, U.S.A.

Rizal became a prolific poet and writer. His most famous works were two novels: *Noli me Tangere* and *El Filibusterismo,* Touch Me Not and Reign of Greed, respectively. Both were a parody of the injustices and suffering doled out to his country-men by the Spanish theocracy. After additional studies at the Universidad Central de Madrid, the University of Paris and the University of Heidelberg, he returned home conversant in ten languages and a polymath.

His contemporaries were the ilustrados, many of whom had studied abroad. As a persuasive group of intellectuals, they spread their observations of a Spain that was backward of its northern neighbor countries. At the time, Europeans were progressively shying from the bonds of autocracy, its citizens benefiting from a liberal socio-economic milieu. The observation contrasted with those befalling the Filipinos who remained oppressed. The theo-cratic rule of the Islas had an administrative structure that was aided by an anachronistic body of select Spanish and Chinese mestizos, elite indios and principales who enjoyed their social privileges and honorific roles as *gobernadorcillos* and *cabezas del barangay*, municipal judges and leaders of a municipality. This favored group tended to retain the status quo. The ilustrados, on the other hand, became the nucleus of activists who lent cohesion of the sporadic rebellious riots of the past and provided direction for the welling popular yearning for self-governance. Rizal, para-doxically, advocated only non-violent reforms. He championed such causes as Filipino representation in the *Cortes*, Spain's leg-islature; the appointment of ordained Filipino priests to serve as parish curates; and the legislation of equal rights of all residents of the Islas before the law.

CONVERGENT CAUSES AND CONFLICTS

Toward the end of the 19th century, there came a confluence of historic events. The colonialists, their hold of Las Islas vis-ibly dwindling, had become obsessed to employ drastic means in order to retain suzerainty. They targeted the most prominent of the ilustrados, Rizal. By accusing him of treason against mother Spain, the rulers were convinced that his death would defuse the populist itch for independence. The reality not withstanding, he was condemned to die. On 30th December 1896 Jose Rizal was executed by a firing squad. His death, instead, became a martyrdom and a powerful catalyst for revolution. On the eve of his execution, Rizal penned *Mi Ultimo Adios*—My Last Farewell. It became an inspiring ode to patriotism and a rallying force for the struggle for independence. School children, especially those Spanish-conversant as I was, would aim to memorize the lengthy farewell. I remember best the first stanza—the copy allegedly of his own handwriting below.

A translation of Mi Ultimo Adios:

> Farewell, my adored Land, region of the sun
> caressed Pearl of the Orient Sea, our Eden lost.
> With gladness I give you my Life,
> sad and repressed;
> And, were it more brilliant,
> more fresh and at its best,
> I would still give it to you for your welfare at most.

The insurrection against the Spanish authorities fulminated by 1898 with the formation of a revolutionary government. The *Acta de la Proclamación de Independencia del Pueblo Filipina*, Act of the Declaration of Independence of the Filipino Nation was proclaimed by General Emilio Aguinaldo, the twenty-nine-year-old acclaimed president on 12ᵗʰ June 1898.

General Emilio Aguinaldo, 29 year old President of
the Filipino Nation, declared on 12th June 1898.

Its army—the *Katipunan*—subsequently engaged in armed confrontation with the Spanish soldiers. They proved equal to the challenge and were credited for a number of victories.

By then, the Islas Filipinas was regarded as an archipelago of islands clustered in three identifiable regions: Luzon, the largest land mass to the north where most of the islands' population resided; Mindanao, the second largest to the south which was the least populated but having the better societal order as a result of Mohammedanism; and, the Visayas, those islands in its midsection whose inhabitants with their multiplicity of languages were historically less interconnected and more alienated from other tribes. Luzon's satellite islands to its north end are less than 150 miles south of Formosa–Taiwan, of today; and, in southwest

Mindanao, a sequence of islands southward, known as the Sulu Archipelago, are a stone's throw proximity to Malaysia.

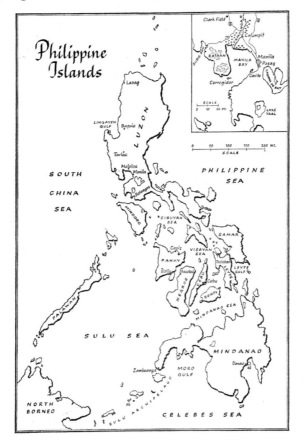

The Philippine Islands circa late 1800s.

The challenges that the fledgling republic faced were overpowering. As subsequent events would point out, the core group of patriots who led the rebellion were from Luzon, weakened by internal quarrels and charges of assassinations. From other regions of the archipelago the military strategies were wanting in synchronous coordination. The indios were problematic, coming as they did from a colonial past that had nurtured a subservient rather than an empowered spirit. They held a tradition of provincialism; they were predominantly poorly educated; and, the multiple dialects among them were a communication hurdle. Furthermore, the core leadership needed to reform a crippled infrastructure in education, transportation, taxation and they had to institute a democratic governance over a population estimated at over seven million. These conditions haunted efforts for a collective sense of nationhood. The pronouncement of independence was ignored by Spain and the United States. The rejection was dispiriting, if not deflating. The patriotic fervor and the unity of the Filipinos to the cause of independence and self-rule would be tested.

Shortly, an international incident—the Spanish American War—erupted on 25th April 1898. In that conflict, the Americans defeated the weakened Spanish armed forces. Among the spoils of victory was Las Islas Filipinas. Initially, U.S. President William McKinley was unclear on their disposition. His uncertainty attracted the attention of other European powers, at the time in search for Far Eastern countries to colonize. Germany, prominent among them and eager to fill a seeming vacuum, sent a flotilla of warships to Manila Bay. The Germans, however, retreated, sensing an American determination to ensure dominion of the Islas. The United States took possession of Las Islas Filipinas—subsequently anglicized as the Philippine Islands. It would induce a powerful nation to partake in the tumultuous domestic events, its own imperialist goals fueled by misguidedly disparaging the wisdom, capacity, and determination for self-rule of the Filipinos. In agreement to the 10th December 1898 Treaty of Paris, Spain received a compensation of twenty million dollars. McKinley, eleven days later, ultimately proclaimed the American intention for the newly-acquired charges. In part, it reads:

> Finally, it should be the earnest wish and paramount aim of the military administration to win the confidence, respect, and affection of the inhabitants of the Philippines by assuring them in every possible way that full measure

of individual rights and liberties which is the heritage of free peoples, and by proving to them that the mission of the United States is one of benevolent assimilation substituting the mild sway of justice and right for arbitrary rule.

In taking control of the country, Americans received a welcoming reception, initially. However, certain of the begrudging issues continued to percolate without satisfying resolutions. There were unresolved issues with Commodore Dewey and senior officials of the McKinley Administration such that Filipinos dishearteningly came to view the Americans as having surreptitiously begot the occupation of Manila when the U.S. involvement was, instead, believed to be the enduring aid in their struggle for independence.

THE FORGOTTEN WAR

The American troops in Manila soon had isolated clashes with the Katipunan. The incidents ignited an escalating shooting exchange and thereby began the Philippine-American War, contrary to President McKinley's benevolent intentions. It was a conflict some historians have dubbed the "Forgotten War" for the paucity of written references on the historic event as taught to today's students of American and Philippine history. In 'The Philippine War 1899-1902," author Brian McAllister Linn covered the American military experiences. I have drawn from his reportage and include snippets of reports to allow my comment on the conflicts in the regions of Mindanao and Samar. They lend insight to the challenges that the protagonists faced. On one side were indigenous people wanting to resist outsider intrusions into their beliefs, traditions and aims for self-rule. Their opponents were Americans who had been ceded dominion of the land as the spoils of war with Spain; they avowedly were wanting to assimilate a native population with benevolence.

While the Spaniards had three centuries to overwhelm the indios, Americans would encounter a more self-assured populace that then had included sizeable groups of ilustrados, mestizos, insulares, and principales, all having a congealing sense of cohesion and communal identity. Collectively regarding themselves Filipinos, they came to view the foreign presence as yet another attempt at colonial domination. Americans, determined to impose their overlord, pursued their goals militarily. The fighting started on 4th February 1899 when President Aguinaldo declared war on the U.S. forces in the Philippine Islands. Although it officially terminated in July 1902, sporadic, isolated uprisings continued for another decade.

As the conflict persisted, Americans responded to the Katipunan attacks and killings by revengeful, indiscriminate shooting of civilians and burning of their villages. Among the military, contrary to their efforts to improve cross-cultural relations, Filipinos were often regarded pejoratively as "niggers" and "savages." Individual American soldiers, notably, on many occasions disturbed by conduct contrary to their personal moral code, sent reflective letters home; a few even opted to desert. Mostly, those letters and reports by field officers became the more insightful record of the conflicting estimates of the progress of battle and the conflicted efforts at pacification of the natives than were the sanitized accounts published for the reading public.

Indeed, strenuous opposition to the Forgotten War and concern over the perceived beginnings of America's expansionist venture became the pervasive issues in the American homeland, in particular the control of the Philippine Islands. The contentious policy had supporters. They were advocates who voiced an obligatory responsibility to promulgate American normative values and, by empire building, bring modernity to the islands of benighted natives. It even begot the advocacy of the pro-imperialist English as epitomized by India-born Rudyard Kipling's poem "The White Man's Burden: The United States and the Philippine Islands". It urged America to shoulder the weight of empire, as Britain and other European nations had done. The opposition was inspired and led by the influential writer, the renowned anti-imperialist Mark Twain. He, together with notable Andrew Carnegie and others, formed the American Anti-Imperialist League. The conservationist group felt the annexation of a land whose people were racially different and living in the distant Orient as an overstretch of constraints set by the U.S. Constitution.

American public opinion was further stirred by reports of the belligerent conduct of the combatants. One episode known as the Balangiga Massacre occured on the island of Samar. The happening was a tale of Filipino premeditative, cunning subterfuge to massacre American troops, reciprocated by vindictive, unbridled killings of men, women, and children of the community on directives of U.S. military commanders. The confrontation took place in the coastal town of Balangiga. The protagonist garrison of soldiers and marines had been stationed as part of their province-wide efforts at pacification as well as providing security for the thriving abaca and hemp industry. The island, it turned out, had an organized, well-led contingent of *insurrectos*, rebels who, in cahoots with the townfolks, plotted a rout of the army garrison using the bell in the church tower to signal the attack. Of the seventy-four-soldier contingent, forty-eight were killed and twenty-two were severely wounded. The carnage shocked the U.S. public. An infuriated military governor of the Philippines, Maj. Gen. Adna R. Chaffee, declared the situation called for retaliatory use of "shells and bayonets against natives who could not be trusted." In response to a correspondent's request for comment on the bravery of the Filipinos, General Lloyd Wheaton barked: "Brave! Brave! Brave! Damn 'em, they won't stand up to be shot!" Assigned to the task was a General Jacob H. Smith who, facing his troops, ordered: "I wish you to kill and burn... the more you kill and burn the better it will please me... I want no prisoners." Estimates of the Filipino casualties included civilian men, women, and children; they varied from fifty to a thousand, the factual number blurred by the bias of the accountant. In the end, the church bells of the town were brought back to the Infantry Headquarters in America as a trophy. Despite recent attempts by the Philippine government to gain return of the bells to Balangiga, they remain under US government control and have become a lingering ire of Filipino nationalists. In May 1902, General Smith faced court marshal for his orders. He was found guilty; for punishment, he was ordered to retire from the service.

Throughout the Islands, meanwhile, the American pacification efforts were being notably avoided by two ethnic groups. First were the *Igorots* who lived in remote, inaccessible highland villages of Luzon; their Aeta ancestors had been driven to the jungle fastness from their riverine beginnings by migrant Malays long before the Spaniards had discovered the Islands. The other group was in Mindanao. They were the *Moros*, so named by the Spaniards after the Moors that occupied southern Spain from the eighth to the tenth century. As Muslims, they succeeded in thwarting Christianization efforts throughout the centuries of Spanish proselytizing programs. Once again, they would battle to stay outside the tentacles of foreign overlord. The American forces, in taking control of the Islands, extended their presence to southern regions of Mindanao as early as 1899. Moro forces in those areas, by organizing recurrent battles, would delay, if not obstruct American efforts at pacification. Their resistance had compelled the U.S. Army to alter their organization and armament. Of the latter, they replaced the 0.38 caliber service revolver with the 0.45 caliber automatic pistol. The 0.38 was found unable to stop a determined Moro warrior in time to prevent him from wreaking havoc before he fell. The 0.45 Colt automatic, on the other hand, threw a slug that would more assuredly neutralize a *juramentado*—jihadist—attack. The pistol was subsequently adopted as the preferred military sidearm thereafter.

Many punitive U.S. Army expeditions continued for several years before they were able to institute lasting reforms. In time, Americans succeeded in instituting the concept of land ownership by private individuals, a contrast to their traditional societal form. They also introduced an educational system with English as its language of instruction; a program to promote agriculture and trade which gradually discouraged banditry and intertribal disputes; and, they were able to organize a streamlined, simplistic legal system. Notably, when President Theodore Roosevelt—on 6th September 1901, McKinley was assassinated—issued a proclamation declaring an end to the insurrection and a cessation of hostilities on 4th July 1902, he pointedly noted "except in the country inhabited by the Moro tribes, to which this proclamation does not apply." Ultimately, 130 Americans were killed and another 500 died of disease. An estimated 20, 000 Moros had succumbed in battle.

As the realities of the Forgotten War conflict bode of certain defeat for the Filipino, their resistance changed strategies by avoiding direct confrontation in favor of guerilla tactics. The approach provided nightmarish unease for the Americans as the population, seemingly behaving as their *amigos,* were becoming openly supportive of the *guerilleros* (guerillas*).* Nonetheless, on 23rd March 1901 President Emilio Aguinaldo was captured at his mountain lair deep in the jungles of northern Luzon. The leader of the undertaking was Colonel Frederick Funston. The capture had required the complicity of a band of *Macabebe* Scouts—indio and mestizo mercenary recruits of the U.S. Army who later would regretfully regard their participation as a betrayal to the Filipino quest for independence. The spurious guerilla resistance gradually sputtered thereafter. Vestiges of the armed struggle, however, would persist for nearly ten more years. The dream of self-determination, its flame now in embers, would remain, covertly seeking for circumstances to re-ignite. Ultimately, the Americans achieved their country-wide program of pacification. More than

4,000 American soldiers and about 20,000 Filipino fighters lost their lives paying the price. Estimates of Filipino civilian casualties killed or who died because of disease or hunger ranged up to one million. Parenthetically, James H. Blount, in writing "The American Occupation of the Philippines 1898–1912," authoritatively provides valuable, insightful account of the times and the roles of the cast of participants of the tumultuous era. His onsite observations of the Philippine Islands gives added details of historic events and the contentious purviews that the participants advocated. The book is recommendable as an informative read.

AMERICAN BENEVOLENCE

On 4th July 1902, U.S. President Theodore Roosevelt closed the annals of the Forgotten War and promulgated the full and complete pardon and amnesty of all people of the Philippine Islands who participated in the conflict. Once again, the Moros were pointedly exempted.

Progressively, the American occupation changed the cultural landscape of the Islands. Filipinos benefited from the implementation of public health programs, seeing a decrease in the rates of death from cholera as a result of poor hygienic measures instituted during Spanish governance. The infrastructure, such as transportation—roads, railways, shipping—improved. The Spanish-imposed theocratic authority was amended by providing a system of government in the mirror of that of the United States. Earlier in July 1901, some 600 U. S. schoolteachers came to the Philippines, transported aboard SS *Thomas*. They were participants of a program to demonstrate American intent to help "civilize the new little brown brothers" not with the force of military rifles but with schoolbooks. Their crowning accomplishment was the training of the nucleus of 25,000 English-speaking Filipino teachers who then staffed the island schools. They would be regarded as the "Thomasites." At this same period, a number of U.S. servicemen also volunteered to participate in the educational systems. Many of those Americans, devoted to the cause, remained as residents of the country. English would thereafter become the language of instruction in schools, government, and business.

In 1935, pursuant to the Tyding-MacDuffie Law enacted by the U.S. Congress the previous year, America recognized the islands as the Commonwealth of the Philippines, able to formulate its own Constitution. They were given a promise to become independent ten years later. On a plebiscite that followed, Manuel Quezon and Sergio Osmeña were voted to lead the country as President and Vice-President, respectively.

In time, the relationship between both countries became indubitably friendly. Filipinos overwhelmingly came to regard the American dominion as far more beneficial than that of the Spaniards. But there was a quid pro quo arrangement. As a signatory with the U.S. to an agreement to partake in their mutual defense, the Commonwealth turned into an important bulwark of the Pan-Pacific extension of U.S. military power. Multiple army, navy and air corps garrisons sprouted throughout many areas of the country, their personnel augmented with American-trained Filipino constabulary units. The pervading lulling mood of the Filipinos was a sense of cuddling comfort by the protective might of the Americans. The bitter memories of the Forgotten War had become clouded, if not tacitly erased. As a student in the primary grades, I regarded references about American benevolence towards the Filipinos to be integral to the scope of such subjects as History and Literature. The subliminal effects that students received, as I did, when learning English, studying American history, enjoying American movies and candies were stimulating, attractive, and enticing exposures. They made students easy converts of American goodwill. In the following years, Filipinos would continue to bind their affinity for America, Americans, and the American overall pursuit of a life of freedom, happiness and liberty. Certainly, in rural Ormoc, the pro-American sentiment was effusive, as was mine.

ON REFLECTION

The natives of the archipelago did come at odds with Spanish colonial interests, which were themselves divided between the compulsion to proselytize and educate the indio or succumb to the temptation of continued rapacious harvest of the islands' resources and rule by enslaving serfdom. Those conflicted conditions prevailed for three centuries. Eventually, their identifiable indigenous culture and tradition, through centuries of colonial expurgatory efforts would become blended in varied degrees of influence by the colonists and other immigrants who included merchants from China, Japan, and other countries of Asia and the Middle East. Today, the cuisine and lexicon of the vernacular speech have telltale signs of the foreigner's legacy. Paradoxically, superstition and a regard for the occult, each vestiges of long-held native life-views remained commonplace. They persisted, even among the educated and despite exposure to the contrarian teachings of the Catholic faith and that of scientific reasoning. It has become imprinted in today's Filipino beliefs.

The American military behavior of the early 1900s reflected the prevailing views held by Westerners of peoples under their colonial oversight and dominance. Racial discrimination in their various manifestations was an overriding behavior among Americans, as it was of the Spaniards. Indeed, even as the Philippine Islands had become a Commonwealth of the U.S. in 1935, it did not displace nor reform the discriminatory class society the Spanish had created. The Americans, in retaining the status quo, inserted themselves at the top of the social tree and allocated economic privileges for themselves. The purview would become a vestigial legacy of the colonial system that, although not by decree, would be implicitly practiced in the ensuing decades. In retrospect, there did seem to me a practice of discrimination based on the Iberian stratification even in Ormoc. At some future time when civilization has come to profit from increased international cross-cultural exchanges and adapts a reasoned societal regard for human rights and dignity, hopefully, people can then shed their many forms of prejudices.

In America, the disposition of the Philippines had ignited contentious debates along opposing ideological belief. On one side were the conservationists who viewed annexation as a stretch of constraints set by the U.S. Constitution. Opponents, in favor of colonization, were advocates who voiced an obligatory responsibility to promulgate the American normative values. The latter prevailed. Filipinos in future decades would become inured, some even feeling themselves citizen-extensions of Americanism in the Far East. It seems to me that the contrasting power, wealth and benevolence of the Imperialist had become so convincing and enviable that in time, the Filipinos came to regard America their beacon of hope for a promising life. Their mother lode? Henry Graff's "American Imperialism and the Philippine Insurrection" reviews testimonies of officials preimminently involved in the Philippines affairs up to 1902, before the US Senate Committee; it is a highly informative source.

The Moros merit attention, even praise-worthy regard. As a people who had achieved well-defined socio-political institutions before the arrival of the Spanish, they succeeded in overcoming intrusive efforts into their society and culture by two powerful imperialist outsiders through four centuries. As a result, today their distinctive ancient traditions have prevailed. A pressing concern remains. It is the past secessionist goal of the Moros and their alienated views of the Filipino community. The predicament will surely pose predictable obstacles to efforts for harmony and cohesion by an independent Filipino nation. In this regard, it is interesting to speculate and wonder how the history of the Philippines would have changed had the Spaniards discovered the islands a century later than they did. Would an unfettered, continuing conversion of the indigenous inhabitants to Islam have spread to other regions of the Islands during the time period? If so, could there have been a more formidable obstacle to Iberian Christianization efforts? Might the Moros have created a Muslin Philippines? More importantly, will the country, in time, succeed in the acculturation of the Moros?

Post-colonial Filipinos often regard their fate in the political and economic spheres as having resulted from three centuries of Spanish reign and tend to ascribe the control of their educational and religious affairs to the Catholic friars. There is an ancient-held attitude that may have had a contributory factor: "*bahala na.*" It is an individual's viewpoint that defers to a superior being the ultimate disposition of any challenge above one's own self-empowered capacity to resolve. Considering that the early society was based on a tradition of restrictive intertribal relationships and a subservience by the individual to a superior *Datu*, might the colonialists have inadvertently found a compliant people suitable to a "divide and conquer" strategy? Could the divisive provincialism have thus allowed Spaniards the centuries of rule before awakening the nativist determination for self-rule? How effectively will future Filipinos marshal "*bahala na*"?

The American dominion thereafter followed for half a century. Their contrasting nation building policies were introduced by a people with imitatively tempting lifestyle: freedom to pursue a life of happiness and self-worth. As a consequence, the combined epoch of Spanish and American rule had ample time to nurture a colonial mentality on the Filipinos. In practice, its socio-economic impact manifested as an instinctive preference for anything American or European over that which was native. The backlash of the outlook had always been a saddling concern since a perception of ethnic or cultural inferiority tended to become a burden and a repressive barrier for aspiring Filipino pride and dignity. The conviction might even have tended to deter progress of the national economy, especially on those industries that produced locally-made merchandises. When reminiscing about my adolescent years, I too admit to have preferred "things" foreign over the local. Indeed, colonial mentality rarely bypasses anyone; it affects the individual, insidiously. In the future, would the Filipinos fashion strategies to empower a passion to optimize ones own potential? Encourage the zest for entrepreneurial know-how? Develop the spirit of intellectual inquiry for everyone? Time will tell.

The extended period of colonization seems to have evolved a duality of Filipino behavior: subservient and provincial on one hand or astute and resolutely proud-hearted of their homeland, on the other. Interestingly, the conundrum might have an intertwining contemporary concern. It is the ubiquitous effort at globalization—aptly proffered in a book by Benjamin Barber, *Jihad vs. McWorld*, as a world coming together in commonality of economic, technological and ecological factors, while at the same time competitively eroding the uniquely identifiable culture and traditions of individual nations. Among countries whose customs are not deeply rooted or have become muddled and indistinctively defined, individual citizens may become confounded as to thereby loosen their sense of identity and pride of nationhood. Had these conflicting influences played a role in defining the Filipino culture of today?

On reviewing the dawning history of the Islas, it seem fitting to surmise that the post-colonial direction of the country's economic, political and cultural aspirations will predictably rest on the actions of the empowered offspring of indios as well as the contributions of contemporary elites, descendants of past peninsulares, insulares, mestizos, ilustrados, and the principales.

Since antiquity, man seems to have harbored a curiosity about the unknown beyond his own confines. It is to the visionary quest of the many explorers of history that we owe much of our contemporary knowledge and advances. Will my reactions to the challenges I face throughout my lifetime similarly nudged me in directions less traveled?

GROWING UP IN ANTEBELLUM

*In every child who is born, under no matter what circum-
stances, and of no matter what parents, the potentiality of the
human race is born again; and in him, too, once more—and
of each of us—our terrific responsibility toward human life;
toward the utmost idea of goodness, of the horror of error, and
of God.*

　　　　　　　　—James Agee (Poet and Author...b1909-1995)

*How beautiful is youth! How bright it gleams with its illu-
sions, aspirations, dreams! Book of Beginnings, Story without
End, Each maid a heroine, and each man a friend!*

　　　　　　　—Henry Wadsworth Longfellow (Poet...b1807-1882)

*Youth is not a time of life; it is a state of mind; it is not a mat-
ter of rosy cheeks, red lips and supple knees; it is a matter of the
will, quality of the imagination, a vigor of the emotions; it is
the freshness of the deep springs of life.*

　　　　　　　—Samuel Ullman (Humanitarian... b1840–1924)

My childhood days, the 1930s, were spent in an idyllic tropical
society. It was a village located on the western side of the island-
province of Leyte, named Ormoc. Even today, when approaching
the town from the sea, one is greeted by a panoramic view of the
community's predominantly agricultural economic base: fields
of sugar cane and coconuts, as far as the eye can see. The land
gradually elevates to the foot of a range of verdant mountains

about ten miles distant that gives the impression of an impenetrable jungle inhabited by a menagerie of tropical animals, exotic birds and reptiles. Looking seaward from atop its hill overlooks is the beautiful, crescent-shaped, fifty-mile wide Ormoc Bay with many lengthy beaches dotting its littoral loveliness. About thirty nautical miles westerly, and barely silhouetted are the sparsely populated Camotes islands; during the seasonal typhoons they often serve to moderate the roiling sea and protect Ormoc from the full fury of the storm. From well beyond those outcroppings, about another thirty nautical miles onward is the island of Cebu, whose provincial capital is Cebu City, the second most populous center of the country.

In those early times, the Ormoc streets, set up with limited vision of the future, were plotted wide enough only to comfortably accommodate a two-way space for the ubiquitous, horse-drawn carriage for passengers, the *tartanilla*. Only a few were paved in asphalt or cement. They were plotted from the seashore to inland, probably not more than a dozen street blocks deep and another couple dozen each on either side of the concrete landing pier where docked interisland ships and passenger-sized out-board motor-powered outrigger boats. The wharf had been a wooden jetty until late 1937, when it was reconstructed of concrete. The improvement jotted past its land base just under a hundred yards. Most commonly, townspeople strolled its length at sunset to leisurely enjoy the cooling outdoor vistas and commune with friends and neighbors, a treat that was inspired by the Spanish custom called a *paseo*. A lighthouse, about thirty feet tall, was anchored on the south side of the pier's land base, adjacent to my home.

Many houses in town were made of *nipa*, an assorted combination of bamboo, coconut and palm tree leaves. My house was made of wood. It was bayside, adjacent to the lighthouse. At a lower floor, few steps below street level, were a medical and dental office, each sharing the same reception room. Prominently

positioned on one of the outside walls was a signage that advertised my parents' respective professions. The rectangular-shaped
family living quarters on the main floor was reached by an outdoor stairway. Inside was a central space occupied by the living
room, dining room, kitchen, and adjacent bathroom. The master
bedroom was separated from two bedrooms for the children on
either side of the living room. The floors, made from the narra
tree hardwood, were uncarpeted. Instead, we had servants who
would keep the floors shiny and clean by polishing the surface
with coconut husks turned scrubbers and brooms made of bamboo and palm. All the windows were unscreened and always open
equally for tropical breezes, flies and mosquitoes.

My home had a modest-sized backyard garden dominated by
a large acacia tree that provided shade. We enjoyed the yard. I was
not aware that the garden was personally tended by my parents; I
only remember them engaging me in conversations in appreciation of the beauty of our surroundings. I felt unbounded playing
there, usually with visiting cousins, unmindful of the shrubbery
and flowers. Also serving as our extended playground were the
paved streets by my house that led to the pier, safe from the infrequent motor and horse-drawn vehicular traffic.

Although I don't recall having animals to pet, there were a
number of cats that seemed to dart around, especially at meal-
times. Dogs, in those times, were not inoculated against rabies
and, more commonly, some did roam the streets unleashed. I was
bitten once when eight years old and received a series of anti-
rabies injections. The scar it left me was not physical but mental
since thereafter, I would hesitate to reciprocate a dog's willingness to befriend me. I have since outgrown my caution.

We had a *yaya* named Patricia, likely in her early thirties. She
attended to us children as the resident babysitter—even tending
as a surrogate mother on occasion, such that we children were
to have a binding relationship with her. Patricia—we referred
to her with deference—acted as the principal supervisor of two

other younger women who cared for household chores. They all were quartered in the house, in a compartmented area behind the medical-dental offices.

MY FAMILY

The sphere of my growing years was far narrower and insular than my own imagination which was wont to wander and wonder. Ormoc seemed to me peopled primarily by aunts, uncles, cousins, other relatives, and friends. Whenever I went out of the house, in town or to nearby communities, it was mainly to be in their company or to go to church or school. On occasions when I crossed Ormoc Bay, it was to sail to Cebu and visit other sets of aunts, uncles, cousins, and grandparents. Some of my relations, although far removed in degrees of kinship, felt close and intimate as we all were factually confined to a small geographic milieu. It was by being with each of them or learning about them that my own worldview was importantly influenced and formed.

Mamá—Adelina nee Alonso, more commonly nicknamed *Indáy (inn-dye)*, was a dentist by profession. Her pre-collegiate studies were at a public school of Cebu, the city of her birth. It had been among many staffed by a faculty of Thomasite Americans. They were volunteers who responded to an educational assistance program promulgated by U.S. President William McKinley. Their participation formed a nation-wide public elementary & secondary school educational system which until then was deficient, if not lacking in many regions. The historic contribution is more commonly referred as the early version of the world-renown present-day U.S. Peace Corps program. Conventional knowledge then held that graduates of such schools were suitably prepared for collegiate studies, as Mamá was by completing her dental education on full academic scholarship until her graduation in 1930. She met my father while attending the University of the Philippines School of Dentistry in Manila.

*Mamá dressed in a Filipiniana gown with bouffant shoulder
sleeves for a dance with Papá during courtship days, 1929.*

Papá—Gregorio, most often known as *Goring*—grew up in
Ormoc. He obtained his high school education at the Colegio-
Seminario de San Carlos in Cebu, a private Spanish Friars-run
institution initially intended for students of Spanish descent. The
exclusive policy ended only by the nineteenth century. He then
enrolled at the University of the Philippines in Manila, where
he completed his medical education. His was a distinguished
accomplishment, coming as he did from a family with limited
resources. Papá would always point out, with deep gratitude, how
much his mother labored to afford his collegiate studies. That he
studied at the University of the Philippines was in itself remarkable considering its prestigious scholastic reputation. He served
his internship at the Southern Islands Hospital in Cebu, a plum
appointment sought after as a premier training center of the
Visayas region.

My parents married in Cebu City on Saturday 5th April 1930. Nine months later, 23rd December, I was born. I was baptized Jaime Alonso Yrastorza. When Mamá would call for Jaime—*high-meh*—it often ominously foretold of some misdeed of my doing, only rarely for a virtuous feat. Otherwise, I would more commonly be Jimmy or Jaime—*jay-mee*. Yrastorza is pronounced phonetically: *era-store-zah*. Filipino personal identification normally consisted of a given name, followed by the mother's maiden name and ending with the father's surname. First names of everyone on both sides of my family were selected after a relative, a saint, or of an icon of biblical times.

By mid-1931 Papá, now a confirmed School of Medicine graduate—diplomas were given only after completion of an internship—the three of us returned to Papá's hometown to reside. Both parents established their respective professional practices in the community: he, a physician and surgeon and she, a dentist.

My parents, newly wed, photographed in their togas as graduates of the University of the Philippines School of Dentistry 1930 and School of Medicine 1932.

Of my siblings, Josefina—*Fenny*—was born in Ormoc on 30th July 1933. Then, on 17th December 1934 Erlinda—*Linda*—followed. Both were delivered by Papá at the town's Pericultural Center and had namesakes of saints. Growing up closely in age, they bonded together as intimate sisters would. Their friends, like mine, were our cousins, relatives, and neighbors. And, in their early years, they had, as I did, similar privileges and limitations that my parents provided. Both received the pampering that parents seemed more prone to enjoy with their little girls; in this instance, deservedly, as both were coquettish and coy. We three did have our share of wrangling and tears. As the eldest and often exerting seniority rights, I surely must have initiated many of the quarrels.

On 20th October 1938, my brother was born at the same Health Center. He was named after my father, who was named after his grandfather. Little baby Gregorio, Junior—*Jun*, a nickname that was commonly used instead of his baptismal name—would grow to acquire the charm and good-looks of his father. He would inherit Mamá's musical talents. Jun later could play the violin with gusto and became a physician in co-practice with Papá. On the 22nd of November 1939, our family had another addition who unlike the others was delivered at home, by Papá. She was baptized Adelina. In time, Indáy, also my mother's nickname, would fulfill the dreams for which she was named: charming, energetic, intelligent, loving, a gifted musician with a pre-destined leadership future in government and education. Later in life, she would bloom with many enviable accomplishments. She grew being a happy addition to our family.

While the delivery of my siblings had the benefit of a physician, the opportunity was not readily available to many expectant mothers in Ormoc, let alone in many regions of the country. Childbirth was more commonly assisted by a *hilot*, a person with midwife experience in supporting a woman during prenatal preparations, labor and post-partum. Not uncommonly, the advise given by hilots was steeped in folklore beliefs that, for example, could include not to eat mangoes to avoid delivery of an overly-hairy baby or cutting the umbilical cord with a sharpened boiled bamboo stick, and binding the hips to aid healing of the vaginal tear. Papá often pointed out that hilot services in the Philippines during the 1930s did participate in about three-fourths of the births per annum but accounted for a higher incidence of infant and maternal mortality rates when compared to physician-assisted parturition.

For each of our birthdays, the celebration invariably started by attending Mass. The unforgettable gifts in those times would include an infrequently available apple, new set of pajamas, and for me, a pair of long pants large enough to last for another couple years' growth. Holiday dishes would invariably include dried codfish brought from Spain or roasted piglet, *lechon de leche* or *inasal* in *Binisayá*. A cake with lighted candles was accompanied by a Happy Birthday songfest in English. On my fifth birthday most, if not every cousin and friend joined in the celebration.

My five year old birthday party attended by cousins and friends, posing in front of my playhouse.

Two days after my birthday is Christmas, a most important festive day. The celebration would begin several days before the twenty-fifth with pre-dawn Mass and prayers. The series, celebrating Mass as the rooster crows—*misa de gallo*—would conclude on the feast day. Until after my late teen years, the custom of giving and exchanging gifts was not associated with Santa Claus. Instead, the tradition coincided with the Feast of the Epiphany. The holiday is usually commemorated at the end of the first week of the new year when, Catholic teachings imparted, three wise men: Gaspar, Melchor, and Balthasar visited the baby Jesus in Bethlehem, presenting him with gifts of gold, frankincense, and myrrh. I grew up feeling overwhelmed when receiving gifts and attention in celebration of both events; they were given me in a single day in recognition of both affairs or, at other times, separately on each of the specific event.

Every Sunday and other days obligated by church doctrine, my parents would gather my siblings and me for the four-block walk to the seven o'clock Mass. The church, structured in the way of early Spanish-held tradition, in the image of a cross, had a main altar at its upper end and a minor altar at each side wing, all separated from the pews by a communion railing. The wooden benches had unpadded kneelers which allowed congregants, including me, to offer the discomfort as a sacrifice for the love of the Lord. Dressed in our Sunday-best, we had repeated the same routine. On arrival home from church there would invariably be a group of huddled poor to whom my parents gave alms in money or food. It was a compassionate donation for the needy that I had taken for granted since a segment of the population was jobless and penniless. My parents had us mindful of town beggars as deserving of our charity, usually, pointing out the rewarding opportunity, if not obligation, to help others less fortunate; even to include the impoverished in distant countries such as China. I would be reminded that our comparative life of ease resulted from education, austerity, and personal industry. The conversation, often at the dining table, would come with urgings to eat every morsel of food on the plate. I do not recall being always able to comply.

My parents, as healthcare professionals, practiced their profession as a calling. Their dedication and zeal were common knowledge. My father's services seemed in demand, even after hours with house calls. Sometimes, he visited patients very distant from town, reaching those places by outrigger boats large enough for passengers. For his services, many of the patients compensated in kind: bunches of bananas, dozens of eggs, baskets of fruits and vegetables, chickens, pigs, sacks of rice; we always had plenty to eat. Although there must have been other physicians in town, in my view, Papá had the premier practice.

One time, he really challenged his surgical stamina. He scheduled six patients for circumcision, using local anesthesia, in a single day: the four Varela brothers, Ramon Moraza, and me. On completion of the circumcision surgeries, everyone returned home to rest, on doctor's orders. I, instead, got out of bed within hours. I sneaked across the street to the Lladoc's house, where I managed to brag about the operation, of course I jostled with Romy and his brothers, all of whom I knew were uncircumcised. In a matter of minutes, I returned to bed rest. Early that evening, Papá discovered my cover sheet blood-stained and my incision wound pendulous and bleeding. He was obliged to control the hemorrhage with the assistance of *Tio Fernando*, a non-practicing physician who rushed to my side from his neighboring house. Aside from that incident, all of us healed well.

The large-scale operations must have enhanced Papa's medical reputation because, in contrast, the non-medical alternative that was practiced at the time seemed unattractive, crude, and fraught with potential complications. In those days youngsters could be circumcised "the local way:" while squatted by the seashore, a knife would be inserted between the foreskin and the penis-head with its sharpened blade facing outward. Then, with a single wooden-hammer blow, it would cause the prepuce to split. Hoping to rely on the hemostatic effect of saline, the "patient" would then get up and run to immerse himself in sea-water. It is tempting to speculate that in Ormoc only a few boys of my age had been circumcised. Whether or when circumcisions for males were an accepted tradition is unknown to me although, it would not seem universally practiced.

The Varelas were among the Spanish families of Ormoc. The parents, immigrants from a northern province of Spain called Galicia, had four sons and a daughter. They lived a distance from town where they owned a large sugarcane plantation, named *Hacienda Galicia*. It was there I first saw a full-sized basketball court and had my first attempt at playing the game. I joined in, not knowing the rules. When I was first passed the ball, I promptly ran with it, without dribbling, and attempted to shoot the basket. I turned around. Embarrassing to me, they all had frozen in their tracks, disbelief and disgust in their faces at my ignorance. I learned the rules thereafter, and the brothers would remain close friends through the years. I did spend innumerable overnight times with the Varelas. Those brothers and I spent a lot of time in a river called Baó, which coursed the edge of their farm. It was a large river that had a section that pooled deep enough to swim in. And, swim we did.

In their parental concern, my parents were no less eager to practice their profession on their children. Papá seemed ever ready to spoon in that disgustingly nauseous castor oil or cod liver oil on the early detection of fever. I did try to feint wellness when otherwise feeling ill but not always succeeding. Once, I tried to escape discovery. I got a lengthy, deep gash on my right knee when jumping a ditch at the rear of the school campus. The culprit—barbwire—was hidden by the overgrowth. With a pocket handkerchief as a tourniquet, I controlled the bleeding and tried to keep from seeking the doctor's attention. Sr. Editha, instead, had me home where the wound was treated with repeated mercurochrome and hydrogen peroxide applications for days. My knee bears the residual scar to this day.

While my mother was an acclaimed dentist, I nonetheless clearly recall those times when as a frightened patient, dreading the anesthetic injections, I would battle Mamá for control at the dental chair. Despite my shrieks and tears, she would win. She practiced in an office complete with state-of-the-art equipment. The dental drill of the times was non-electric to suit its use where electricity was unavailable. The drilling burr revolutions were effected by a foot pedal. Often, on return home from school, I provided the pedal power in her stead. I wonder today how well my foot might have contributed to her patient's comfort. Mamá also was a gifted pianist, a talent that she tried hard to develop in her children; all my sisters practiced their lessons religiously and could play the piano far better than I. She also doubled as disciplinarian. In those early years, children's misdeeds incurred penalties and corporeal punishment. She dispensed mine by either manually spanking my butt or by having me kneel before a crucifix, located in their bedroom. Although I didn't question her justice, I did succumb to plotting mischievous ways to neutralize the penalty. Once, feeling abused by being at the butt end of her spanking, however infrequent and mild they actually were, I announced at the dinner table that I had bundled up my favorite short pants together with a can of sardines and was prepared to "run away" after supper. However, the thought of trudging in the dark on the way to Tio Fernando's house for refuge and having to pass by the large acacia tree where elves or ghosts reputedly lurked at night did test my mettle. A few steps out on the street, I changed my mind. I don't recall a rousing welcome home. Nor can I say that I got the "I told you so…" lecture.

THE RELATIVES

My maternal grandparents were José Alonso and wife Crispina nee Reynes. I would refer to them as *Lolo Otíc* and *Lola Empíng*, *lolo* and *lola* being terms of endearment and respect for grandpa and grandma. Quite notably, Lolo Otíc, a local politician, was among those selected to the Philippine Assembly of 1907 to draft the Philippine Legislature, after the country became an American colony in 1898.

They had four other offspring besides my mother. Each was educated in the professions. The eldest, Eugenio—*Tio Nené*—was a physician and my godfather; the youngest, Nestor—*Tio Nestór*—was a veterinarian; and, sisters Anunsacion—*Tia Anún* and Elnora—*Tia Noríng* were school teachers. All my uncles and aunts were addressed as *tio* and *tia*; notably, in their stead, "tito" and "tita" would find more universal use by post-WWII generations of Filipinos. They resided in Cebu where the Alonso family had lived for a long time. Tio Nené and his wife, a daughter of the politically prominent Sergio Osmeña who would become president of the Commonwealth of the Philippines in 1944, were separated shortly after the birth of their second child. The two children, Raul, who was a year younger than me, and Diana, thereafter lived with my grandparents. I regarded Raul as a city-slicker and always felt obliged to defer to his aphorisms. What seemed incongruous to me, over which I would snicker in secret, was his fear of the actors projected on the movie screen, enlarged as they were. He had mentally encoded them as super-giants. For the longest time, Raul would watch only Shirley Temple movies, covering his eyes most of the time when having to see other actors. We attended movies at my favorite theater, the delightfully air-conditioned Vision Theatre.

My grandparents always seemed to have a houseful of company, particularly on Sundays when the many aunts, uncles, and cousins would gather. The adults clustered around tables playing *mahjong*, a game of chance and betting using finely carved ivory tiles, a legacy from the Chinese. Their house was large enough to make hide-and-seek games with oodles of cousins very interesting, fun and challenging. They enjoyed having grandchildren putter with them in the food preparations. Meals were well-attended and sumptuous. I always looked forward to the *lechón de leche*, vying to be among the first of the cousins to taste the crispy skin and the brain. We all believed the latter as the unquestioned food that added immeasurably to one's brain power and intelligence. Those of us who helped the most, particularly in hand-cranking the ice-cream maker, or was it simply those who misbehaved the least, had priority to the brain. Aside from the roasted piglet, there were dishes of squid cooked in its ink, snails, lobster, shrimp, pig's blood, rice-based *paella*—each a derivative of Spanish cuisine; and, of the Chinese dishes were recipes of rice noodle-based preparations named *pansit* and soups in a mixture of rice, vegetables, chicken, pork and seafoods. Filipino preparations of the seemingly infinitesimal variety of fishes were a frequent part of the meal, always accompanied by boiled rice and, on occasion, corn meal.

Lola Emping was extravagant with her love and tenderness. However, those qualities did not keep her from twisting ears of any errant grandchild. Since those years, I have often ascribed my pendulous ear lobes to my youthful antics and Lola Emping's endearing form of discipline. Many decades later, on a poignant visit with her, after years of absence for reasons I clarify on a later chapter, she would tweak a sentimental cord in me when she lovingly greeted me by pulling and twisting my ear. My Cebu visits would usually be capped by Lolo Otic taking me to a favorite 5 and 10-cent store where there was a counter filled with trinkets. He would let me choose any two of the knick-knacks of my liking, usually toy mechanical vehicles made in Japan.

*Seated, L to R: Eugenio Alonso, MD, Lola Emping, Lolo Otic,
Nestor Alonso, DVM
Standing: Lenora A.-Jesus Paras, DDS, Anunsacion A.-Juan
Alburo, Adelina A., DDS-Gregorio Yrastorza, MD*

To visit them took an eight-hour seafarer's crossing from
Ormoc. Arriving in Cebu was always so impressive. The wharf was
expansive, busy with varied-sized boats and steamers moving in
and out of the harbor, their horns at times sounding like a cacoph-
onic brass band. Awaiting the disembarking passengers were the
tartanillas, and even, taxis for transportation. *Cargadores*, those men
who physically unloaded and loaded cargo were everywhere, out-
bidding each other to carry the load. The beehive of activities always
added to the anticipation of a different, more modern community
and an exciting visit away from Ormoc. The streets of the city were
wide, paved. Extra wide ones were called avenues, one of which was
a delightful sight for being lined on both sides of its length with
one mango tree after another: Mango Avenue. The well-decorated
tartanilla gave the traffic an ogling mix with that of the automobiles. I did not get to ride in one of the latter until I was eight years
old; it was a Studebaker owned and pampered by Lolo Otic.

The farthest car ride I took was whenever my grandparents
packed a load of cousins for a vacation to Asturias, a sleepy seaside

village on the opposite, northwestern side of the island, about fifty miles from the city. It was a day-long journey and a hazardous trip. We traversed through craggy mountainous ridges that jutted in-between the narrow, serpentine roadway which, at some points, was a mere ledge carved on the side of a deep precipice. Nonetheless, it was the company that always made the trip exciting and had preconditioned each of us to savor those delightful pastoral interludes. I recall that along the way in that crowded car, there were the periodic breaks that had everyone scattering by the roadside for personal relief. Also, there were the unexpected stops to care for the nauseated, which invariably included my sister Fenny. Of course, the din of the passengers would range from boisterous laughter to serious crying. Another attraction which Lolo Otic felt obliged to show was located downtown. It was a structure that housed a Christian crucifix that Magellan—actual or replicate is still unresolved in my mind—had planted on April 1521. Meanwhile, in Ormoc, Papá finally bought a used model-T Ford when I was nine years old. Then, the car rides were mostly limited about the town's environs. They were thrilling and titillating. I was always seated in the rear rumble seat and looked forward to a joyfully wind-blown rumpled hair on return home.

My paternal grandparents were Ricardo Torres Yrastorza and Fortunata nee Carillo or, as they were always addressed, *Lolo Cadó and Lola Tatang*. Although my maternal grandparents had lived well past my adolescent years, such was not the case with Papá's parents. They had both died before I was old enough to remember: my lolo on the 20th June 1932 at 78 years of age and Lola Tatang on 6th January 1937 when 53 years old. Much of what I know about them came from storytelling, from accounts recounted in get-togethers of relatives and from photographs. One of the photos well-impressed on my mind was of a group dourly looking at a casket in which Lolo Cadó was to be interred. I was among the observers, a child just one year old. I was held at Papá's waistline and he appeared to be directing my attention to the visible countenance of Lolo Cadó. I, of course, have no recollection of the event.

As mournful as the rest of those in the photograph appeared to be, I always imagined how easily they could have been emoting raw trepidation of the macabre. You see, in Ormoc where story-telling was practiced to an art form, there was a ghoulish anecdote which circulated freely. It was an account of a person who upon being declared dead was prepared for burial. While laid in an open casket, surrounded by mourners praying at the wake, he suddenly arose. Everyone scattered in horror, fright and disbelief. The yarn attributed the person to have only lost consciousness, perhaps in a coma. He had been declared dead in error by the doctor whose limited expertise was very likely no worse than that of his peers of those times. This was a well-known anecdote I repeatedly heard throughout my elementary school years. It was a favorite story recounted by *Tio Luis* Carillo, who was Lola Tatang's brother. It must surely have been a choice yarn long before Lolo Cadó's fune-real group gathering. It became my convenient excuse since I grew up wanting to avoid funerals. On those rare, inevitable occasions, I would sneak a vigilant eye on the corpse, leaving a respectable distance between the casket and me, the better to outrun others in case of a surprise reawakening. The yarn actually went on to declare that after living a few more years, the person subsequently died, truly died. This time, however, the customary gathering of mourners were sparse; most people in town, although bereaved, hesitating to risk re-witnessing a mere mortal's resuscitation.

Lolo Cadó was a Spaniard, a Basque. Tracing his heritage is akin to becoming familiar with Spain's historic relation to the Philippines. His family was known to have come from their ancestral region of northern Spain's Basque Country, commonly referred as *País Vasco*. There, in areas of the beautiful mountain ranges of the Pyrenees are frequent fields of fern; it is by the abundance of the plant that the early kin had originally adopted the Yrastorza surname to signify the land of ferns.

As did many fellow-compatriots who envisioned adventure and a better life in the colonies, Lolo Cado's grandparents had cho-sen the Islas their destination. On a ship then plying its way to the colony, his Papá, Gregorio, is said to have been born on 2nd March 1820. Had the family been among the Spaniard residents in Mexico for a period before migrating to the Islas? With Mexico embroiled in battles against Spain between 1810 to 1821 before it declared Independence, could one reasonably speculate that some Spaniard residents, concerned for their own safety and well-being, would uproot and chose the Islas as their safe harbor? Or had the family immigrated directly from Pais Vasco, transited via Mexico and boarded a ship to the Islas? But the Galleon trade terminated in 1815. Had shipping continued between Mexican and Filipino ports? In either event, the trip would have been lengthy and arduous. Did Gregorio have siblings? Sadly, even if Papá had known of his grandfather's beginnings, I don't recall any attributive conversation. The answers to the puzzles will remain a mystery.

Gregorio's parents settled in Ormoc where he grew up and married another Spaniard, Ana Torres. They had seven offspring: Ricardo-Lolo Cadó, Manuel, Maria, Guadalupe, Rosa, and Luisa. Emilia, the seventh, would marry Paulino Aboitiz whom Gregorio had initial employed to manage his enterprising shipping and trading enterprise. Subsequently, Paulino established his own shipping business which, in time, importantly contributed to the development of a major commercial and maritime network of today. The Aboitiz family was destined to join the rarefied few, important, and powerful trail blazers of the Philippine economic foundation.

Lolo Cadó himself remained in Ormoc. During his adulthood, it was a port for the transport of hemp and abaca processed in Leyte for use in Cebu; he likely was employed in the enterprise. He sired a total of seven children with two separate lovers before marrying the last of the Filipina flowers he was to gather: Lola Tatang when she was twenty years old and he was fifty years old. He was ever-ready to charm them all by serenading with his concertina accordion. A photograph of Lolo Cadó that survived the decades was of a handsome face with a paintbrush moustache that well projected an imposing look of one descendant of colonists of the era;

Ricardo Torres Yrastorza, circa 1920s.

Lola Tatang was a demure woman of small stature with the kind features of a Filipina. She was of the Carillo family whose ancestry seemed to me had no foreign mixture. As his wife, she bore my father on 10th July 1903. Papá always described her as a hard-worker, committed to providing every assistance necessary to ensure her son's successful, extended education, even taking in laundry to augment income.

Also, by Papá's account, she was at once generous and motherly to her stepchildren. Of her stepdaughters, Lucrecia married Andres Polancos, and *Tia Luisa* married Edward Greene. They were alive during my adolescent years. Maria and Cristita were spinsters and unknown to me. Her two stepsons were Teodoro—*Tio Dinoy*—and *Tio Joaquin*; both tied their future work to the Aboitiz conglomerate in Cebu. The third and oldest, Rafael—*Tio Paeng*—remained in Ormoc as a sugar planter.

Tio Dinoy and his wife *Tia Julia* lived in Cebu. I looked forward to staying at their house. Their four boys and two girls were my close friends. Eriberto—*Berting*, the second eldest was one we all agreed showed early promise. He had constructed a scale model of their house out of matchsticks; the finished work of art was thereafter prominently displayed in their living room to our amazement. This feat he accomplished at a time of our lives when the rest of us were content to have made a kite that could fly or felt ingenuous to have fashioned a sling-shot from fairly symmetrical branches of a guava tree. Berting would join the Aboitiz conglomerate before establishing his own furniture manufacturing enterprise. He married a gifted, intelligent, energetic pediatrician who would be among the elite leaders of the Philippine medical world: Vivina Chiu. Of his other siblings Mariano, the eldest became a mariner, to his father's delight; Julian married a U.S. Peace Corps volunteer, Cathi Collar; Norma married Eddie Porter and together would found a successful anchorage and dockside maintenance facility for private yachts in the city outskirts; Andrea, now resides in California. The youngest of the siblings, Benjamin, as did Mariano, Eriberto and Norma, died before or shortly after the turn of the twenty-first century. Those cousins always made the sojourn livelier and not without mischief.

Tio Joaquin and his wife, *Tia Mediong* also lived in Cebu. They had six offspring: two sons, Carlos now deceased and Joaquin, Jr. The eldest of the girls, Milagros, married Teofilo Tan and remains in Cebu. Another, Cecilia—*Celing*—married Romeo Hermosilla and raised a family in Ormoc; Mario, one of their now orphaned children, joined the US Navy and on retirement led an influential organization of expatriates in southern California: Ormocanon Circle U.S.A. The third, Ana Maria—*Maring*—married a lawyer from Mindanao, Honorio Villaranda; she would become a faculty member of the Xavier University of Cagayan de Oro, once the Ateneo de Cagayan. One of their daughters, Yvonne, would become a stewardess for United Airlines, marry and reside in

Colorado. The youngest of the females, Remedios—*Remy*—now resides in California.

Tio Paeng and his wife Maria nee Kierulf—*Tia Mary*, lived on the block next to my house with their family of six children. The youngest of the girls and boys, Alicia and Ricardo, nicknamed *Baby* and *Dadíng* respectively, were a couple years on either side of my age. Baby was more Fenny's playmate and Dadíng mine.

Beside Tio Paéng's house lived the Moraza family. The parents, Basque-descendant physician Tio Fernando and his Spaniard wife *Tia* Elena nee Miciano were related because his mother was my paternal grandfather's sister. They had six children. Three, Angel, Lupe, and Eduardo died before their adolescent years. Two girls, *Rosarito* who was my schoolmate and *Teresita*, a playmate and friend of my sisters had an elder brother, Ramon—*Ramoning*—who was three years older than I. He was to spend his elementary school years in Cebu City living with one of his Aboitiz relations. I was with him infrequently. But our paths would cross years later. For the school term in 1947-48, we were fellow-boarders at a Jesuit high school located in Cagayan, a town of northern Mindanao. Even more heartwarming, and quite by serendipity, decades later we would again reconnect while settled in such disparate continents as Australia and North America, respectively.

ST. PETER'S ACADEMY

Ormoc had a number of public elementary schools and a single high school. Fr. Cataag, the parish priest, succeeded in attracting Benedictine nuns from Germany to staff a parochial school, the St. Peter's Academy. It was built adjacent to the Church in 1914. The nuns had earned the reputation as dedicated educators and no-nonsense disciplinarians. The latter threatening renown, even if dubious, was not lost on me since the town gossip had it efficiently circulated as to reach anyone within earshot of storytellers. Families able to afford the tuition did prefer to enroll their children in the private school. At age six, I was matriculated a first grader, fearful of those nuns. My first day of school, I compelled my mother to take leave of her dental patients in order to accompany me and my caretaker, Patricia. They escorted me all the way to the classroom. I did not want to go to school. On hindsight, however, the environment the "sisters" provided was valuable. It influenced my personal growth, deportment and upbringing.

Of the many nuns on the faculty, Sister Editha had a most lasting impact on me. It prevailed throughout the elementary-grade years. As the teacher of English, presenting grammar with a special flair for spelling and phonics, she was uncompromising and thorough. Most of the time, however, everyone in school felt she relished more her role of school disciplinarian. For instance, with a ruler in hand, she begun the first class of the morning with everyone seated while she passed in review to check for dirty hands; off to the washroom the offender would go, after getting the whack on the hand. In the classroom, idle chatter among classmates while the teacher was busy chalking and erasing the blackboard with important information, was often an inviting distraction. This would annoy Sr. Editha to the point of losing her saintly virtues. With the same ruler, she was ever ready to whack an errant student in the back, the butt her favorite site; and, she would twist an ear with a glint in her eye that she couldn't always succeed in hiding.

To this day, I vividly remember how my classmates and I were convinced that in the back of her head, hidden behind that white veil that encircled her face, was an extra set of eyes. How else could she have known which of us she would turn around, take a deadly aim, and throw the eraser right smack at our head—all in the blink of an eye! At merely five feet tall with horn-rimmed eyeglasses to complete a stern-looking face, Sister Editha's penetrating eyeball-to-eyeball admonitions were occasions to be avoided. Only a few evaded her attention. I did not. Once, for having been caught talking to a seatmate while she discoursed about how certain words were to be pronounced, I got to kneel by the doorway during recess, having already tallied enough demerits against my good behavior. What might have only been minutes seemed to me hours, made worse by the taunting jeers of schoolmate passers-by.

Recess was our favorite time. It was spent mostly in the square enclosed by the C-shaped, 2-storey building which was filled with classrooms, the library, and the nun's cloisters. Not only were the chatter and jostling at their peak, despite the constraints imposed by the nuns' disciplinary edicts on good conduct, the elder boys liked to parade slowly among girls seated on benches that wrapped around the shade trees. Each one hoping to spy those not wearing underwear—more often they were schoolmates coming from the rural barrios. I only got in on the gossip, never actually witnessed the "thrill" even once, despite the trying.

At home, Binisayá and Spanish were the *lingua franca;* I spoke them as a matter of course without the benefit of formal lessons or books. Throughout the seven thousand islands, which in time would be organized into seventy-nine provinces, Binisayá is one of seventy-two spoken dialects. However, at St. Peter's Academy and within Sr. Editha's earshot, conversational tones among students would understandably hush since on campus we were compelled to converse in English. Speaking the dialect risked incurring a demerit. Demerits would accumulate to beget the penitent a variety of penances that included saying the rosary and having a contemplative timeout before the crucifix on bended knees. My sisters and I spoke English as we acquired the know-how at school.

Sr. Editha rarely excused anyone found wandering the hallways aimlessly except at recess. Having already determined how long it took to leave the classroom and return from the communal outhouse toilet area, she was implacable. Once there happened an exception. It was on an unforgettable mid-morning when I was nine years old. A solitary airplane flew across the Ormoc skies. It had been the first such sighting for most people of Ormoc, even for the town elders, who were to retell the event for years thereafter. Where the airplane came from or where it was going seemed unimportant. What was captivating, so enrapturing was the sound of the whirling propeller forward of the starkly beautiful flying object that seemed so high in the sky. The entire student population, en masse, threw discretion to the wind and rushed out of the classrooms to cluster around the inner yard in utter awe. I, for one, excitedly witnessed the happening, following its silhouette and sound till it disappeared in the distant horizon. If memory serves me right, the remaining morning classes were canceled to allow us all ample time to savor the momentous milestone.

The school curriculum and the extra-curricular activities of St. Peter's Academy were ambitious, if not complete. In addition to the prescribed courses, the arts were taught, beginning with fourth grade. There were classes in drawing, piano with recitals, choir and plays. I looked forward to drawing but found excuses to miss piano lessons though I participated in piano recitals, without distinction; opted out of choir to become one of the acolytes in its stead. I was a cast member of a few musical plays. Of the few lay teachers I had, I only remember one other, Mister Moncada. I recall him as a dedicated, patient and caring individual. He taught third grade.

The most extravagantly produced play that remains in my memory showcased a minuet. I was cast along with two other boys and three girls. All of us fourth graders were costumed in Victorian outfits, complete with wigs; two others of the cast I recall were my cousin Rosarito Moraza and a friend, Alicia Serafica. Romy Lladoc, my closest friend, was also included. From the rousing applause that the performance received and the repeated bows we took in response, that play must have been a resounding success. I have often wondered if today, some of us cast members can boast of having had thespian ventures thereafter. Of course, our audience then was well-peppered with, if not mostly attended by parents, cousins, relatives, and friends.

Students from Grade I to Grade VII of the elementary years and those of the four-year High School began the day assembled in the yard. There, in front of two flag poles, the standards of the Commonwealth of the Philippines and the United States of America were raised as we sang both national anthems. Throughout all the years at school, neither I nor any of the other schoolmates ever thought odd that the American anthem began by asking, "Oh José, can you see…" Sister Editha never returned to her native Germany. On her request, she is interred in Ormoc.

HALCYON TIMES OF ORMOC

Kitty-corner from our house was a free-flowing artesian well that provided potable water and served to rinse off salt-water after a dip in the sea. I preferred rinsing there to showering at home, contrary to Mama's wishes. The Lladoc family of five children lived beside the artesian well. Their pharmacy, run by pharmacist Mrs. Lladoc, occupied the first level; the family quarters were on the second floor. Romy was my best friend. We shared countless hours resting on branches of their fruit tree or flying kites at the beach in front of my house, discussing mundane concerns as other school children elsewhere must likewise have done, or so we had imagined. It was with Romy that, one day, we stretched a thread between our houses, both end of which were tethered to an empty talcum powder cardboard box. The devise was our telephone. We thoughtfully hoped the innovation would bring us to the level of Cebu City's modernity. Actually, our vision of the world went past Cebu. A favorite fantasy we often shared lying on the beach was to turn into birds, fly away, land on a cruising ship to rest, then continuing on to distant lands where wonders of the world were located. On return to Ormoc, we then imagined transforming back to our physical selves to share the excitement of the tour with envious relatives and friends, when congregating on the late afternoon paseó on the pier.

It was on one of my pier walks that I had my first real life-threatening scare. I had just turned eight. On that early afternoon, I had yanked free a stalk of sugar cane from a slow-moving truck loaded with cut canes on its way to the southern outskirt of town where the sugar-mill was located. The product the cane produced at the mill was sugar in varying degrees of refinement; one particular by-product was a gooey toffee of molasses that we ate as candy called *tira-tira*.

The hauling trucks did customarily drive by our house. As I had done on other such occasions, I used my teeth to peel the tough, segmented covering skin, thereby un-husking the cane fibers. Once un-husked, I would then bite off and chew portions of the cane to express the saccharine-sweet juice in the process. It was a deed which would lead to decay of my front teeth. On that afternoon, I was happily gnawing on the cane, daydreaming with the images the clouds overhead had formed. As I was walking down the steps on the side of the pier to get closer to water's edge, I slipped. And promptly dumped into the water. Although I felt I was bobbing in and out of the surface, my arms were vainly swinging to reach for something to grab. Instead, all I managed to do was to swallow briny water. I was drowning. After a seemingly interminable interlude, a kindly samaritan passerby reached over to grab me by the hair, pulled me upright so I felt my feet touching bottom. To his surprise and my embarrassment, I found myself standing in water no deeper than my neck! Not yet knowing how to swim, I apparently was kneeling while frantically trying to stay above water. After thanking my savior for sparing my life, I hastily returned home before a crowd of onlookers could gather. I nodded in meek agreement with his parting advice to learn how to swim.

Later that year, I had learned to swim and the table would turn on me. My cousin Eddie came from his home in Manila to stay for a visit. His father was Edward Greene, an American soldier who was stationed in the Philippines where he remained after the end of World War I, as did many of his veteran colleagues; Tia Luisa was his mother. They named their only offspring after him. One day Eddie and I went for a swim. We jumped off the pier close to the steps from which I had accidentally fallen years past, not too far from shore. We were floating lazily toward shallow water when Eddie started flailing his arms in a panic. His stomach muscles were cramping, and he was doubling over in pain. He yelled for help, afraid he was going to drown. I was frightened. Being two years younger and built far lighter than he, my instinct was to avoid getting caught in his embrace. Instead, I found myself nudging him from behind, urging that he keep paddling with his arms. Thankfully, we didn't have to tread long before touching bottom. Safely at home, Mamá would admonish us with the advice handed her by her parents who may have likely heard it from her own parents: swim no sooner than one whole hour after eating or risk abdominal cramps. Eddie and I had filled up with sugarcoated fried bananas before taking the swim. Decades later, I would find myself repeating the same advice to my children, amused to garner the same questioning look I must have given Mamá.

LORES AND TRADITIONS

Anecdotes of ghosts are a part of Filipino folklore. One recounted a scene that involved the town cemetery located on a hilltop just outside of town. Back then, the cemetery plots were unclearly marked. If there were entombment policies, they were laxly obeyed. As a result, there were occasional graves dug too shallow so that with the annual torrential rain storms, the eroding top soil would uncover the coffin, which was sometimes in varying degrees of decomposition as to expose its insides. The same rains cascading downhill pot-marked the unpaved road such that the ascent was near impossible for motor vehicles; walking was more the common mode. The roadway and the cemetery itself was unlit. A night-time visit was uninviting and foreboding. Further, the whistling winds coming from the sea tended to compete with the crickets and other such noises to add to an eerie mood.

One night, the story was told, a group of Spanish soldiers encamped in town during the colonial era, were drunkenly boasting of their bravery and skepticism of the supernatural. On a bet, one of them agreed to go to the cemetery and hammer a nail in a known wooden cross in the center of all the grave sites. To further prove his daring, the act was to be accomplished by beginning his ascent as the church bells rang at midnight. The following morning with the betting soldier now absent at roll-call, a search party climbed to the cemetery. They found the soldier, pulse-less and sprawled with his coat-tail nailed to the cross. It was deduced that by having accidentally nailed his coattail in the dark, the victim had mistakenly believed a ghost had held him to the cross. A heart attack from fright had caused his untimely downfall. A tragic-comedy!

Story telling in those times was not only to scare children. It was also a way by which we could escape from our insular environment and take vicarious delight in imagining the fascinating happenings away from Ormoc. So it was, for instance, that someone returning from a trip to Cebu would feel imposed to share the experience with awaiting friends and relatives. Those lucky enough to have taken in a motion picture show would assuredly attract a ready crowd eager to hear about the movie, in detail and with dramatic storytelling aplomb. Tio Fernando, who went to Spain to pursue graduate studies in obstetrics, was a favored story teller. With such impeccable credentials, he always attracted a large gathering of nephews and nieces. His anecdotes and yarns invariably included tales of distant lands and their different customs. We often sat on the front steps of his house, enraptured by accounts that invariably included references to Spain. He would rivet our attention, challenge the imagination, and, to me, tweak my continuing longings to travel.

Fiesta in most towns was an annual celebration. It was another custom ascribed to the Spanish. It held religious connotations and civic importance. Our Fiesta, coinciding with the feast day of the patron saints Peter and Paul, would be on the last weekend of June. The church bells brought on the festivities by ringing with abandon. The church itself would be brim-full with celebrants at each of the multiple Masses. A special procession for the occasion would start and end by the municipal building, just opposite of the church. The parish priest invariably led the march, preceded and trailed by a body of altar boys. Floats of religious statues, a platoon of Army soldiers, the full complement of high-school cadets from St. Peter's Academy, and, the troops of Boy Scouts and Cub Scouts completed the parade participants. I became a Cub Scout at age eight and joined the parades thereafter. All participants would trail the floats with church statues, marching to the accompaniment of a band. Those out-of-step marchers invariably were the object of friendly teasing from the onlookers. And, of course, from the reviewing stands, the town dignitaries waved and smiled their approval.

Other attractions were the traditional folk dances performed accompanied by music of indigenous renown. Among them was the *tinikling*: a hop-skip dance made tricky by jumping in rhythm before slapping bamboo sticks; it was open to participation by anyone of the audience willing to risk trapping non-synchronous ankle between those slapping poles. Then, at yet another exhibition, the dancers would gyrate and whirl gracefully with a lighted candle atop the head and contorting their arms while balancing liquid-filled cups held steady on open palms. The folk dance was named *Kuratsa*. The entertainment was popularly awaited and always assured a giggling audience, adding to the festive ambiance.

Another was the "Talent Show," a show-case for local amateurs that was a prelude to the principal attraction of the day, invariably, a traveling troupe of show-business talents brought to town from Manila or more likely from nearer Cebu City. One year, Romy and I were among a group of contestants. We had practiced for days in preparation for our singing debut. Romy was confident he could mask his off-key voice by grabbing and wiggling his throat-skin to produce a vibrato sound; I was the tenor. Because of the number of entrants, the judges were permitted to ring a bell at any time they felt a contestant could be justifiably disqualified, thereby curtailing completion of the avowed talent number. We were outfitted with caps fashioned like those worn by sailors to set the mood of our song: Anchors Aweigh. On cue, we came on-stage. There, facing the crowd assembled in that block-square in front of the church, we sang. We stole side-glances at each other and feeling sure winners, particularly since we had begun the song, *a capella* and in unison. The judges reasoned otherwise. Before we had completed the first stanza, we got the gong! Crushed and dejected? Maybe. Enjoyed the opportunity? Yup! In addition, our pals rewarded our effort with extravagant back-slaps. Adequate reward!

Another popular Fiesta that was celebrated every twenty-fourth of June is in memory of yet another saint considered the patron of swimmers; appropriately, St. John the Baptist. On that day, town folks would swarm to the seashore, prepared to feast and bathe. Picnicking meant food to last the day for everyone. The selection of viands and piles of cooked rice would be laid on large banana leaves and eaten by hand, squatted. Grownup drinks, for the adventuresome, included the fermented coconut liquor, *tubá*. Many of those going for a dip in the sea carried with them a banana tree trunk cut from its roots and the leafy end. On water, the buoyant log would serve as a float to straddle or tread beside. I think lounging in that manner may have been preferable to active swimming in order to allow feasting and avoid cramps from a full stomach.

MOMENTOUS PRE-ADOLESCENT YEARS

In 1939, I was eight years old, ready to take my First Communion, the culmination of hours of preparatory catechism sessions. Not the least of the preparations was for the First Confession. To be ready, I had listed my venial sins on a piece of paper, anxious not to omit any of them; my examination of conscience had failed to uncover any mortal sin. Father Cataág, our parish priest, had granted First Confession candidates the privilege of kneeling, not in the privacy of the curtained side cubicle of the confessional booth but rather in front of him. While nervously whispering my sins, I can still see him reach into my shirt pocket and unfold my prepared list of sins. It allowed him to corroborate the extent of my transgressions and even helped me recall others I failed, unintentionally, to mention. Confession tête-á-tête was a privileged concession that I have ever since declined to exercise, preferring the privacy and anonymity of the cloistered section of the confessional.

Romy Lladoc also was among the First Communicants. That day, we affirmed our long-planned wish to be ordained parish priests although I also harbored a wish to be a chaplain in the army, fascinated as I was with yarns of their heroic exploits in Mindanao. They were described in mythic, epic-like clashes with Moros, Muslims who then we regarded with suspicion and fear for their allegedly professed secessionist ambitions and Islamic jihadist proclivity. Conventional thought of the time regarded them as distant from Christianized Filipinos with a historic propensity to raid vulnerable communities of the islands to capture non-Muslims for slave-trade with nearby Brunei to the south. Once, I recall sighting a vinta—a Moro vessel powered by a

colorful sail for inter-island passenger transport-harmlessly plying across the bay. Admitedly, a peaceful non-event but our mis-
informed views prevailed. Long-held suspisions seem difficult to
erase. Regardless, longing to become a priest or a nun was a most
likely ambition among male and female youngsters being raised
Catholics. The yearning would be the triumphant, captivating
return for the avid catechism instructions, and, the answer of the
prayers of parents. But, like yearling cubs finding other pastures
as they mature and broaden their horizons, most would eventually favor other life choices.

First Communion Sunday the day after First Confession,
was very special. I deported the day with piety, feeling blessed
for having swallowed the host whole, conscious to keep from
chewing the body of Christ, which had been transubstantiated through the sacramental blessing of Father Cataág.

Dressed in white on the occasion of my First
Communion at St. Peter & Paul Catholic Church.

My parents rewarded me an unusually large amount of *turron*, a nougat specially imported from Spain, to eat all day long. I surely must have shared with my sisters. Treats from foreign sources I particularly regarded as delicious. Actually, native desserts were abounding and delectable, their ingredients ranging from coconuts, pineapples, bananas, yams, corn, guava, to sticky rice cakes.

In late 1939, Ormoc's first movie house with talking pictures was inaugurated. The only theater until then was a cramped, nearly suffocating place where personal comfort was gained only by fanning one's self. A pianist at the front row provided music accompaniment to the otherwise silent moving pictures with the actors' dialogue in succinct English sub-titles. I had gone there once. The modern movie house, located a couple blocks from our home was a joint venture of my parents and Tio Paéng.

Being the children of the co-owners of Ormoc's movie house did have its privileges. There were many days when I would stop by the theater after school for a few minutes, if only to catch a quick glimpse of a cowboy series, usually starring Ken Maynard or Tom Mix. Some weekends, I would be allowed to catch a full-length show. One I particularly remember watching with cousins Dading and Baby. It featured, the always frightening Boris Karloff. It scared each of us so much we trembled out of the movie house. We all went straight to their parent's bedroom, hid under the covers and each of us finagling to be between the others. We expected Boris to appear at any moment to haunt us. I got home that evening escorted by my parents rather than risk the one block walk home alone. I must have slept with them that night. The memory now seems hilarious.

Happily, it was from watching a Tarzan movie one day that I eventually learned to swim in the sea in front of our house, spending many after-school afternoons mimicking the breast stroke, ala Tarzan. Mamá did discourage prolonged exposure to the sun, afraid more that I would tan darkly than that I would have a mishap swimming all by myself. The sea then seemed free of pollution, the bottom sand transparent to the naked eye and when wading by the shore, I could easily trap live tiny shrimps by scooping water with an empty saltine cracker tin container.

It was comforting to have some of the modernities that the nearby big city of Cebu enjoyed. In town, electric power was now available from noon up to the early evening hours. It added to the gas-powered flammable lamps albeit, food refrigeration would remain using the icebox. One day, coming back from school, I noticed a large rectangular wooden box in the living room. Both parents were in the lower floor attending to their patients. Alone, I curiously opened the panel doors and tinkered with the circular knobs. By miracle, a choir almost instantly came singing from inside the box. I must have tuned in toward the end of the song because the announcer then identified the station. I turned the knob some more and shut the radio off. I did not want to get caught playing with something I wasn't supposed to. That evening, before I could share my misadventure, my parents proudly announced the new possession and explained how it was able to tune in to the Voice of Cebu. Thankfully, I got informed before I could describe my own suspicions about the radio. You see, I had heard the announcer to say "The Boys" rather than "The Voice" of Cebu and promptly imagined that housed inside that big wooden box were miniature, gifted midgets—perhaps elves—singing the tune. To shed light on my misinterpretation, Binisayá, like all the other dialects is based on an alphabet that, without the letter "v" or "f" may cause substituting "b" and "p," respectively. For instance, the word *voice* to the Filipino ear may sound or is mispronounced as *boys* and *favor* as *pahbor*. Even today, the Filipino alphabet differs from the English by not having the consonants: c, f, j, q, v, and x. When speaking in English, the Filipino speech may manifest the peculiar difference by having difficulty pronouncing "f" or "v". Paradoxically, it may cause a "p" to "f" or "b" to "v" inversion. Additionally, the dialects do not use distinguishing personal pronouns; when speaking English, "she" and "he", "her" and " him" may be misused. Regardless, having another of the advanced technological inventions, as the radio was, did add pleasure to our lives. My family spent many evenings together around the dining room table, our ears perked to the music it emitted while shelling and eating mounds of freshly roasted or boiled peanuts.

Later that same year, the Aboitiz conglomerate inaugurated a fifty-passenger ship to ply regularly between Cebu City and Ormoc. Tio Dinóy was its skipper. On Sundays the bells of the campanile seemed to strike more melodiously than on other days, rousing the town at six in the morning; on daily occasions, the bells would also signal the noonday, the *Angelus* at six o'clock, and finally midnight. The horns of the interisland ship would blow in competition with the early bell-ringing, to announce its arrival from Cebu as early as six-o'clock. Since the ship did not depart till the late evening hours, Tio Dinóy would sometimes undock the ship and drop anchor a nautical mile or so into the bay. There, complete with a live band, Ormoc's invited society people would spend the day in dance and feasting while we children frolicked with abandon, diving and swimming off a platform starboard-side. Those dance steps, probably imported from Cebu, would include the rhumba, the congo, the waltz. Many of the invitees were the Spanish-descendant families so that the conversations were invariably trilingual: Binisayá, Spanish and English. Tio Dinóy, the skipper, enabled his family and my cousins easy, frequent visits with us. In turn, I traveled to Cebu, shipboard, to visit my grandparents and the various relatives more often.

Perhaps, planning to profit from the anticipated increase in the number of out-of-town visitors that the inter-island trade would bring, my parents opened a modest-sized, two-storey business establishment called the Seaside Hotel. The ground it was built on was between our house and the beach; it provided guests, in our stead, the magnificent bay view. I recall its grand room with tables along its edges, a center space for dancing, and a piano and phonograph in one corner. There were many evenings when

I would sneak a peek at grown-ups dancing the latest craze, most often the tango or the waltz, depending on the tune the phonograph was playing. On more than one Sunday, in the quiet of the afternoon, I sat in the large dining room of the Seaside Hotel transfixed by the sight and sound of Mamá playing the piano to accompany the brothers Tio Dinóy and Papá singing song after song. I always felt comforted by their fellowship and togetherness as well as the affection for each other. The memory of those occasions is brought afresh today when in my home, my own children would gather by the piano in song and glee.

The hotel did lead to changes in many communal activities of Ormoc. One of them was by our beach-front. In the past, daily, a group of fishermen would paddle two outrigger *bancas*—narrow-beamed canoes made of select native tree with bilateral outriggers of bamboo to balance and improve floatation. On reaching some distance from shore, they would lower a gigantic net, the ends held by each banca. Slowly paddling to shore, they would land in that stretch of beach by our house. Two land-based larger groups about a yelling distance apart would then gather the netting, pulling on its ends. From the crowd that often gathered in anticipation of the catch, many would lend their brawn to help bring in the haul. Youngsters were always eager to join in the action; whenever possible, I did. That net always seemed loaded with wiggling fish of varying sizes. Although the custom continued, the boats later landed at a rocky shoal some distance from our house, after the hotel was built. Beside the group fishing, there were solitary fishermen who ventured in a smaller banca. Anchored overnight in the middle of the bay, they would weather rain, wind and waves. Their presence, a single flickering oil lantern, would dot the bay expanse. Their collective catch likely added to the fish supply.

The year 1939 ended with my ninth birthday. It was only days after when I became aware of Mary Sala. She was easily ten or more years older. I was infatuated with the most beautiful woman in the world. Right then, Mary added another to my many reasons for choosing the priesthood. In my world and naiveté, it was only by becoming a priest, returning to the Ormoc parish and having Mary come to the confessional could I envision having the chance or temerity to converse with her. Silly puppy love! That's how my best friend Romy dismissed my invigorated yen for the priesthood, not thoroughly impressed with my newfound motive. I always regarded him, even in those early days, as the more level-headed. Nonetheless, three decades later Mary and I would cross paths, and I did have a chance to recount with her my youthful infatuation.

1941

By my tenth year, the beginning of 1941, Papá would leave and return to the house in an Army uniform: khaki breeches and highly polished knee-high boots with a matching khaki tunic, leather belted with a diagonal chest strap looped under the right epaulet which was topped with shinny silver bars of a captain and, a caduceus clipped to its collar sides. He was among the citizen soldiers conscripted for reasons not then clear to me. In Ormoc, these uniformed men would gather at a military enclave just outside town named Camp Downes where he participated as the group's physician and surgeon. At mid-year, he was gone for about two weeks to an Army barracks in Cabanatuan, hundreds of miles north of Manila in the island of Luzon. Papá returned to a routine Ormoc family life that gave nobody, at least not me, any premonition of a foreboding future.

On 8th December 1941, the church was festively decorated. It was the Feast Day of the Immaculate Conception. Flowers abounded around the altar. Among the many religious icons were statues of the namesake saints and the crucified Jesus. That of the Blessed Virgin Mary stood high above the central altar. The ladies of the Altar Society had adorned its surroundings by lacing strategically about her feet fluffs of cotton to symbolize her being suspended among clouds—a beatific intent that was sure to please the congregation. Added all around the altar were candles of varying sizes. The extra decoration was merited since the church was expected to be packed at each of the three scheduled Masses, the attendance being obliged under pain of mortal sin which is a transgression more grievous than a venial sin, according to the catechism. As the church began to fill with devotees, above their muffled cadence hum from reciting the rosary devotion, here and there one could overhear the admiring comment on the decorations: *"ooyyy"* and *"sus"*—a constriction of "oh boy" and "Jesus" in the vernacular. On that morning, I was one of the two acolytes scheduled to serve the seven o'clock Mass. My partner was Romy Lladoc.

That day, Romy and I were not worrying, nor were we aware in the slightest about the dark clouds of conflict gathering before us. Ours was indeed a simpler time, a childhood of blissful innocence. We had a naïveté that would upturn when, at the end of the Mass, news rapidly spread that the American Naval Base in Pearl Harbor, Hawaii, had been bombed by carrier-based Japanese war planes. Unbeknown to any of us, tragically, World War II would soon be fought on our land, and we would be thrown into a whirlpool of unimaginable bondage, destruction and death. It would abbreviate my brother and sisters' early adolescence. To them, the coming war would become a turbulent phase in their innocent lives. Their coming experiences, however, I felt they would absorb in awesomely cognitive innocence. Their memories of the following traumatic years, I would learn in later years were hazy and innocently incomprehensible.

ON REFLECTION

I grew up in a family that had a mixture of Spanish and Filipino bloodlines in a rural community that was principally agrarian, insular, and oligarchic-based. It retained a tiered class society—in practice rather than by decree. I look back now and imagine that my early exposure to people with tales of distant travel must have fueled a longing to reach out to a broader worldview, to wonder of a life guided by visions of unknown places with attractions still to uncover.

My early education was at a parochial school. To me, the foundational education that the nuns of St. Peter's Academy (SPA) espoused included a belief in the basic values of life and correct behavior. José Palma, Archbishop of Cebu, in 2012 sent a pastoral letter on the occasion of the 400 Years of Catholic Education of the Philippines. Notably, contrary to a commonly-held belief that keeping the indio ignorant was attributed of the colonialist's policy, he cited that the missionaries of the early centuries not only taught Church doctrines but extended contributions in scientific and ethnographic studies as well as the preservation of the dialects. The nuns of SPA discouraged students from speaking the vernacular on campus as a policy intended to optimize familiarity and competence with English. Will future Filipinos accommodate a bilingual aptitude as personally advantageous and valuable?

My upbringing was the societal norm of the time. It bears clarification. Although my family was patriarchal, my father's responsibility teamed with my mother's role to provide safeguards for a family life vested in its social prestige and adherence to the sanctions of a Catholic moral and religious tradition. We had an in-house caretaker—yaya—who would importantly contribute to the mix. She attended to the babysitter chores. While our parents were freed of those trivial aspects of parenting, the custom engendered an intimate, multi-faceted yaya-child psycho-social relationship, as regards: meting discipline, extending caressing comfort, providing supportive companionship, even receptive ears of personal sentiments. If my parents also shared a similar inter-relationship, there had to have been a difference.

It was a difference that might have been the underpinning of at least a couple observations I retain from my youth: our love and care for each other had a sense of being more considered and *de rigueur* rather than deep-seated and intimate; and, in social functions, adults tended to separate themselves with their concerns from those of the children who more often than not were with their yayas. Everybody, it seemed to me, was comfortable with the arrangement. The long-held characterization of the close-knit Filipino family may undoubtedly be conditioned by multiple factors; might my observations be regarded an aberration? I am tempted, however, to posit that our parent-sibling kinship would temper my views about intimacy and interplay with love ones, a dynamic I would carry into adulthood and wanting to modify in time. The custom had lent me liberties to be on my own, unconsciously encouraging the outgrowth of a keen sense of inquisitiveness and carefree independence. The coming era, rumbling with experiences of war and post-adolescent years in a foreign land, would further teach me to cope with hurdles and changes, malleably.

Above all, my parents provided for their family well; we lived comfortably, if modestly. To us children, they imbued principles of ethical behavior and cultivated a sense of responsibility to one's self, to fellowmen and to the community. They comported with those beliefs as parents and as practitioners of their professions; and, as participant-members of our society. Just how effectively their values had permeated to their children and me in particular, would well manifest as I review the course that my life has taken in the subsequent pages.

That the sphere of my social world would appear limited to cousins, uncles, aunts, grandparents and relatives is a happenstance common in the Philippines. Customarily, Filipinos view family relations as a dyadic bond of members of both the father's and mother's lineage. The kinship relationship—*parientes*—and their interactions may be expanded by a *compadre* system—a tradition of Spanish origin known to them as *compadrazgo*. It is a behavior by which a family related by blood and marriage coalesces with a fictive-kinship unit acquired by being god-parents, sponsors of weddings and/or religious rites, such as baptism. As the convenient source of social inter-relations, protection, and support, its members come to define the "us" from those on the outside as the "them." The custom can give rise to clan-formation that, in turn, may exacerbate fractionalization of the populace, particularly when politicians seek and exploit the relationship to partisan advantage. Could the compadre custom be utilized to energize the yearning for nationalism, so essential to the well-being of the country? Would it obstruct efforts at curbing the potentially discordant effects of provincialism? The coming decades will be informative and transformative.

SURVIVING THE WAR

When people speak to you about a preventive war, you tell them to go and fight it. After my experience, I have come to hate war. War settles nothing.

—Dwight D. Eisenhower
(Soldier, US President... b1890–1961).

War will exist until that distant day when the conscientious objector enjoys the same reputation and prestige that the warrior has today.

—John F. Kennedy
(Navy Veteran, US President... b1917–1963).

I hate war for its consequences, for the lies it lives on and propagates, for the undying hatred it arouses, for the dictators it puts in the place of democracies, and for the starvation that stalks after it.

—Harry Emerson Fosdick
(American pastor, writer...b1878–1969)

"Yesterday, December 7th 1941, a date which will live in infamy..." so declared the president of the United States of America Franklin Delano Roosevelt before the Joint Session of the U.S. Congress that 8th December 1941; he urged a declaration of war against Japan.

The whole world would soon experience the cataclysmic consequences that the American president's grave warning and avowed comeback implied. Then, his admonition did not seem to me that foreboding. Although like those select seminal events of history, the memory of the day that had triggered the rejoinder was an aggressive act and the days that followed would be unforgettable. I was ten years old. Living as I did on the eastern edge of the Pan-Asiatic region, Sunday 7th December east of the International Date Line as America and Hawaii are was already Monday 8th in the Philippines. Being a predominantly Catholic populace, it was a day to celebrate the feast of the Immaculate Conception. That day, however, would be unlike any other. I was getting an earful of news reports and rumors. The ominous and catastrophic events that my family, my country and I would soon endure were beyond my imagination. I would soon learn more.

The "infamy" that President Roosevelt had attributed to was a sneak attack by carrier-based Japanese war planes on the American Naval Station at Pearl Harbor, the Hickam Air Base and the Army Schofield Barracks of Honolulu, Hawaii. Unprepared, the losses in sunken battleships, disabled airplanes, casualties of military personnel as well as innocent civilians were enraging although yet to be tallied. Until that day, I had known Hawaii only as a land filled with graceful women dancing the hula-hula in grass skirts. My world felt un-nerved and shaken, having to absorb a horribly shocking and alarming news.

As if to underscore the peril to us Filipinos, by noon there followed similar destructive bombing forays on American military Air Corps and naval installations located in parts of Luzon and Mindanao, even on bases surrounding Manila, which placed the nation's capital and inhabitants at risk. Disturbingly, the raids in the Philippines were reported to have met only niggardly opposition. What was disquieting and worrisome were the gossips that ascribed the damages to have rendered inutile a number, perhaps the majority, of American and Philippine Army aircrafts. Had the poorly contested bombings represented a kink in the defensive armor of the combined Filipino and American might? Had the American Command not received or failed to react to intelligence reports forewarning attacks in the Philippines? Were there actually a covert army of Japanese spies? They were questions less entertained. Instead, at the time, the country-wide paramount response that I shared was that of contempt and hatred for a devious enemy that I naively believed lived in paper houses and were only merchants of shoddy toys. Nonetheless, as people voiced the fear of a Japanese invasion, I wondered what tragedies could befall the country, the people, and my family. And, our family prayed for Papá's safety.

At the Mass I served as an acolyte early that morning, an elder while lighting one of the candles had accidentally ignited the cloud decoration made of cotton. The commotion only lasted as long as it took to douse the fire with a pitcher of Holy Water nearby. Our sages were quick to point to the incident at the church as the omen, a message delivered by the heavenly hierarchy forewarning us in Ormoc of impending doom. Never mind that the altar fire occurred hours after the Japanese attack on Pearl Harbor. The foibles of war!

PERLA DEL MAR DE ORIENTE—A BATTLEFIELD...THE PRELUDE

In the decades before and after I was born, early twenties to 1941, there was unrest and instability the world over. The League of Nations, adopted in 1919 following World War I as an international body for the peaceful settlement of disputes by arbitration, was having early difficulties with its credibility. While it was an instrument "to end all wars," instead, one by one its members flaunted their disregard for its peaceable goals.

In Europe, by 1923 France forcibly occupied the Ruhr area of defeated Germany in reparations as a victor of the War; it accelerated the latter's economic collapse and hardened their revengeful enmity. In Spain a civil war erupted in the second half of the 1930s. In conflict were the Spanish Republic ideologues against rebel forces led by General Francisco Franco. Before the bloody civil war had ceased, the world would be provided a preview of the brewing dissension between the major European powers as Russia favored the former while Germany and Italy supported the latter. In 1940, Germany and Italy, joined by Japan, signed the Tripartite Axis Powers Pact; the unity would bind them against a feared-for conflict against the British and their Allies. The bombing of the Basque city of Guernica by German military planes would harden the divide. In the Philippines, the Spanish and Hispanophile community would reflectively split their moral and financial support for the conflicting groups, their disagreements subsequently eroding past communal harmony.

In the Orient, in 1931 the Japanese Army occupied Manchuria and invaded China. There, they incubated a callous breed of combatants that brought about the infamous wholesale rape and wanton killing of civilians at every community they occupied. American agitation, meanwhile, was further stoked when the USS Panay gunboat plying China's Yangtze River was sunk by attacking Japanese planes in early December 1937. To Japan, on the other hand, the subsequent U.S. embargo of oil exports from the Dutch East Indies posed a threat to their expansionist policies, sufficient to ratchet their anti-American fervor and raise the specter of armed conflict between them. Only a dozen years earlier, US General Billy Mitchell, who was a consummate advocate for development of an air force, forewarned of an aerial attack by Japan on military bases in Hawaii, even the Philippines. An enraged War Department belittled his views, instead, brought charges of insubordination and found him guilty. Michell died in 1936, his country yet to regard the importance of an air force. Was Japan emboldened by a "sleeping giant" America?

To the outbreaks of aggression and deteriorating global instability, America would add its own worrisome economic depression. Joblessness was ubiquitous, its devastating consequences had rippled worldwide. The recovery was slow and lasted well into the start of World War II.

During the same period, the Philippines was in consuming debates and political negotiations with America on the disposition of the Filipino crusade for independence and concerns over its economic survival, its security from foreign invasion, and its future relations with their overlord. On 24th March 1934, the United States responded with the Tydings-McDuffie Act, signed as a federal law by President Franklyn D. Roosevelt. In its provisions, the Filipinos were charged to draft a Constitution for, and inaugurate the Commonwealth of the Philippines by the following year. At the same time, it mandated the United States to grant independence ten years later. Not well known, nor its implications clearly understood by many Filipinos, least of all to me, the Act allowed the United States to maintain bases of its armed forces in Philippines soil and call to its service all military personnel of the Commonwealth. America thereby seemed to have obligated itself to the defense of the country against foreign invasion and ensured the committed involvement of Filipinos.

Between 1935 and 1941, the experiences with the governance of the Philippines were attended by unceasing harangue among partisan politicians; while, at the same time, Washington policymakers continued to vacillate over its military strategy in the Orient. In frustration, President Quezon, when once asked to choose between having an extended American dominion or receive a prompt, outright independence, was quoted as saying, "I would rather have a Philippines run like hell by Filipinos than a Philippines run like heaven by the Americans." One is tempted to recall a cliché of caution that warns be "careful what you wish for… it may come true." The president, however, was believed to have agonized over the choice of gaining immediate independence, which risked dislocating the fragile economic well-being of the country against the counter-pressure worry that delay would bind the fate of the nation away from neutrality. To compound his dilemma, there was the American quandary over tessellating its policy for the Far East. Their strategic planners had voiced concern, in assessing military assets, that the Commonwealth was vulnerable to conquest, its defense lasting for only a limited time before capitulation. Any plan to ameliorate the deficiencies were estimated to take until 1942 to complete, a process that to initiate would have needed prior approval by the U.S. Congress. Quezon was said to be left confounded and irresolute while finding the means to safeguard Filipino interests at his disposal unclear. Through diplomatic channels, he sought assurances of non-intervention from the Japanese. However, Japan had come to view the country as an American citadel in the Orient, thereby negating negotiations with Filipinos whom they viewed as subjects tightly trussed to American interests. Inexorably, as tension kept growing between the United States and Japan, like a ticking time bomb, an exploding war between them was all but inescapable; regrettably, a battlefield would be on soil of the Perla del Mar de Oriente. At harm's way were the seventeen million Filipinos.

...THE PROTAGONISTS

Wars between nations are an aggressive armed conflict that employ armamentaria of destruction. They are combats with potentially ruinous and morbid consequences to man and treasure. History has repeatedly pointed out that the individual warriors who bear the burnt of the conflict get called to commit the ultimate sacrifice and, sadly, innocent non-combatants inevitably find themselves in the midst of the fray, even if unintended. Thus, everyone in the theater of war invariably becomes victimized by the atrocious toll of the experience. Most prudently then, wars ought to be carried out only as the last recourse, after political and diplomatic discourse have failed to settle adversarial issues. Opposing leaders owe humanity and civilization an awesome responsibility for the underlying principles of their decisions and for the consequences of the conduct of their protagonists. I point to individuals who, in my view, had crucial roles in the battles that were fought in the Philippines, recognizing that the cast had included thousands of nameless combatants, innumerable innocent civilians and unfathomable destruction of property and treasure. It is also important to recognize that, from the onset, U.S. military forces were augmented by Commonwealth of the

Philippines military units; they would fight valiantly at great sacrifice and despite wanting in combat preparedness.

The principals of the opposing armies were General Douglas MacArthur and General Tomoyuki Yamashita. Both Generals, it seemed, were inhibited by the resources at their disposal and objectives of the conflict. I further point out that, in the early phase of the battle, MacArthur relegated command to General Jonathan Wainwright who ultimately would declare defeat by surrender; and, Yamashita, in turn, would replace General Masaharu Homma who, despite having commanded the victorious invasion forces, was forced into retirement for alleged conduct incongruent with those of Tokyo policy makers. The commands of MacArthur and Yamashita, then, would face combat toward the last phases of the War.

General Douglas MacArthur (L), General Tomoyuki Yamashita(R). The principal protagonists of the Philippine Battlefield, fought between December 1941 and 2nd September 1945 when VJ Day was declared.

President Manuel Quezon, as President of the Commonwealth of the Philippines and leader of the Filipino quest for self-governance and neutrality, was sandwiched in between. Above all, he aimed to avoid battle in Filipino soil, fearing the catastrophic consequences on his people and treasure. His efforts, however, were constrained by the intricate interdependence the country had with America.

President of the Commonwealth of the Philippines Manuel Quezon, his concerns sandwiched between two conflicted major powers who would battle in the Philippines, putting at risk the safety of his countrymen and their treasure.

...THE UNFOLDING EVENTS

My family and I were among those at peril. The events that follow are an amalgam of my reminiscences and of the tales of others who shared in the experiences.

By mid-afternoon of that Monday 8th December, a platoon of Army soldiers led by a sword-carrying lieutenant was marching in step into town from the military base just south of the town's edge, Camp Downes. In column of twos. They looked impressive with their rifles on their right shoulders and bayonets hung by their webbed belts. They were on a mission. The buzz of their purpose was preceding them by several blocks. By the time they had marched past the Church, the gathering curious had grown to a sizable crowd. Many who joined in the march were students, off for the feast day of the Immaculate Conception. By now, I was aware of the talk of impeding war and the excitement the marching troopers were generating, yet not fully understanding their dire consequences. Excitedly, I donned my cowboy outfit— my mother had ordered it from a Montgomery Ward catalog— and strapped a cap-pistol to my waist, prepared to be in the mix. After getting Mamá's permission, I went hopping along with the soldiers on their way to the commercial street, only four blocks away, where the business shops included one owned by Mr. and Mrs. Ito. They were Ormoc's only Japanese family. Until that day, they had been unobtrusive.

The army officer confronted and advised Mr. Ito only that the Commonwealth of the Philippines and the United States of America were at war with Japan. As an enemy alien, he was to be detained. At best, that was the essence of the message rather than the verbatim denunciation. The exchange, after all, had been passed backwards to those of us crouched a safe distance away, in case of any shooting or some such desperate act by the prisoner, who instead, acknowledged the soldiers cooperatively, courteously and compliantly. Mr. Ito was confined to a room at the Army barracks during the day but spent the nights with his family. Not to be repressed was a rumor circulating even that very day, whispered through covered mouths, that Mr. Ito was suspected to be an undercover officer of the Imperial Japanese Army, sent to Ormoc for a mission as yet to be uncovered. I do not recall anyone speculating on the strategic secrets that Mr. Ito might have spied on and gathered in Ormoc for transmission to his superiors. Nor did the subsequent Japanese occupation reveal Mr. Ito's espionage role, if any. Factually, the number of Japanese immigrants in the Philippines during the decade of the 1930s had exceeded that of the Chinese who were historically the largest of the ethnic demography. In Davao, a coastal city of southern Mindanao, they had built a cultural and commercial enclave. Their entrepreneurship led in the development of hemp, lumber and fishing trade. Were the Japanese presence justifiably posing a security risk? Sadly, in retrospect, Mr. Ito and his family had nonetheless unjustly suffered a travesty of War.

After the United States of America declared war against Japan, the Japanese Imperial Army did not tarry. Within a couple days, I heard massive numbers of their troops begun landing at multiple points of Luzon. The American and Filipino combatant defenders, jointly known by the acronym USAFFE, United States Armed Forces of the Far East, were rapidly mobilized and deployed to reinforce those engaging the enemy at their invasion points. Papá was among those called to duty, going up to Camp Downes for preparations not well known to me. Sometime a few weeks later, he left Ormoc with the Army troops as newly sworn-in members of USAFFE, their destination somewhere in Luzon.

By the Christmas season, Ormoc itself was on a war-footing. With each news report of the raging battles by radio, I would hear new names of towns, their locale elsewhere in the Philippines not clear to me: Aparri, Corregidor, Lingayen, Cavite, Bataan; the list would go on. In town, there was a palpable state of apprehension, particularly since the Army unit had left for battlefields somewhere to the north. While Papá's departure must surely have had my mother concerned and worried, I recall only welling with pride by the bravery of our soldiers and of their daunting might.

The deployment of troopers from Camp Downes to the north served to strengthen the town's own patriotic resolve, now left without military defense. At dusk, I would watch male volunteers of the organized group of air-raid wardens take daily turns climbing the lighthouse ladder to its top. There, armed in each hand with a flashlight powered by four D-batteries, they remained for hours scanning the darkening skies. To complete the early-warning strategy, other volunteers were assigned to reach the belfry of the church where a prescribed series of bell-ringing was to denote an impending air-raid or, on completion, all clear. I do not recall hearing reports on how effectively the flashlights searched the darkening skies. Never mind that the ambit of the flashlights in the hunt for attacking Japanese planes were so limited as to be useless. Nor was the relay of information from the air-raid wardens atop the lighthouse to the bell ringers at the church that well clarified. Perhaps there were volunteers nearby the pier who planned to run the four blocks to church to ring the bells in reasonable time. As yet another defensive ruse, at night our window shades were drawn down to help darken the town. In fact, all motor vehicles had partly covered headlights at night-time. All these patriotic endeavors were in compliance to orders for a nationwide black-out. I was certain it was a strategy to baffle attacking Japanese airplanes.

One day in January, the town's preparedness was put to the test. It was a clear, cloudless morning. Without any warning, from one side of the horizon came the drone, with each ticking second increasingly louder. There, for anyone to see were three planes flying in formation, their red Rising Sun insignia increasingly visible to the naked eye. Clearly, the Japanese Air Force was headed our way. The town was in a frenzy. People were scurrying in every direction. I was with Romy, whiling our time at the beach when the loud drone frightened us as well. We ran to our homes for safety, convinced I was about to witness and suffer the town's first bombing attack. In a matter of minutes and before everyone could get to where they were scurrying, the planes had flown past beyond eyesight. Shortly, the chattering was broken by the church bells. They were ringing to signal an air raid. Then, after brief minutes, the chiming bells were announcing the all clear message. Apparently, the volunteer warden in charge had panicked with the rest of us and only collected his wits much later, well past the feared attack. But, now aware of his assigned responsibility, he climbed to the belfry and decided to precede the all clear tolling sequence by ringing the "air-raid warning to be thorough." Rather than disparagement, he got cheered for providing the community comic relief. The collective sigh of relief and thanksgiving had to have been audible. However, anxiety and fear were feelings that would soon permeate the community.

By early January 1942, an evacuation had been recommended to depopulate Ormoc before the anticipated occupation by Japanese forces. They were rumored to be ruthless, their atrocities had not excluded women and children. While awaiting the Japanese troops, Ormoc was under the care of a skeleton crew of elected officials, the mayor then was Catalino Hermocilla. Meanwhile, one by one throughout the weeks of March 1942 those men, conscripted into the army and who had been a part of the battles raging in northern Luzon, were filtering back to their homes, dispirited. In Ormoc, among them was Tio Paeng's son José, who served as an infantry Lieutenant. He recounted the horrors of fighting against superior numbers of combat-veteran enemy forces while our troops were equipped with meager supplies of ammunition and food, some bare-footed, armed with archaic rifles. He went on to describe how the Japanese were attacking with ferocity, filling the air with repeated yells of "banzai, banzai, banzai." Fearless the enemy were. There were many other related battle encounters that I now less clearly remember. What is hard to forget were José's sketches of the gravity and depravity of armed conflict. They made me recoil in repugnance and, sharing with those of my elders' concern: fear. What would become a seemingly growing realization was that the country's defenders were facing a highly seasoned military of purposeful warriors, well-prepared, well-equipped and battle-tested.

Meantime, another soldier who had returned a few weeks later was Papá. His unit was ordered to disband as Japanese victory seemed imminent, only Bataan and Corregidor the hopeless resistance. He found us living in a nipa house on the hillside village of Dolores, about ten miles north of town. It was owned by a dear and close friend of the family—so intimate, she was affectionately known to us as an aunt, although she was unrelated by blood. Generosa Kavanaugh, *manang Gener—manang* being an endearing, affectionate tribute to an elderly person—was a widow; her American husband had left her a "pensioner." For years until her demise, manang Gener would remain attached to my family. To Inday and Jun's good fortune, growing up as they would orphaned of a mother by early 1945, she would assume a consummate surrogate auntie role.

The farm on which the house was built had the redolent hint to the fresh air from the abundant fruit trees, known by their native names: *lanzones, ceriguelas, balimbing, tambis, manga, piña,* coconuts and the nearby sugar cane plantation. For this move we had, of course, brought with us only bare essentials, leaving our possessions locked up in Ormoc. I remember the accommodations comfortable although there was no running water or sanitary facilities. The former was drawn from a river a half mile away and manually carried back in two 10-gallon cans hanging at either end of a sturdy length of bamboo borne on the shoulder. I don't recall having the duty so I assume there may have been older helpers. The river, additionally, was where we bathed and washed our laundry. Since there was no out-house, we would scatter into the depths of the rows of sugarcane for those privacy moments. We were ensured adequate subsistence while sheltered in that mountain preserve.

Relatives and friends of our family had also found refuge in similar abodes in nearby farms. Others, such as the Moraza family, moved to Baybay, a small rural coastal town about 15 miles south where the Japanese would extend their authority only sporadically. I would later learn that the Morazas too had harrowing experiences. The Lladoc family departed to be with relatives in the province of Occidental Negros, another three islands distant. Tio Paeng's family found their mountain hideout a mile uphill from us. In the weeks that we spent in Dolores, his eldest son Emilio would leave his mare in my care to graze by our home site. He commuted to Ormoc on foot for some undetermined business. I rode that horse bare-back as often as I could, learning to stay astride while trotting and galloping. The country living meant carefree days spent on horseback and without fifth grade classes to attend. They were a sabbatical moment in time that belied the cruel nature of the warfare surrounding us. Soon the interlude would end.

THE HOMELAND UNDER OCCUPATION

News of the war strategy was of a last ditch effort to prolong the battle while awaiting reinforcement in troops and materiel from the United States; none, however, was forthcoming. General Douglas MacArthur, President Manuel Quezon and their close associates together with a sizeable complement of military commands were reported to have retreated to Corregidor island, situated at the mouth of Manila Bay. It was a fortress, believed impregnable by its copious artillery defenses and an elaborate tunnel that was turned into an underground military encampment with its own hospital facility. From his headquarters, the General directed the limited battles that by then had concentrated on the province of Bataan.

There were some notable events, little known and effectively secreted from the public. I would come to better know them well after the War. One was that during the early weeks of November 1941, a disguised ploy was hatched aimed to inflame Filipino disdain for the Japanese and tighten their wavering allegiance to America. It involved a pleasure craft crewed by American and Filipino off-duty U.S. Navy sailors, dressed in civilian clothes. They were encouraged to venture into waters of the China Sea. With the crew unaware of their sacrificial role, the subterfuge objective was to lure the Japanese to attack and sink the boat. With the anticipated death of the sailors that included Filipinos, the incident would then have provided a newsworthy report of an allegedly unprovoked Japanese aggression against the Philippines. The sailors ventured but returned to home base safely, the ploy unfulfilled. There also was a plea by President Quezon before

President Roosevelt, just days after 7th December, to grant the Philippines its immediate independence, intending thereafter to declare the country's neutrality so as to spare itself the destructive toll of war. The petition and Roosevelt's rejection were hidden from public notice.

On 11th March, the eye-opening chitchat was that General MacArthur and President Quezon together with their families and close associates had left Corregidor by U.S. Navy PT boats, aided by the darkness of night. They arrived in a Mindanao port, successfully weaving past mine-infested Manila Bay and eluding Japanese Navy patrol boats. From there they ferried by airplane to Australia. Subsequently, we would know that President Quezon and his associates found their way to the safety of Washington, D.C. where the Commonwealth of the Philippines established a government-in-exile. The sum of all those escapades added to a despairing sense of inescapable, ultimate victory and occupation of the country by the Japanese.

Quezon, on his departure, had apparently covertly instructed the remaining officialdom to adopt a policy of cooperation and collaboration with the invaders, his alleged motive was to minimize, if not avoid the feared atrocities to civilians and wanton destruction of property and treasure. Only years later would the secreted records of those emergent times be opened to corroborative scrutiny. Unnecessarily, those officials who had implemented the instructions received the needless ire and accusation of treason by an uninformed citizenry.

On arrival in Australia General MacArthur proclaimed to Filipinos and the world, "I shall return." It was a promise, surely surreptitiously picked-up by short-wave radio and spread as rapidly as wildfire, that Filipinos viewed with hope as the country faced the imminent peril of occupation. Others, better informed, would recall the General's boastful declaration a month earlier when Manila newspapers reported him to say "nothing would please me better than if they—the Japanese—would give me three months and then attack here." Of course, the General did not have the extended time he had wished for. Instead, at a U.S. Navy investigatory session on the Japanese attacks months later, Rear Admiral Edwin T. Layton Chief of Pacific Fleet Intelligence opined that the General's deportment: "...by failing to initiate his war plans after the Pearl Harbor attack... during the seven hours before Japanese bombing of the Philippines, he ensured swift retribution and disaster." To add to the intrigue, the General, by having accepted a large sum of money of the Philippine Treasury before escaping to Australia, lent suspicion of a conflict of interest between his role as a U.S. soldier and his close relations with Quezon whose well-known desire was to declare his nation's neutrality. Was it a duplicitous behavior of the General?

By early April, the enemy had come to Ormoc without meeting armed resistance. They had already taken control of Tacloban, the provincial capital located 60 miles on the eastern side of the island. Meanwhile from the warfronts came accounts that described a morass of confusion and breakdown of the USAFFE defensive strategies. On 9th April, the highest ranking officer General Jonathan Wainwright broadcast the surrender of all the soldiers and sailors in his command. He ordered the cessation of armed resistance and termination of the battle for the Philippines. With the surrender, the Japanese Forces would face the challenge of imprisoning the thousands of Filipino and American troopers. Their experiences have since been immortalized as the Bataan Death March in books and the cinema. Listed on the Index that I recommend for added reading are those authored by Stanley Karnow and Edwin T. Layton. From those sources, I synthesize below the salient conditions both the Japanese and the Filipino-American combatants faced, aware that more detailed accounts are beyond the scope of this tome.

The Tribune

THE WEATHER
Yesterday's Max.: 92.0 C. or
96.0 F. at 1:40 P. M. Min.:
73.5 C. or 74.5 F. at 6:55 A. M.

5 Centavos
4 Pages

MANILA, PHILIPPINES, FRIDAY, APRIL 24, 1942

YEAR XVIII

BATAAN COMPLETELY OCCUPIED BY JAPANESE

Japanese Forces Take Cebu

15 Generals Among War Prisoners

TOKYO, April 11 (Domei)—
Imperial Headquarters announced at 4:10 o'clock this afternoon that Japanese forces since the commencement of the general offensive against the beleaguered Filipino-American forces in Bataan Peninsula up to Sunday captured a total of 40,000 war prisoners, including 15 generals and 8,700 American troops.

The officers captured included Major General Edward P. King, Jr., commander of United States forces in Bataan Peninsula; Major General Albert Jones, commander of the First Army Corps; Major General George Parker, commander of the Second Army Corps; and Major General Guillermo B. Francisco, commander of the Filipino Forces.

The communique said that the spoils taken by the Japanese during the same period amounted to 196 guns including heavy artillery, 230 machineguns, 900 automatic rifles, 13½ tanks including armored cars, 230 automobiles and many other arms and munitions.

The entire Bataan Peninsula is now under the control of the Japanese Imperial Forces, the Propaganda Corps said in an announcement on April 13.

Bataan came under Japanese control following the surrender of Major General Edward P. King, Jr., commander of the eastern front, due to the fierce attack of the Nippon forces. Major General Albert Jones, commander of the western front of Bataan, has also been captured, according to the Propaganda Corps. Captured with him were his staff, composed of Colonel Mara, military chief of staff, Captain Cross and Captain.
(Continued on page 2)

RELIEF—Japanese officers and soldiers shown distributing food to Filipino civilians whose homes were caught between cross firing on the Bataan front. The Japanese also gave medicine for the sick and helped war refugees in all other ways possible, showing great concern for their welfare. (Photo taken by the photography section of the Japanese Propaganda Corps.)

Gen. Homma Thanks Officers And Men Under Him for Heroism

BATAAN FRONT, April 11 (Domei)—Lieutenant General Masaharu Homma, commander-in-chief of the Japanese forces in the Philippines, told the press yesterday evening that "it is still too early to identify myself to the world as commander of the Japanese forces in the Philippines in view of the fact that the war has just begun."

Gen. Homma revealed that "Our battle has been one against difficult terrain rather than against American forces." He recalled that the fight started with the routing of American troops in the plains of Luzon, followed by the general offensive against the American forces who took shelter in the Bataan fortresses. He expressed gratitude to his officers and men for their heroism and bravery which led to the complete occupation of the Imperial Japanese forces here.
(Continued on page 2)

Lt. Gen. MASAHARU HOMMA
First photograph ever published of the commander-in-chief of the Imperial Japanese forces here.

Surrender Of Bataan Praised

The occupation of Bataan by the Imperial Japanese Forces will bring back peace and tranquility in many Filipino homes and will enable the Filipino people to undertake in earnest the rehabilitation and reconstruction of the country, Jorge B. Vargas, chairman of the executive commission, declared in a statement issued yesterday.

The statement read:
"The surrender of Bataan is a wise decision on the part of the Filipino fighting forces. It means the stopping of further sacrifice in futile and unequal resistance as many young lives of which the nation is sorely in need during these critical times. With the occupation of Bataan and the rest of the Southern Islands, peace and tranquility will be returned to many Filipino homes disrupted by the war.
(Continued on page 2)

Japanese Flag Planted In Cebu City

ABOARD A JAPANESE WAR-SHIP, April 11 (Domei)—Crashing of Japanese bluejackets at 10 o'clock yesterday morning effected successful landings near Cebu City, Cebu Island, Bacid, on the western coast of Cebu, and Argao, a town 42 kilometres south of Cebu City.

The Japanese forces which landed from Cebu bay in the face of enemy resistance are now engaged in violent street fighting with the enemy in Cebu and are rapidly expanding their operations.

Cebu City is shrouded in smoke as the enemy has set fire to vessels in the bay and other establishments in the area. Located south of Mindanao Island, Cebu forms a key strategic point in the southern part of the Philippines.

LISBON, April 11 (Domei)—The United States war department issued a communique today stating that Japanese forces supported by bombers and heavy naval gunfire effected a landing on Cebu island, north of Mindanao, according to report from Washington.

The communique added that Japanese forces continued their intense attacks on Corregidor and Fort Hughes, one of the fortified islands in Manila Bay.

FROM AN UNDISCLOSED BASE IN THE PHILIPPINES, April 11 (Domei)—Alert units of the Nipponese naval forces maintaining an air-tight blockade of Manila Bay captured three American transports attempting to escape from Bataan peninsula on April 9. It was learned today.

CEBU ISLAND, April 12 (Domei)—It was learned that Leon Abad Santos, former secretary of justice of the Philippine Commonwealth.
(Continued on page 4)

SURRENDER—The surrender of Filipino-American troops on the eastern front of Bataan was effected in this historic scene somewhere in Bataan when Major General Edward P. King, Jr., second from left, accompanied by Col. Williams (with face covered), expressed his wish to a representative of the commander-in-chief of the Japanese Imperial Forces.

Manila newspaper, The Tribune, report the
Surrender of Bataan, April 1942.

The Bataan Death March. It begun 09th April 1942. American and Filipino troops on the Bataan Peninsula were low on food, ammunition, and morale; some were dying from lack of nourishment more than enemy fire. On orders of General Jonathan Wainwright, designated Commander by General MacArthur who had escaped to Australia, they turned themselves over by raising white flags, T-shirts, and whatever other white articles.

Lt. General Masahuro Homma, Commander of the Japanese Forces had chosen Camp O'Donnell in San Fernando as the stockade, 70 miles north. But, his command had discovered that the available transport was severely shortened by their purposeful destruction as ordered by General MacArthur. And, that there were many more prisoners than anticipated, some of whom were in poor health and malnourished.

The Japanese guards were battle-tested warriors from years of war in China where they committed random beatings and killings without provocation. The guards were at liberty to bayonet prisoners, specially if found with a souvenir of an item that could be assumed came from killing a Japanese soldier. Of the 75,000 prisoners of war, ten thousand Filipinos and over 600 American prisoners of war died before they could reach the Camp. Sixty-four thousand reached their destination.

In Manila, General Masahuro Homma, supreme commander of the Imperial Japanese Forces celebrated the victory with a military parade. His leadership and contrarian liberal implementation of Imperial General Headquarters policies, it turned out, were regarded with skepticism in Tokyo. Nonetheless, to the Filipino advantage, he had apparently ordered his troops to treat Filipinos not as enemies but friends and respect their customs and religion. He also was said to have saved lives of Filipino leaders such as Manuel Roxas from execution as pro-American stooges. In time, he was replaced by General Tomoyuki Yamashita.

Among the marching participants of the parade were Filipino, German, and Italian groups. The spectacle was witnessed and attended by officials flown from Tokyo; the commanders of the Imperial Japanese Army, Air Force and Navy; and, a large group of school children and government employees waving the rising sun flag of Japan.

In time, a mounting, increasingly organized guerilla opposition to the Japanese interlopers followed. The band of American and Filipino soldiers who defied orders to surrender lived by stealth in mountain hideouts. In the province of Leyte, the hillsides of the island including those of Ormoc offered many hideouts for the guerillas. As their activities became better coordinated throughout the country, they became a pesky challenge to the Japanese occupation's dictate, stability and security.

In Luzon, a well-organized group of peasant and agricultural workers formed. Their anti-Japanese skirmishes were recurrent, disruptive and casualty-effective. The organization was named Hukbalahap—Huks for short—the acronym of the Filipino *Hukbong Bayan Laban sa mga Hapon* or Peoples' Liberation Army, led by Luis Taruc. They had originally begun as a movement against the *encomienda*, a Spanish system of grants established in 1521 that was designed to exploit indigenous inhabitants of the colonies by abrogating their land holdings, forcing them to work for low wages and imposing high taxes. In the Philippines, the Spanish grants had created large land holdings and with them, tensions between tenants and landlords. For the duration of the Japanese occupation, the Huks took advantage of the opportunity to advocate and rally for resolution of the festering problem. In fact, their fight for agrarian reforms did target large landholders, a few of whom were reportedly killed on the guise of being pro-Japanese. After the War, their contributions to the resistance movement would become obscured by being successfully labeled as communists, a group perceived at that time as a dreaded opponent to oligarchic and national interests. As a result, they were hunted as insurgents by the Philippine constabulary, with American aid, until 1949 when the brunt of their armed resistance had been effectively quelled. The American attempts to reform the landlord-tenant inequities would not succeed; the oligarchy opposed the efforts. The unresolved agrarian problem would fulminate in the near future.

On the whole, the resistance movement proved helpful to American liberation battles. The Japanese, meanwhile, would learn that the guerillas could blend with the civilian population with ease. Identifying the unorthodox enemy became difficult, if not impossible. Shortly, a pro-Japanese Filipino military group to counter the anti-Japanese resistance was formed: Alliance of Philippine Patriots or *Makapili*, an acronym of the name in the vernacular, *Makabayan Katipunan Ng Mga Pilipino*. Through subterfuge, they became instruments of espionage against their countrymen. Meanwhile, as the Japanese came to regard the vanquished population with increasing distrust and as their own casualties mounted from interdiction by the resistance movement, they became more easily prone to vent their ratcheting cruelty on innocent civilians. As a consequence, there occurred vindictive beheadings, killings by bayonet, rapes, burning of villages—a vicious and brutal iron-fisted policy that merely estranged the populace, inexorably. Guerillas, on the other hand, when courting sympathy and collaboration from the civilian population were occasionally constrained to apply coercive ploys to compel support; refusal invariably risked retribution to themselves or their families. The citizens, it seemed to me, felt compelled to adapt a behavior of deceit, graft and corruption. Sadly, there also developed a schism of the national patriotic fervor as some citizens cooperated with the enemy. It was a cascading eye-for-an-eye phenomenon with cruel consequences to the non-combatant. Once again, Filipinos would find themselves fighting each other to pursue objectives of foreign overlords.

Yet another subjugating imposition was travel between towns and cities; passes were required. Permits were provided by the Japanese. They limited intra- and inter-island travel. In Ormoc, the horse-drawn conveyance, the tartanilla became the prevailing mode of transportation. Car, trucks, and buses were allowed only by expressed approval. Radios were to be surrendered. Of course, in short time, there were courageous, defiant individuals who kept contraband radios in secret locations, tuned to short-wave stations. Their word-of-mouth reports would become underground sources of news from the outside world. When contraband radios were successfully hunted, the enemy exacted punishment of unlimited cruelty, even death although I have no recollection of anyone caught in possession of the radio. There were other instances when I witnessed a civilian being exhibited, tied to a post exposed to the searing sun for behavior suspicious of being a guerilla sympathizer. Perhaps the victim may indeed have been a *guerillero;* I often wondered how effectively and how cruelly the Japanese obtained a confession. On those occasions I felt best to observe the regrettable spectacle without being discovered.

...MY FAMILY IN RISK

Apart from goings-on elsewhere, one day in April, Papá and I trudged back to Ormoc from Dolores. The mayor had sent word that the commanding officer of the Japanese Forces garrisoned in Ormoc wanted to meet my father. There were good reasons to confer with Papá. The troop complement did not include a physician and the Seaside Hotel had been commandeered as the headquarters. The commandant was probably also anxious to avail of his medical services.

One day, arriving within two blocks of my house by secrecy, I shared more than the cautious regard which Papá had of the impending meeting with the commandant. From our vantage point, hidden behind the partly-open door, we could see our house and the front of the Seaside Hotel beyond. There were sentries guarding the intersection leading to the hotel, their rifles fixed with bayonets. I was scared but amused. Gathered around the artesian well next to the Lladoc home were Japanese soldiers in varying degrees of disrobe, enjoying the refreshing bath and splashing each other like children. Some wore the army issue underwear, a form of G-String; others walked about with funny-looking rubber shoes.

Papá must have summoned an extraordinary amount of courage to walk to the hotel and meet the commandant. I stayed behind. He soon returned to fetch me for the hike back to Dolores. There, conferring with Mamá, he revealed the details of the conference. The commandant had spoken in halting English and was surprisingly differential. He sought my father's return to town with his family and resume his medical practice, allowing his use of our car. In return, Papá would provide medical care to the Japanese troops numbering fewer than a hundred, as needed. I do not recall hearing that the commandant had offered to pay for use of the Seaside Hotel.

Our family shortly prepared to leave Dolores and go back to our house. Most of the townspeople gradually returned as well. Soon, community activities begun to resume a rhythm we had known before the Japanese occupation, with some changes. For instance, as schools eventually re-opened, it became apparent that the curriculum had been altered, particularly by removing references of advantage to the United States. Adults and children were compelled to learn Nippongo, the Japanese language. I was amused at having my parents among my classmates. Everyone would learn that the Japanese were eager to dispel pro-American sentiments and portray themselves as liberators rather than the heavy-handed occupiers that everyone in Ormoc seemed convinced they were, including me. Concurrently, truckloads of soldiers would periodically foray the foothills seeking skirmishes with guerrilla groups. When those vehicles rumbled back to town, on occasion with soldiers noticeably injured, they spread an ambiance of insecurity, fear, and suspicion; my imagination would conjure scenes of heroic hand-to-hand combat.

Eventually, our family packed up, boarded a small inter-island motor launch and left for Cebu. There, we housed with my grandparents. Unbeknown to me, Papá had labored with increasing tension the months before. The guerrilla activities had been exacting heavy casualties on both sides. During the day, Papá would minister to the Japanese wounded. And, under cover of darkness, he would get escorted to secret hideouts to provide the same care to guerrillas, sometimes in nearby houses in town. Convinced that the situation would continue but rife with peril to his family and self, he must have hoodwinked the commandant into granting a rare family pass to visit my grandparents in Cebu for the Christmas holidays. It was a dangerous and mendacious gamble that succeeded. My own sixth grade education would be on hold.

Left to care for our Ormoc abode was our longtime yaya, Patricia. Parenthetically, she retired shortly after the war to be with her own family. Years later, on those reunion occasions with Inday, she reminisced about how I was a particularly challenging charge in my youth. Full of mischief. Helping me bathe when a toddler, she recalled, almost always got her equally soaked from my splattering. By 1937, we had installed a shower. However, I would not realize that showering could be more comfortable with heated water, which was a convenience we did not have.

The motorboat we sailed in that day in December was filled with Japanese troops ostensibly being transported from one garrison to another. Civilian passengers joined only on space-available basis. The ship was so small it took a littoral course along the northwestern perimeter of the bay, away from high waves and closer to land for safety. At some point, a few hours from Ormoc, the transport was fired upon by guerrillas hiding near the shore. Bullets were splashing the water surface on the starboard side. To get out of firing range, the ship altered course toward the open sea, risking our safety in another way and adding to the stress of the adventure. We arrived in Cebu safely at long last. To ensure a convincing illusion of our Christmastime visit intentions, we had left our possessions at home and brought only suitcases of clothing.

Our interlude would not really free us from tension. Next door to my grandparent's house was a brothel. It was frequented by Japanese troopers. They came in groups, at all hours of the day and night, some inebriated, others boisterous. On occasion, a few missed the address and found themselves knocking on our front door by mistake. Those were times when my sisters and I were left alone shaking in fright while hiding as those soldiers would rap at the door impatiently. Fortunately, the neighbors, anxious to ply their trade to the maximum, invariably yelled and motioned the soldiers their way.

One day a couple of samurai-carrying non-commissioned officers gave me a scare I would long remember. I was alone playing marbles in the dirt of our front yard, just beside a fruit tree with low-hanging branches. From the street they sauntered in. In basic Nippongo, I indicated that their objective was the house next door. Perhaps amused by my rudimentary use of their language, they each lingered. At some point, they unsheathed their swords, one had me feel its sharp blade. Then, in mock demonstration of their swashbuckling prowess, both proceeded to hack at tree branches in their two-fisted form and sharp grunts. I was squatted by the trunk, frozen in fear that I attempted to hide. I felt that those swishing blades, missing my unprotected head by inches, would at any moment catch my neck and end my very existence right there and then. When those swords finally returned to their scabbards and the soldiers took leave, I was limp in thankful relief. They had shown off at my own neck's risk! They went next door.

There was another memorable moment, however, that portrayed a humane twist to the earlier ruckus experience. It happened at Tia Anun's ice cream parlor. My role there was to help crank the ice cream maker. In exchange, I had un-rationed servings, so much so that I once actually swore off eating ice cream for life, a vow that lasted no longer than a few days. One day in that parlor, with my back to the front door, I heard approaching footsteps by a person who started cussing in English. The accent was decidedly un-Japanese. American? I turned around, and to my surprise, he was a youthful Japanese soldier. On one of his later repeat visits, now comfortable with me and getting past our salutatory chit-chat in Nippongo, he settled in a booth and disgorged his life history, in English. He was born to Japanese parents in the State of Washington. In the summer of 1941, just after high school graduation, he departed by ship to visit his grandparents in Japan, apparently a traditional custom among offspring of immigrants. It was a welcome gift from his parents. On disembarking, he found himself forcibly detained and conscripted into the Japanese Army, without regard of his de facto citizenship. He would fight in a war on the wrong side. He felt mistrusted by his superiors and ignored by his platoon-mates. And, being frequently assigned to patrol guerrilla-infested countryside made him justifiably paranoid and pessimistic about his well-being.

He continued to frequent the ice cream parlor and befriended me. I came to regard him as a pleasant young man caught in a most unpleasant, tragic predicament. After a while, he quit coming and I wondered about his ultimate fate. I have long since forgotten his name. But I would remember him as a person by whose acquaintance I was to often grieve. I wondered how many untold tragedies befell individual participants on both sides of that war, arose from simply being in the wrong place at a wrong time? How were their individual beliefs and moral compasses tested? How readily do the pathos of the conflict subsume an individual's identity into oblivion? Those reflective questions always left me saddened, their answers beyond my comprehension. Nonetheless, I felt certain that among the millions of souls that were in the throes of the global inferno there must have been countless who possessed traits in common which were both genteel and humane.

After a few months' stay in Cebu, we would uproot again. This time for the anonymity of Manila, arriving there by one of the few inter-island ships allowed by the Japanese. In my mind, our move was likely fueled by my parent's paranoia, suspecting that the commandant, awaiting our return to Ormoc in vain, would soon search us out to vent his wrath for having been tricked, outfoxed.

THE MANILA INTERLUDE

Shortly after America had gone to war against Japan, the Philippine Commonwealth government and USAFFE declared Manila an Open City, an internationally recognized proclamation that an invading force, on consent, agrees to occupy without resistance. By intention, it thereby avoids destruction and devastation while ceding its resources to the caprice of the occupier. Indeed, the decision to declare Manila an Open City spared its wonders, its beauty, its treasures, and its populace from destruction and harm. Accordingly, the Japanese Army entered Manila un-opposed.

By mid-1943, we were in Manila. To the then twelve-year old visitor from the provinces, a *provinciano*, the city was a marvel. It had a beauty that had inspired others to rave in poetic exultations. It was the showcase of the country's modernity, the repository of the nation's rich cultural treasures, and it was the attractive maritime center of the Far East. It deservedly represented the country as the Perla del Mar de Oriente. I agreed as it struck me of a magnificence that I had not seen before; a vision of a promisingly modern country but now in uncertainty.

The city was laid out with abundant broad avenues and many tree-lined streets, all paved. Large buildings were everywhere, many of which housed legislative and judicial offices of government. They were awaiting Japanese control. In some sections of the city, homes—mansions really—looked opulent with their expansive, manicured gardens. The traffic was a mixture of cars of varied sizes and shapes; horse-drawn *calesas*—akin to the tartanilla—made of polished wood that could accommodate up to four passengers; buses; and, even streetcars. Unlike those of either Cebu or Ormoc, people spoke a dialect different than Binisayá; it was Tagalog, one of eighty-seven dialects spoken throughout the Islands that would eventually be designated the national language. The Pasig River that divided the city in northern and southern sections was large enough to accommodate commercial transport. There were many magnificently structured bridges that connected both sides. One spanned adjacent to an islet named Isla de Convalescencia that was accessed from its side opening. It housed the Hospicio de San Jose, an expansive convalescent home for orphaned children and the aged. Many of the former had been abandoned at their gate. The facility was run by nuns belonging to the Daughters of Charity and Vincentian Fathers— all of Spanish extraction—since before the turn of the century. Soon, I would become better acquainted with the islet.

North of Pasig River, along the river's edge near the bay, was the principal business district, the downtown known as the Escolta. The harbor was envied for its assortment of docking facilities, said to be beyond compare in the Orient. Also on the same side was the University of Santo Tomas. In educational excellence, it would rival the University of the Philippines whose campus was located south of the River. Further upstream sprawled Malacañan Palace, the past residence of Spanish colonial Governors and the American High Commissioner. Since 1935, it had become the home of the president of the Commonwealth of the Philippines.

South of Pasig River, fronting the bay was a large park, Luneta—the venue of a number of significant and historic milestones that included the martyrdom death by firing squad of the national hero Dr. Jose Rizal. Beside the mouth of the river was Manila Hotel, the landmark world-class facility. General Douglas MacArthur had resided there, but it was now headquarters of the Japanese High Command. Just nearby was Old Manila, a city within the city surrounded by a heavy stonewall, named Intramuros. The Spaniards had constructed the wall in 1585 and taken twenty-one years to complete. Within its walls were centuries-old churches erected by laborious efforts of past colonialists and subjugated Filipino labor; academic institutions and museums that were the hallmarks of foreign missionary contributions; and hospitals as well as public buildings that were the showcase of the country's advances. Many of the residential homes were owned by Manila's elite families. Intramuros was a veritable trove of the country's treasures. It also had an ancient garrison known as Fort Santiago. The fort had notoriety for its dungeons dug with side openings to the River. In colonial yesteryears, chained prisoners in those cells were condemned to death by drowning with the rising tide. The Japanese Kempeitai—the military police similar to Germany's Gestapo by reputation for cruelty and torture—had its headquarters in the fort and held its prisoners in those dungeons. They were to be feared, even by the regular Japanese soldiers as their prisoners reputedly rarely came out alive.

The large bay is bordered by multiple provinces. Well past eyesight near its wide aperture is the island named Corregidor; it had historically served to guard the sea-lane approaches to the Manila harbor. At its fortified encampment, Filipino and American combatants fought their last bloody, desperate fight after the losing struggle in Bataan, that provincial projection of jungle area to its north.

In Manila, we lived in an apartment in the district of Paco, south of Pasig River. It was pleasant. There was a playground nearby and a marketplace within a short walk. Adjacent was a drugstore stocked with comic books—Superman, Batman, and others, none of which I had read before. I could browse for free. Our area was connected to downtown Manila by a streetcar; its many distractions were not available in Ormoc. So, overall, I felt that we had a likable rhythm of day-to-day living that had been absent in Cebu.

MAMÁ...THE UNDERGROUND BACKLASH

My parents were unaccustomed to involving children in decision-making. In matters viewed of adult concern, seldom did they feel inclined to include their children in the conversations. For instance, I do not recall ever being party to deliberations about household matters, family goals, or even decisions revolving around daily activities, including mealtime menu choices. I would later recognize the custom not to be an aberration of the country's societal norm. And so, it came as a frightening surprise to me when one November morning in 1943, I opened the front door to the apartment in response to loud pounding. I had been in the living room at that moment playing with my brother and sisters. Both my parents were out of the house. Two stern faced, uniformed members of the Kempeitai stood before me. They wanted Mamá. Why? "For questioning" was the limit of their retort. They returned that afternoon and took her to Fort Santiago, their dreaded headquarters. Much later, I would hear that she was one of several who were arrested in a coordinated roundup of suspects. Of course, as people often behave, conversations that related to events involving the Japanese, rumors about the war or tales bordering on espionage and treason were topics to whisper in confidence but more likely avoided. I became informed by keeping my ears open for tidbits overheard out of casual talk or interpreted from non-verbal exchanges.

When Mamá returned home three days later, she appeared disheveled and disconsolate, pained and weak, her body bruised and welted. Throughout her confinement, she was unfed, denied sleep, and lashed. All of this, I would learn, was for engaging in money-exchange: buying and selling of pre-war Philippine currency in exchange with Japanese-script. The latter was printed without credible legal tender; valueless after the Japanese defeat. Use of the former was illegal, unusable during the occupation. Inevitably, exchanging currencies became an underground business. Mamá, I would realize, was engaged in an illegal enterprise: the black market. Her commissions were partly a means of our livelihood. Her arrest made me anxious since I had been a willing although unwitting accomplice. I was a courier delivering wads of paper bills, either Japanese printed script currency or pre-war Philippine Peso stuffed in my pants pocket, to named parties some walking distance away. Vividly, I recall purposely taking a route that passed by a guard, relishing in the daring and danger. I do not remember being a courier after Mamá's imprisonment.

"Collaborators," "quislings," were individuals who would abet the invaders of one's own country. These people were scorned and denigrated by their compatriots for their conspicuous participation with or suspected sympathy for the enemy. In the Philippines, many years later when events of those war times were better understood and judged with objectivity and compassion, history would establish that but a very few Filipinos betrayed their country by embracing the totalitarian goals of Japan. Instead, many had served as double-agents, and most had performed acts of kindness and humanitarianism. Each of their contributions was for the welfare of fellow-citizens; they had to have been undertaken at great risk to their personal safety. Sadly, those turns of heroism were more often unrecognized, under-appreciated. One such person who lived in Manila was tagged "pro-Japanese." Her failing was that she was a lover of an enemy officer, a colonel of the Kempeitai. Their dalliance had been fodder of derisive gossip. She was shunned and ostracized for her amorous complicity. My parents, however, remained among her dwindled circle of confidants. It was through this tangled web of human interrelationship that my father sought—or more likely begged—her assistance in pleading for Mamá's release. After spending three days imprisoned in Fort Santiago, she returned home. The lady friend must have used her wiles on her colonel lover to good advantage. For this act of charity, my family was certainly in her debt. Neither she nor the colonel survived the war. Since then, I have believed that others such as she, tagged a collaborator, must have also extended assistance to their fellow-citizen, without fanfare and with anonymity.

We surely had ample grounds to be thankful by Christmas of 1943. Our family was intact and surviving the constraints brought on by the occupation. More importantly, Mamá must have healed from her trauma sufficiently by then. My parents celebrated our good fortune such that about nine months later, on the 29th August 1944, their sixth child, Antonio, was born. He was delivered at the Philippine General Hospital. His namesake Saint is believed to be the patron of lost souls. Baby Tonio, we called him, was a great joy and not lost in any way. He, like his father, was born with wavy hair and was very attractive. Not a few months later, a barber cut his hair close to the scalp. Years later, I vented my disgust and incomprehension as sadly, the re-grown head of hair lost much of its curls. Papá explained the practice as a native belief that doing so ensured a healthy head of hair for life, avoiding baldness. I could not believe that his scientific education would not triumph over indigenous belief lacking supportive evidence.

PUPPETS...FOREBODING DAYS OF LIBERATION

Meanwhile, telling consequences of the occupation became increasingly evident. The country, now governed by a de facto puppet leadership, was cowered to declare the Philippines an independent republic, the second time in its history. It was proclaimed on 14th October 1943, tacitly approved, if not on covert command by the Japanese. Jose Laurel, the imminent Chief

Justice of the Supreme Court, became the president. We later would learn that he and a corps of politicians, on direction of President Quezon before departing for Australia, were entrusted the leadership of the government with instructions to cooperate with the enemy. The collaboration was hoped to spare the citizenry harsh and cruel conduct by the Japanese. But was the country now independent of the United States of America? What of the subjugation by the Japanese? Would it abate? A paradox. A conundrum.

From posters that flooded Manila for everyone to read, Laurel stated, in part:

> Today we have proclaimed our independence. This independence is real, complete and total. The Republic of the Philippines is to be run by Filipinos for Filipinos. This is true independence and freedom never before offered by any other people in the history of the world. It is very clear, that the role of the Philippines is one of collaboration with all member peoples benefit, under the leadership of Japan. Distribution, it goes without saying, will be fair and compensation always equitable, under the benevolent leadership and direction of Japan.

The proclamation gained recognition only by countries of the Axis powers. An exception was a congratulatory message from General Francisco Franco of neutral Spain. Nonetheless, the Japanese propaganda machine went on overdrive. It was geared to convince the Filipinos that America was the enemy and Japan the protector, savior, and liberator. It reminded the Filipinos that they were Asians, as were the Japanese. Propaganda billboards were pasted in many places, easily viewed by the public. Of course, marring the signs was a harshly punishable offense. The republic was welcomed to the Greater East Asia Co-Prosperity Sphere, a "one for all and all for one" concept of collaboration. But there was a disquieting addition, "under the leadership of Japan." It implied the complete and total willingness of the Filipino people to submit to the guidance and leadership of the Japanese Empire.

Events of the subsequent months would prove the pronouncements vacuous. Laurel's government functioned as a puppet of Japan, a failed camouflaged instrument of its strategy of enslavement. The ubiquitous posters before the public served only as a mockery of the atmosphere of terror and enmity. However, there were pro-Japanese groups. Prominent among them was the *Makapili—Makabayan Katipunan Ng Mga Pilipino* or Alliance of Philippine Patriots—a militant volunteer group which formed without President Laurel's approval. There were important Filipino members of major business enterprises who collaborated with the Japanese as did some of the Spanish community. They earned suspicion and vile. Many of them, however, were active participants of the guerilla movement and covertly anti-Japanese. Most Filipinos overwhelmingly regarded the Japanese as the enemy and held America as the benevolent protector and benefactor. Even President Laurel refused to comply with the Japanese urge for the Philippine government to declare war against the United States of America.

Veiled to the world, sometime in late July1944, U.S. President Roosevelt had conferred with General Douglas MacArthur and Navy Admiral Chester Nimitz as commanders-in-chief of the Army and Naval Forces of the Pacific theater, respectively. The object was to clarify the island-to-island strategy of battle leading to the invasion of Japan. What would be of profound relevance to the Filipinos was that MacArthur had persuaded President Roosevelt to agree to the re-conquest rather than the bypass of the Philippines in the march to Japan. At the same period, increasingly, news about the continuing battles in Europe and the Pacific were the ecstatic object of whispered conversations, their sources the contraband radios. Risking imprisonment or death, the always un-named sources fed everyone's insatiable curiosity about current events, the news passed from ear to ear.

The Allies were winning. General MacArthur's forces were inching their way from Australia to the Philippines, fighting their battles in island after island of the South Pacific.

Emboldened by the improving fortunes of the Allied Forces and encouraged by General MacArthur's "I shall return" promise, the guerrillas were becoming increasingly effective in restraining Japanese troop movements and sabotaging their military fortifications. In revenge, Japanese aggression took to randomly terrorizing and incarcerating civilians suspected of guerilla sympathy, a convenient and easier target than engaging the elusive guerillas in combat. Nowhere was the terrorism and carnage more commonplace than in Luzon, worsening with the continuing victorious campaign of the Americans against the enemy in island garrisons of South Pacific. On the guise of avenging the death of Japanese soldiers or, sometimes by declaring entire villages as inhabited by guerillas, the Japanese turned to rampant killings by bayonet and sword, rape, and burning of villages.

In Manila, as elsewhere in the country, a climate of heightened tension, distrust, and fear pervaded. It was becoming more palpable toward the end of the year, as the Japanese ratcheted their adversarial policies against the Filipinos. In many areas of the city, their defensive anti-aircraft gun placements visibly multiplied. Unknowingly, the city—indeed, the country—would soon suffer the unimaginable wrath and fury of its unbridled interloper. In the meantime, the populace was increasingly burdened by the deficiencies brought on by the occupation. Where there were food distribution centers, the queues of the hungry were becoming longer; rumors abounded of some restaurants serving dog, cat or rat meat, largely underscoring the depleting food supply. Or were they rumors fanned by competing businesses? Walking barefoot became the vogue, leaving shoe-wear only for special events such as going to church. I remember sparing my shoes in favor of going barefooted, on occasions. They were times that gave me a feeling of sharing, in empathy to those barefooted not by choice.

My family would suffer set-backs as well, the kind and extent of which I did not then fully comprehend. The trauma of her imprisonment at Fort Santiago, the period of pregnancy and delivery of baby Tonio in an atmosphere of instability and strife were immeasurable strains Mamá must have endured to preserve her family's welfare. All these circumstances would have a cumulative ill-effect on her cardiovascular system. She did get medical care at the Philippine General Hospital and was prescribed medications for heart troubles. Additionally, Linda had alarming periodic seizures and headaches, symptoms not clearly diagnosed but would later be discovered as a growing brain tumor. As much as she got our more pointed doting care, her malady had to have added to the mental strains which both parents were experiencing in the midst of all the chaos but especially, it would turn out, on Mamá.

THE DARKENING CLOUDS OF DANGER

The 21st September 1944 was just another sunny day. The tension in the air was no different from any of the previous days when leaflets had dropped on the city. I read one. It warned of impending air-raids by American war planes and advised civilians to stay clear of military objectives. Indeed! An anti-aircraft gun had been positioned in a small park mere blocks from the drugstore I frequented that had all the comic books of choice; but how was one to distance from those gun emplacements? By mid-morning I was browsing through a comic book with a neighbor friend when, all of a sudden, the air-raid sirens started blaring, filling the air with their characteristic piercing, whirling sound. As we prepared to run to the safely of our homes, I scanned the sky. To my utter amazement, the northeast horizon was blanketed with black dots. There were hundreds of them. They were fighter planes of the American Navy, carried within striking distance by aircraft carriers in Philippine seas.

The droning sound of those planes grew loader as they approached their targets bringing an endless booming, echoing blasts of exploding bombs. They mixed with the staccato-crackle of the anti-aircraft gun replies, one of which emanated nearby. The sky was awash with puffs of smoke from exploding shells. There were live dog-fights, the defending Japanese and attacking American planes each spewing their machinegun fire. The riveting scenario was short-lived, perhaps lasting under an hour. I recall taking my time reaching home that morning, thinking the experience I had during the feared three-Japanese airplane attack of Ormoc several months earlier paled from the frighteningly astonishing exhibition I had just witnessed.

The American air raid that day was only the first of many more to come in the following days and weeks. With the air raids came the inevitable dogfights between the Japanese Zeros and the U.S. Navy Grumman fighters. There always appeared to be planes exploding in air from machine gun or anti-aircraft firings. On occasion, an ejected parachuted airman would float languorously as if unfazed by the surrounding battle. The frequency and the time of day of the sorties was unpredictable. Propaganda leaflets that continued to float from American airplanes warned civilians to stay away from major airfields and military installations, promisingly the limit of their targets. I would come to assume that we, the civilians, were not at risk. It was a guess my anxious parents did not share, nor did it spare me their chastening. Evolving circumstances in the coming days would justify their concern.

Meanwhile, more defensive fortifications were placed at various sections of the city. Their dispersal within neighborhoods was evident as they marched in large groups to their destinations, scary in their battle gear with rifles and fixed bayonets.

They entrenched themselves in large school houses and government buildings, commandeered at will; their ammunition depots were fearfully within population centers. More alarming were the rumors of able-bodied Filipino males being herded and forced to labor side by side with American prisoners-of-war to repair bombed airport runways and other such destroyed military installations. They were often unprotected from the firefight exchanges overhead and the shower of falling bombs. Would women and children come in harm's way next, probably by intention?

Equally concerning were the economic well-being of the man in the street and the common family of Manila. They were increasingly bridled. Everything seemed on ration. Little was available for purchase and what was sold would take box-loads of Japanese printed scripts to obtain. I recall pieces of coconut meat being sold at inflated prices by street vendors when whole coconuts would have been available for much less in times past. The Japanese, of course, took priority of the food supplies.

One day in early November, our family vacated the apartment. I never knew if we lost our apartment lease or quite simply if my parents felt the need to find a safer haven. Or perhaps, Papa was offered a better position than what he may have had or didn't have. I am also unclear which furnishings came with us or how they were disposed. It is more likely that we brought with us only the barest of possessions. We found ourselves quartered at the Hospicio de San José, located on the Isla de la Convalescencia, adjacent to one of many bridges across Pasig River. Our living quarter was a single room on the second floor, just above the nuns' cloistered area. The bare wooden floor was planked unevenly, so light filtered from below. I slept on the floor as did my siblings, lying atop one of those palm mats. We dined with the nuns and the resident cleric while other evacuees, who seemed to continually filter in to the compound, slept in more confined accommodations and fended for their own provisions. In what I believe to have been the barter, Papá was the designated medical officer.

There was an infirmary where those in his need were tended. His services seemed to me had complemented the spiritual needs of the congregated mass of people which the priest provided. I was among the acolytes who served mass at the chapel.

The Hospicio itself was spacious. It sprawled the islet as its only man-made structure. The ambiance was tranquil and safe, isolated from the turbulence brewing outside. In short time, there developed a communal bond between the resident orphans, the smattering of elderly widows, the staff, and us, the outsider refugees. The orphans, reputed for their artisan knitting training, were made busy with requests for hand-made articles of clothing. My siblings and I each had a pair of knitted cotton socks. I prized mine so much; they were always among the dwindling personal possessions that came with me in the months to come. There shortly organized plays and musicals that were scheduled for entertainment, perhaps to detract us all from the realities of the continuing horrors committed outside the compound. I was flattered when asked to play the violin for the Christmas time production. My participation, I overheard was more in deference to the medical officer rather than my talent. Oh well...

Families kept coming to the Hospicio as refugees. Their children were always my source of stories about happenings outside of the compound. With passing time, the picture which they described, albeit separately as they came from different sections of the city, depicted a desperate enemy force intent on a battle without retreat, without capitulation, and without regard for the safety of the civilian populace. Now and again, there were stories of soldiers herding defenseless males to be shot or beheaded for suspected sympathy for the guerrillas. There were stories of families having to scrounge for food to augment their already meagerly rationed provisions. Indeed, I felt our family quite fortunate for having been provided sustenance by those nuns and for living in the islet, isolated from the mayhem and away from harm's way. Travel to outside the institution was limited and mostly done by adults; we youngsters, however, did not feel confined and would not lack for diversions within. In the ensuing weeks leading to the Christmas holidays, I witnessed and experienced a number of events that made me consider I was part of history in the making. There were the aerial dogfights, American and Japanese war planes coming at or tailing after each other. Some of the former sometimes flew so low I once waved at a pilot who was visibly grinning at me. There were the infrequent parachutists who had bailed out of damaged aircrafts; they always seemed to be floating to earth so gracefully as to belie their perilous fates. All these scenes I witnessed oblivious to the risk the deafening sounds of firepower exchanges portended.

A few days after New Year 1945, by order of the Japanese, everyone then living in the islet was given only hours to vacate. The facility would be converted into an armed fortress; by then, the adjacent bridge was sufficiently mined to blow the structure to pieces. Everyone was to relocate to another schoolhouse, a couple miles distant. The priest was caught in a conundrum: carry the quantity of Hosts, already blessed so that each represented the transubstantiated body of Christ and risk desecration or ask communicants to swallow not the customary single Eucharistic Host but countless so as to empty the reservoir. The priest chose the latter; I was among those who partook in the most unusual departure from traditional regard of the sacrament.

U.S. FORCES RETURN...THE PRICE OF LIBERATION

Several weeks before, on 20th October 1944, the American Forces landed in Leyte. It was brother Jun's birthday. Leading the initial group of invaders was General Douglas MacArthur, wading to shore on the western beachside south of Tacloban, seemingly unfazed by the attendant firefight. That day, before a bevy of microphones and whirling cameras recording the occasion, the general did proclaim:

> People of the Philippines: I have returned.
>
> By the grace of Almighty God our forces stand again on Philippine soil—soil consecrated in the blood of our two peoples. We have come dedicated and committed to the task of destroying every vestige of enemy control over your daily lives, and of restoring upon a foundation of indestructible strength, the liberties of your people.

Almost lost in the grandiosity of the occasion was the Commonwealth of the Philippines President Sergio Osmeña. He was part of the wading party of Filipino officials returning from exile in America. Osmeña had assumed the position following President Quezon's demise from tuberculosis while in America. If President Osmeña spoke at that occasion, he was not the main feature of propaganda leaflets that dropped in Manila. The details of the eventful day, although appropriately censored, were reported in Manila newspapers; more reliably accurate were the whispered accounts picked up from covert, illegal short wave broadcasts emanating from radio stations in America and Australia. The jubilation and the hope of liberation that came with them must have been held within. I do not recall any outbursts of celebration. Instead, there developed a sense of trepidation mixed with a pervading resolve to survive the suffering as allied victory—as if able to see a light at the end of a long harrowing, dark tunnel—now seemed deliverance in sight. The ensuing battle to wrist Japanese control of Leyte, however, would prove more challenging and costly to the American forces than anticipated. The Japanese defensive strategy was to engage their land, sea and air resources, which included the infamous kamikaze sacrifice, suicidal pilots crashing their airplanes into enemy naval vessels.

AIRBORNE EDITION

FREE PHILIPPINES
PUBLISHED WEEKLY

Manila, Sunday, March 25, 1945

MACARTHUR LANDS ON PANAY
NAVY "CRIPPLES" JAP HOME FLEET

Nearly 11,000 Tons Rock Main Arsenals

Carrier Planes Blast At Least 17 Warships

Iloilo Liberated Within 3 Days; 70% Destroyed

All Traffic To Move To Right

5th Airforce Planes Rake Jap Shipping

Allies Free Mandalay, Sweep South of City

Moratorium on Debts

12,000 Marine Wounded May Regain Health

McNutt Suggests Postponement of Complete P.I. Independence

YANKS DESTROY 100,000 NAZIS IN WEST

Newspaper published during early phase of liberation. Note item on McNutt's recommendation to delay Philippine independence.

121

On 9th January 1945, the Americans landed in Lingayen, a coastal town on the western side of the island of Luzon, no more than two hundred miles north of Manila. Thereafter, I would hear of landings in other islands. Meanwhile, the fighting in Leyte would continue for months, both sides suffering heavy casualties as the Japanese put up a determined defense. Ormoc itself, the newspapers reported, became the site of intense battles as ground won and lost would see-saw back and forth. We worried over the fate of relatives and friends we had left there, not knowing that we too would soon be party to the excesses of the warring sides.

When we left the Hospicio compound, Linda had by then become increasingly more disabled from a suspected tumor in her brain. Leaving on foot, Jun, Indáy, and Tonio were too young to trudge along on their own. They all required added care and physical support. All of these concerns limited the material possessions we could bring with us. I do not recall bringing my violin. For my person, I only had clothes stuffed in a pair of long pants, the legs wrapped around me as a waist-pack, my favorite pair of knit socks among them. What was frightening everyone was the knowledge that at the same side of the city, atrocities were being committed on civilians, at random. We felt imperiled by the reaction our group of refugees might provoke should we confront Japanese soldiers in our path. Besides, overhead there were the sporadic firings from American artillery positions north of us that would thunder, aimed and blasting at points unknown to us. We walked, trailing a large number of islet residents to the south side of Pasig River, toward one of the Manila districts called Paco. The streets, now devoid of civilian vehicular traffic, had a jumble of makeshift barricades; litter and shards of broken glass and burnt sidings of houses from the artillery shelling, ostensibly by the Americans, made the trek slow and cautious. Eerily, there were the occasional corpses. They were in ghastly states of decomposition, yet to be disposed. We ended up at the *Colegio de la Inmaculada Concepcion de la Concordia*, simply Concordia College, a Catholic institution founded in 1868 for girls, now deserted. It was also run by nuns of the Daughters of Charity. Thankfully, we arrived safely; it may have been a three-mile walk. At the college, we joined the elderly and the very young Hospicio residents who had crossed the river by barge. Unbeknown to the many of us refugees, months earlier the College had been requisitioned as a headquarters of Japanese soldiers.

The school house now was serving as an evacuation center, attracting large numbers of other families coming from surrounding points. Some related being forced out of homes that had been set afire by Japanese soldiers, who were said to be running amok. Others described the horrors of witnessing civilians herded and summarily executed by rifle fire or the sword. The atrocities appeared to be ominously mounting. Then, there were the American shells aimed at buildings suspected to be command posts of entrenched Japanese soldiers. Where were the liberation forces? How long would the fighting continue? Would we survive? Those were the questions whispered back and forth in that large room among the many huddled evacuees: hungry, terrified, desperate, praying.

We shared a small area of a large ground floor room with strangers, perhaps numbering a couple of hundred. We were overcrowded but the sense of intimacy was less annoying and not so depressing to me as it might have been to my parents. Surely my parent's compounding concerns for the unraveling tragedy must have been indescribably heart wrenching. Meanwhile, Papá continued to serve as the medical officer of the growing evacuee population. Maybe it was in this capacity that his family somehow was provided its mealtime rations since I do recall always having food to eat for each of us, even if severely rationed. Exactly what the grub consisted of, I do not remember. It mattered less when knowing that others lacked food.

The grown-up males came to organize a volunteer group to provide an all-night watch for fires in the building. Perhaps, the concern was in response to the tales related by newcomer refugees about the enemy troopers wantonly setting fires to residences and then shooting at the escaping residents. There did not appear to be any armed defense against the carnage. Additionally, the sound of exploding artillery, now a daily occurrence, did suggest an intensifying exchange between the warring armies; they seemed suspiciously aimed nearby. Our hope and salvation, it seemed, would have to come only from the approaching American troops, now already precipitously close, on the north side of Manila. My parents would talk of looking forward to an era of reconstruction, of rehabilitation, of peace. Instead, the swirling clouds of hope would give way to a more sinister outburst of inhumane brutality and wanton destruction of the country's treasures and human lives.

THE BATTLE COMES TO MANILA

Intent on liberation, a vanguard column of US Army soldiers arrived in Manila on 3rd February 1945. They rushed to the University of Santo Tomas compound, which had served as the internment camp for civilian Americans and allied nationals. It included Edward Greene, husband of Tia Luisa and cousin Eddie's dad. That joyous news spread around our huddled group, lifting our spirits and venting hope of freedom. Our family, fortunate for the blessings that our togetherness maintained, prayed for the warfare to cease shortly with Japan's surrender.

Our revelry would prove short lived. That very day, as the liberators reinforced their hold on north Manila, they brought with them artillery guns and begun shelling suspected Japanese strongholds on the south side, our own La Concordia domicile included. Their bombardment would continue for days.

Ironically, four days later even as Manila was suffering the consequences of intense battle between the combatants, General MacArthur did boastfully declare to the world that the Japanese had ceased fighting in the city. Neither the soldiers of both sides, still engaged in armed conflict as they were, nor the civilians dying and wounded when caught in the crossfire would surely have agreed with the General. Instead, unbeknownst to us, US Army intelligence had erroneously mistaken La Concordia College as a Japanese stronghold, as it once was actually occupied by troops. Accordingly, a more aggressive shelling of the compound, to be continued day and night for days on end until totally destroyed, was planned. Many of the evacuees, in the process, would have been innocently killed or maimed by friendly shelling.

Thankfully, good fortune was on our side. On mid-morning of Saturday 10th February, a number of people, crowded in that ground-level large room, were gazing out the window that fronted the quadrangle garden. I was among them. Unbelievably, some of us soon spied soldiers in olive-green fatigue uniform darting from tree to bush, advancing toward our side of the building, their rifles on the ready. Aware of the atrocities that Japanese troops were committing elsewhere, the scene was frightening. Many believed at that very moment the soldiers were Japanese, intent on invading our premises and killing us. The room was charged with fear and near panic. Until that instant, our last-held remembrance of the American soldier uniform was khaki, not the olive-green we saw that we familiarly associated with the Japanese; and, the American steel helmets from our memory were more flat-topped than what we now had sighted. Suddenly, someone, boldly gambling that the soldiers were American, urged the women to show their faces by the window in an overt demonstration of our civilian presence. The ploy succeeded. The soldiers were, indeed, Americans. We were thankful, particularly since they had been sent to scout the building and confirm its military worth before intensifying the shelling of the college.

The Americans had come at last. The sporadic shelling of days before their presence ceased. There followed a celebratory mood that lasted well into the evening of the following day. It was a relief, but only temporarily. On Sunday 11th February, sometime close to midnight, alarming news spread among the evacuees, awakening everyone. Our building was set ablaze at multiple points. Without any fire-fighting resource, the blaze rapidly got out of control. Unbeknownst to everyone in the compound, Japanese troops had somehow infiltrated the walled campus and set the inferno. They were destroying the building by fire in a manner that the American shells could not. Had they mistakenly assumed the building was now occupied by American soldiers? Or were they intent on committing atrocities on civilians? I had slept that evening with my waistpack of clothes for a pillow. I looped the bundle around me, ready to join the escape. As my family prepared to evacuate the worsening conflagration we resolved to stay together holding hands. The darkness faintly lit by the glowing flames, which were accompanied by the crackling noises of burning wood and breaking glass. My parents were guiding my younger siblings through the dark, amid bewildering cries of people, with me tailing our human train. People were shoving, shouting, crying, everyone scrambling hither and yon forcing a slow pace. There were dozens of people ahead of us who had headed for the main gate. Surprisingly and pitifully, their rush out was savagely greeted by machine gunfire, the weapons set up by awaiting Japanese soldiers. Just as civilians were being killed or wounded in that atrocious act, others of us fortunate for being at the back of the crowd and now aware of the danger ahead, turned around and back-tracked. In that ghastly moment, desperate to escape but believing that one route would lead to certain death while any other risked an unknown fate, we opted to wiggle ourselves out through a side window at the back of the room. Miraculously, everyone in my family got out of the burning building safely by having chosen to avoid doorways and gateways. Others who followed us would as well. Just how many escaped to safety and how many others became casualties of that incomprehensible act of inhumanity, I would not know.

Our escape route led us outside of the college campus, on the side adjacent to railroad tracks, no more than thirty yards away.

As we crawled our way from the campus, ever fearful of running into Japanese soldiers, a backward glance confirmed the enormity of the flaming inferno. The raging fire was made eerie by crying sounds of the dying and wounded, while overheard was the unceasing report of machine guns. I never knew how many were trapped between the flames and rapid-fire bullets from those machine gun nests. I am certain that everyone who had escaped to safety decried their helplessness to assist, to bring everyone to safety. I was left to imagine doomed companions in the bull's-eye of harm's way. What astounded me, as I stood there away from the firestorm, was that the sides of the railroad tracks were lined with American soldiers, bivouacked in their dug-out foxholes. I recall being momentarily disturbed and irritated by the unexpected encounter. In a brief eye-to-eye contact, I asked one of those soldiers to account for their seeming inaction to the imbroglio before their eyes. Of course, there was no time for discussion. I may have consoled myself by empathizing with their helplessness. Perhaps they had a strategy that had compelled the demeanor. Overall, they were a sight to behold. Being among them gave me a sense of safety, of liberation, of a relief from danger. They were feelings surely shared by my family and every one of the escapees.

The group that had now gathered around the American troops was then herded along a circuitous path toward the Pasig riverbanks, another few miles distant. By dawn, we saw a pontoon bridge. It had been installed by the Americans across the river, the many beautiful bridges of the past now in ruins and impassable. All of us trudged across that makeshift bridge in quiet celebration. We moved toward the north of Manila, feeling grateful to have survived. At least, I felt that way. The Japanese troops more determined to stage a savage resistance, meanwhile, had retreated from the north-side of Pasig river in favor of entrenching themselves on the south-side. Well before the fighting showed signs of ending, General MacArthur summoned a provisional assembly of prominent Filipinos to Malacañan Palace in mid-February. In their presence, he declared the Commonwealth of the Philippines permanently reestablished; in part, he announced: "My country kept the faith. Your capital city, cruelly punished though it be, has regained its rightful place—citadel of democracy in the East."

As if to belie General MacAthur's myopic assessment of the intensity of the battle, both the American and Japanese combatants would set horrific records of mayhem and destruction. The campaign to liberate the south side of Manila became increasingly desperate; fighting went house-to-house, building-to-building, razing private homes and historic government edifices in the process. Undisciplined Japanese soldiers and sailors went on a wanton spree of barbaric killing and rape. Intramuros was particularly victimized as American artillery targeted the centuries-old stone ramparts, underground edifices, and villages within the city walls, all of which were perversely providing defensive cover for the Japanese. The US Army artillery cannonade, directed from several yards away to point-blank would be massive and last from 17th to 23rd February. More than 4,000 civilians, fearful of the mortar barrage, remained within the wall as if held hostage. Fewer than 3,000 civilians, mostly women and children, were freed on 23rd February. One thousand men, women and children were killed.

I would much later understand that General Yamashita had taken overall command of the Japanese forces in the Philippines only on 10th October 1944, ten days before the American landing in Leyte. It was just days before the invasion by overwhelming U.S. Army units in Lingayen, Luzon that Yamashita had ordered his forces to evacuate Manila and retrench in the mountain fastness of northern Luzon. Left tailing the retreat were naval and marine units in command of Admiral Sanji Iwabuchi who, feeling trapped by the advancing American troops, stayed in the city to battle and commit atrocities. Had the admiral disobeyed orders? How complicit was Yamashita in the massacre?

American artillery barrages would compound the Japanese suicidal defense, which wrought the blasting and burning of homes, buildings, and bridges. Many of the handsome public and private buildings were pulverized. Of utmost inhumanity was the mindless brutality of the massacre of innocent children, women, and men of all ages by Admiral Iwabuchi's troops. Indeed, few battles in the closing months of World War II would exceed the destruction that occurred in Manila. The city was laid in ruins, its treasured relics, monuments to its historic past destroyed, irreplaceably.

Among the many missing and presumed dead was my cousin Eddie Greene. He had been herded with other males from his district as a laborer needed to repair damages at the airport.

He failed to return home.

At the final phase of the fight, which ended on 3rd March 1945, 1,010 U.S. and 16,665 Japanese soldiers had died. Dreadfully, an estimated 100,000 Filipino civilian had lost their lives, victims of the shooting exchanges, strafing from the air, artillery bombardment from both the American and Japanese troops, and wanton massacre by the Japanese.

The Battle for Manila, as it was regarded, became the first and fiercest urban fighting in the entire Pacific War. The "Battle for Manila" by Connaughton, R., Pimlott, J., Anderson, D. is a recommended reading for an exhaustive description of the horrendous events, aptly beyond the scope of this tome.

A 1930s view of Manila, capital of Perla del Mar de Oriente. Painfully, the destruction of property and treasure inflicted by Japanese and American forces in a two-month period of 1945 were allegedly worse than the Londoners had suffered from the German bombing of 1940. The human casualty and suffering were comparable to that resulting from the atom bomb dropped in August 1945 on the residents of Hiroshima (war scene photos in the book are courtesy of Flickr and John Tewell).

Destruction of the capital. Death of innocent civilians would be an onerous yoke as was the country's oncoming herculean reconstruction undertaking.

A section of Manila along Pasig River. The Battle for Manila between 3rd February to 3rd March 1945 caused death and suffering of innocent Filipinos and utter destruction of the city. It is regarded to have been the fiercest urban fighting in the entire Pacific War. General MacArthur was denied his hoped for victory parade in Manila to crown his promised "I shall return."

The noted author Alfonso Aluit wrote "By Sword and Fire—the Destruction of Manila in World War II." His accounts detail the human suffering and wanton destruction that befell on Manila. He quoted a survivor, Ana Mari Calero's heart-breaking experience that led her to say, "The American artillery shelling and mortar fire caused loss of lives and properties in Manila. Survivors, however, were all happy to see the Americans. The constant shelling and street-by-street fighting was a high price to pay for freedom."

Not all survivors felt the same way. In the account of her ordeal, Aluit noted Carmen Guerrero Nakpil's observation thusly:

"Once again, as in Bataan, we had put our faith in the myth of the benevolent protector who did not materialize until fire, shelling from both sides had reduced Manila to the last circle of hell and its people to wide-eyed, shivering madmen. Those who had survived Japanese hate did not survive American love. Both were equally deadly, the latter more so because we had sought and longed for."

ORPHANHOOD AND OTHER TRAGEDIES

Our trek to freedom ended at a school house, also run by nuns of the same order that had earlier cared for us. We had a room to ourselves, in the second floor. Like the flooring at the Hospicio, the floorboards were laid with spaces through which one could hear conversations from below and see any of its occupants. By chance, the lower floor was occupied and used by Americans to interrogate captured Japanese soldiers. One day, in the room immediately below ours, I spied a couple of detainee Japanese soldiers. I got a revengeful thrill out of yelling down to them cuss words in their language. I can still see their bewildered, irritated reaction as they searched in vain for my identity.

That school building became a refugee haven. There we were provided food, complements of American aid organizations and the U.S. Army. In contrast to the meager ration with which we sustained ourselves while confined to the La Concordia compound, the provisions now seemed in great abundance. There were cans and cans of powdered eggs and milk, corned beef hash, Spam, Vienna sausages, and chocolate candies with long-forgotten names like Babe Ruth and Butterfinger. And there were packaged meals issued American soldiers, the K-Ration. In so many ways everything tasted delicious and savory. I remember eating with relish at each mealtime still worried of a relapsing time of severe rationing. Would this heavenly manna continue? There would, of course, be more. For years thereafter, I would crave those canned foods, equating their availability with abundance, the end of war and suffering, the hoped-for return to normalcy. Some of us living in that refugee center, now early teen-agers, could wear the khaki uniforms and shoes that American soldiers wore, acceptably well-fitting; we were issued the cloth-ing. For several years, they were my primary wardrobe. We all regarded them luxurious, and I felt fortunate. At that same time, many of the children would learn to repeat American phrases when surrounding the ubiquitous G.I.s: "helo Joe"… "gimmee tsokolet Jo."

Although now safely in the north side of Manila, not all of my family fared well. Mamá was still caring for suckling baby Tonio; she had not produced adequate milk, almost since birth. It was a deficiency that was likely aggravated, if not induced, by the cumulative traumatic ordeals she had experienced. Despite having had to move from place to place, quite by luck, perhaps providential luck as we all certainly offered a lot of rosary nove-nas, Mamá had found a surrogate breast-milk feeder from among her friends who also had recently given birth. I never knew how the arrangements came about, but it was fortunate for Tonio, who would receive his basic sustenance. Not from his mother but through an unusual act of compassion that only mothers can truly understand and provide. Our infant soon would also benefit from the abundance provided by the liberator forces: baby food.

Mamá continued on a downhill course, despite the meager heart medications and the knowledge that the horrors of the war were in our past, and the palpable hope of a more stable, more peaceful aftermath. On 14th March 1945, she expired. She was forty-one and it was a little over a month after our escape from the holocaust at La Concordia College. All of us were present during her last moments, mournful of the devastating prospect of orphanhood. It was a tragedy that had heaped on top of all the carnage and destruction that I had encountered the days and weeks before. It bothered me that I did not cry when everyone about me did. I felt the immense loss, and I sensed the heaviness in my heart. Perhaps I had been drained of emotion. Today, I am comforted to know that then, despite my eyes dried of tears, we each had prayed consoled that Mamá had departed from a life wracked with agony brought on by the horrors of war to an everlasting rest, deeply secure in the knowledge that she had loved and cared for her family as best she could. In her eternal peace, I sometime search the night sky for a star twinkling to let us know that Mamá knew her brood was grateful for her love and devotion. The next day, we had her laid in a simple wooden coffin, which we balanced precariously atop a borrowed bicycle. Papá, Fenny and I then pushed the bicycle, slowly walking our way to the cemetery, about five miles away. A priest accompanied our private procession. We passed through streets hollowed and torn up by the shelling, past houses and buildings in rubble. They were a stark residual evidence of the nightmare, which had not abated until two weeks before. The cemetery itself had been a battleground only weeks earlier. Many of the tombs were destroyed by mortar shells or pot-marked by bullets. Unbelievably, some coffins had been pried open; Japanese soldiers were believed to have removed gold-filled teeth from the exhumed dead for booty. I saw family groupings who appeared to have camped among the tombs, most probably having been displaced from their destroyed abodes. The whole ghoulish, depressing scene only added to the sadness of our loss. I was eager to leave the premises, as painful as the thought was of Mamá alone in that burial ground. Inday, after graduating from the Philippine Women's University with a Bachelor of Arts degree in Home Economics in 1960, had Mamá's remains exhumed; they now rest in the Yrastorza Family Mausoleum in Ormoc, where many of our deceased family members are interred.

The American military presence was everywhere, enough so that at one point in my excursions, I was actually stopped at a corner as a convoy of jeeps passed by. Among those soldiers, one had a familiar figure, seated erect in the passenger side of a jeep with a flag mounted on its front end having a cluster of five stars. To me, by his dark sunglasses and cap with the braided visor, although they had covered eyes and head, he was undoubtedly General Douglas McArthur himself. I recall that he was applauded as he traveled past the onlookers, including by me.

I had occasion to become acquainted with American soldiers who were likely of the Intelligence Corps as they were the interrogators of those captured Japanese soldiers retained in the rooms below our living quarters. I was fascinated by the seeming parity of appurtenances and privileges that the enlisted G.I. and the officer corps shared. They were uniformed similarly, they smoked and chewed gum alike, they handed candy and bars of chocolate with the same facility, and they all talked as passionately of "back home." I would learn that the soldiers were conscripted to join the military from every societal segment of America. In their civilian life, they were from urban and rural communities. They were farmers, mechanics, laborers, teachers, and business leaders; others were from the health and legal professions. If there was a hierarchal distinction among themselves, as was the tradition of our military, it escaped my notice; they seemed to me as ordinary as they were extraordinary. At the time, they were my intoxicating paradoxical observation with fascinating soldiers, if only perfunctorily.

Little known at the same time was a covert raid by a select group of U.S. Army Rangers who, with the valuable aid of a band of Filipino guerillas, successfully rescued American prisoners of war by overwhelming their Japanese guards who were believed preparing to kill their wards in retribution for losses of their fellow warriors. The concentration camp—once a Philippine Army base that Papá had been assigned to in 1941—was three hundred miles north of Manila named Cabanatuan.

Americans would lose their iconic President Franklin D. Roosevelt. Harry S. Truman became the new leader on whose watch a number of watershed events occurred. The war in Europe ended with the surrender of Germany on 4th May 1945. The war with Japan raged on. Fierce fighting escalated as island after island was invaded ever closer to the Japanese mainland. I would soon add another word to my lexicon besides kamikaze. The other, of historical import was: *atom*—atom bomb! On 6th August 1945, it was dropped on the Japanese city of Hiroshima, and again three days later, on nearby Nagasaki. It was a devastating thermonuclear devise released from a U.S. Superfortress bomber named Enola Gay to float earthward by parachute and detonate at a prescribed distance above ground. The radius of total destruction was about one mile, with resulting fires reaching across four times the area. Japanese officials determined that some 30 percent of the population at each city were killed immediately. More would die from long-term mal effects of radiation. Just as the shooting and shelling by Japanese and American combatants had resulted in wanton destruction of property and loss of non-combatant lives during the Battle of Manila, the atom bombs would cause massive damages of property and civilians to die or be maimed in Hiroshima and Nagasaki. It seemed to me, innocent children, women and men once again were being cruelly victimized by the warring adversaries. Had they become the intended piece of war plans for the defense or for the victory of combating forces? Did a vengeful policy justify the killing of non-combatants? The world would soon split into opposing ideological camps, engaging in a dangerous arms race that was to last for decades.

On 15th August 1945, Emperor Hirohito broadcast to the Japanese his decision to end the war against the United States of America and its Allies. Snippets of his declaration, translated and broadcast by radio stations and printed in the daily newspapers of Manila, read as follows:

> To Our good and loyal subjects... We have ordered Our Government to communicate to the Governments of the United States, Great Britain, China and the Soviet Union that Our Empire accepts the provisions of their Joint Declaration. Moreover, the enemy has begun to employ a

new and most cruel bomb, the power of which to damage is indeed incalculable, taking the toll of many innocent lives. Should We continue to fight, it would not only result in an ultimate collapse and obliteration of the Japanese nation, but also it would lead to the total extinction of human civilization.

...Let the entire nation continue as one family from generation to generation, ever firm in its faith of the imperishableness of its divine land, and mindful of its heavy responsibilities, and the long road before it. Unite your total strength to be devoted to the construction for the future. Cultivate the ways of rectitude; foster nobility of spirit; and work with resolution so as ye may enhance the innate glory of the Imperial State and keep pace with the progress of the world.

Over a half century later, the U.S. government opened archived secret documents from World War II. There, documents were found to reveal the contentious nature of the policies that surrounded the decision to use the atom bomb. A number of books, newspaper reports and popular magazine articles thereafter reviewed and quoted the opinions of military and civilian leaders of that time in regard to the use of the bomb. I have selected two of those who favored using the Bomb and four others who expressed dissent.

Foremost of the advocates was President Harry Truman. He inherited the weighty decision after President Roosevelt's untimely death propelled him to the presidency. He said: "Having found the bomb we have used it. We have used it against those who attacked us without warning at Pearl Harbor, against those who have starved and beaten and executed American prisoners of war, against those who have abandoned all pretense of obeying international laws of warfare. We have used it in order to shorten the agony of war, in order to save the lives of thousands and thousands of young Americans. We will continue to use it until we completely destroy Japan's power to make war. Only a Japanese surrender will stop us."

The other commentator, perhaps compelled by his military obligation, was General Carl "Tooey" Spaatz of the US Army Air Force. He was ordered to deliver the first atom bomb. He said: "...dropping of the atomic bomb was done by a military man under military orders. We're supposed to carry out orders and not question them."

Some of those not in favor of using the Bomb included Ex-President Herbert Hoover. Author Richard Smith: Triumph of Herbert Hoover relates that on 28th May 1945, Hoover shared with President Truman a way to end the Pacific war quickly. He advised: "I am convinced that if you as President, will make a shortwave broadcast to the people of Japan—tell them they can have their Emperor if they surrender, that it will not mean unconditional surrender except for the militarists—you'll get a peace in Japan—you'll have both wars over."

Admiral William D. Leahy, Chief of Staff to Presidents Franklin Roosevelt and Harry Truman, was a skeptic. From his book, "I was There", he warned: "The lethal possibilities of atomic warfare in the future are frightening. My own feeling was that in being the first to use it, we had adopted an ethical standard common to the barbarians of the Dark Ages. I was not taught to make war in that fashion, and wars cannot be won by destroying women and children."

General Dwight Eisenhower, in his book "Mandate for Change, 1953-1956; The White House years" related his reaction to the atom bombing thusly:

> ...in 1945... Secretary of War Stimson, visiting my head-quarters in Germany, informed me that our government was preparing to drop an atomic bomb on Japan. I was one of those who felt that there were a number of cogent reasons to question the wisdom of such an act. ...the Secretary, upon giving me the news of the successful bomb

test in New Mexico, and of the plan for using it, asked for my reaction, apparently expecting a vigorous assent... during his recitation of the relevant facts, I had been conscious of a feeling of depression and so I voiced to him my grave misgivings, first on the basis of my belief that Japan was already defeated and that dropping the bomb was completely unnecessary, and secondly because I thought that our country should avoid shocking world opinion by the use of a weapon whose employment was, I thought, no longer mandatory as a measure to save American lives. It was my belief that Japan was, at that very moment, seeking some way to surrender with a minimum loss of 'face'. The Secretary was deeply perturbed by my attitude...

General Douglas MacArthur's views were recorded by his biographer William Manchester: American Caesar: Douglas MacArthur 1880-1964. He wrote:..."the Potsdam declaration in July... that Japan surrender unconditionally or face 'prompt and utter destruction'—the General was appalled knowing the Japanese would never renounce their emperor, and that without him an orderly transition to peace would be impossible, because his people would never submit to Allied occupation unless he ordered it...on the decision to drop the bomb, he had not even been consulted...he saw no military justification for the dropping of the bomb...he felt, the war might have ended weeks earlier if the U.S. had agreed to the retention of the institution of the emperor."

In the late years of the nineteenth century, reflecting on the aftermath of wars of the American Revolution and that of the impending Spanish-American of 1898, the influential scientist-inventor Thomas Edison, perhaps envisioning the atom bomb, had hoped that one day there would "spring from the brain of science a machine or force so fearful in its potentialities, so absolutely terrifying, that even man the fighter, who will dare torture and death in order to inflict torture and death, will be appalled, and so abandon war forever."

Ironically, for a period of weeks in Autumn 1944, representatives of the United States, the United Kingdom, the USSR, France, and the Republic of China were discussing the values and purposes of a United Nations organization. Its member nations would be tasked the lofty aims of maintaining peace and security through international economic and social cooperation. On ratification of its charter, the organization was officially formed on 24th October 1945.

On 2nd September 1945 VJ Day was declared—victory over Japan. It was solemnized by General Douglas MacArthur in a ceremony aboard the battleship Missouri anchored in Tokyo Bay. He had accepted on behalf of his country and its allies the unconditional surrender of Japan. Whether any high-ranking officer of the Philippine Army or an official representative of the Philippine government was among the assembled witnesses, I am uncertain. Surely the sacrifices which Filipino soldiers and innocent civilians endured for the Allied cause would have more than justified their inclusion. If the Commonwealth of the Philippines was unrepresented or under-represented, the omission ought to be regarded in history as inexcusable and insultingly reprehensible!

Just weeks after the atom bomb was dropped on Hiroshima and Nagasaki, the well-respected correspondent George Weller became the first American to enter and observe the devastating effects on the cities. He arrived after Japan had surrendered but before American troops had set foot on Japanese soil. The trip was unauthorized, and his reports were censored. A secret copy, however, was ultimately uncovered by his son who published the documents posthumously half a century later. The military, Weller surmised, fearing that American POWs would be discovered to have shared the same fate that Japanese civilians sustained, wanted to procrastinate the unhampered public scrutiny of the resultant damages of the bomb. Could early depiction of the horrible killing have risked the disdain and ire of the American nation, if not of the world? The worrisome questions on the morality and prudence of the atomic bombing as well as the dangers of the proliferation of its acquisition by other nations would, predictably, be concerns in the future.

In memoriam to the horrific aftermath of battle in the Philippines, on a hilltop of Ormoc, which clearly overlooks the Bay that now is a cemetery of men, ships, and planes of the combatant forces stands a solitary shrine. It was set and maintained by Japan in tribute to their fallen soldiers who participated in the Battle of Ormoc. Regularly, groups of Japanese come to pay homage and, remarkably, have become the incidental contributors to local tourism. Another monument is located in Intramuros for easy viewing. It was erected on 18th February 1995; the Shrine of Freedom known as Memorare Manila Monument; it is dedicated to the memory to the Filipino war victims. The inscription reads:

> This memorial is dedicated to all those innocent victims of war, many of whom went nameless and unknown to a common grave, or even never knew a grave at all, their bodies having been consumed by fire or crushed to dust beneath the rubble of ruins.
>
> Let this monument be the gravestone for each and every one of the over 100,000 men, women, children and infants killed in Manila during its battle of liberation, February 3–March 3, 1945.
>
> We have not forgotten them, nor shall we ever forget. May they rest in peace as part now of the sacred ground of this city: the Manila of our affections.

In Metro Manila, the American Cemetery and Memorial in the Philippines occupies 152 acres and contains the largest number of graves of American military dead of World War II, a total of 17,202, most of whom lost their lives in operations in New Guinea and the Philippines. A plaque lists 36,285 names of the missing-in-action. In the province of Leyte's municipality of Palo is the Leyte Landing Memorial Park. It memorializes the landing of General Douglas MacArthur and his men at

Red Beach on 20th October 1944. The anniversary of this event is commemorated annually with a reenactment of the famous landing, attended by local and foreign dignitaries.

For Filipinos, as the whole, the war had left nightmarish wounds, inflicted yet once more in their centuries-long quest to unshackle themselves from foreign dominion and become the independent masters of their future. The traumatic loss of life by warriors and innocent civilians, cannot be forgotten. For the survivors, the loss of loved ones, as my family and I had with the demise of Mamá, will always be remembered.

ON REFLECTION

Just as the Spanish had viewed the Islas and its inhabitants as valuable fodder to their colonial aggrandizement, the Americans with foresight of their global reach would succeed in turning the Philippine Islands into an important bastion of their avowed national security interests in the Far East with the Filipinos their duty-bound wards. Inevitably, the country became a battleground.

Pondering on the ravages of the war and, in particular, its debasing consequences on the culture and traditions of the Filipino, Alfonso Aluit pointed out bitter lessons. He wrote: It created the saboteurs, the vandals, the looters, the profiteers... they exacted a toll by taking advantage of scarcity, unconscionably ignoring titles to property by looting, and worst of all there were those who would betray any person and any cause, for lucre.

The mores of the Filipino would undergo changes. During the immediate post-War years, the country's envisioned path to prosperity, peace, and well-being had thorny war-related issues to resolve. They included the vexing hurdles of providing subsistence to a devastated populace living in an otherwise deficient, ravished economic milieu. The reconstruction of a damaged infrastructure, facilitated by foreign aid, needed to manage an overwhelming process to the best advantage of the Filipino and the country. Finding solutions to those questions were, and would become, among the challenges before the Filipino throughout the coming decades. Would the country's leaders feel empowered to overcome the ubiquitous temptations of cronyism, graft, and corruption? Will those depraved behaviors of deceit, subterfuge, corruption, and graft be overcome and corrected? Or, as Aluit wondered, will they find permanence in business, politics, and every sector of the community, and represent the mores of the Filipino?

Defying explanation, the unconscionable disregard for the safety of innocent civilians appeared to be tolerated, if not likely advocated, by leaders of each of the warring nations. The perpetrators, while valiantly partaking as patriotic warriors, were also being motivated by vengeance or a payback, aggravated by racism and xenophobia. The adversarial propagandas, which often dispelled distrust, hostility, and demeaning regard for human life, did compound the combatant's attitudes and fueled the commitment of atrocities, murder and mayhem. Undoubtedly, noncombatant civilians had to be equally prepared to provide support. Indeed, I recall being persuaded by similar propagandas, despising the inhumane conduct of the Japanese enemy and rooting for their defeat.

Nonetheless, having lived in an environment of insecurity and fear, I would come to believe that among warriors—whether American, Japanese or Filipino—were those imbued with ethos of kindness and compassion. I found those qualities among the many soldiers I met. However, those same individuals, overwhelmed by the brutal character of armed conflicts, could quite conceivably take ownership of their particular crusade in random ways. It is the response, either voluntarily or by force of circumstances—be they manifest as feats of courage, urges to survive, even being overcome with fright or cowardice—which may explain a compelling behavior which is otherwise extraordinarily deviant to their person.

Some studies do provide encouraging support for my views of the innate character of human beings. Jintaro Ishida interviewed Japanese officers and soldiers who had served and participated in the massacre of babies, children, women and men on a policy of "guerilla subjugation" in the Philippines. While some of the subjects tried to justify their barbarous behavior as "complying to orders," notably, most expressed personal apology for having participated in the bloodbath. They all admitted to a recurrent nightmare that their conscience had continued to haunt them over their role. Many felt that the Philippines, either willingly or not, had placed their civilians in harm's way by becoming a battleground of the conflict. The Filipino interviewees who were either survivors of the carnage or their descendants, told of having long since shed their hatred and, instead spoke of forgiveness. Interestingly, forgiveness has been proven beneficial as a process of concluding resentment, indignation or anger because of a perceived offense or mistake or unceasing demand for punishment or restitution. In contrast to people who hold resentment, studies have found the forgiving individual to be happier and healthier.

The willingness to forgive is a quality that George Weller also heard among many U.S. POW survivors of the internment camps in Japan. From writings of authors Weller and Ishida, they appear to have found many veterans who had etched their wartime actions—whether for good or evil—indelibly in their conscience in the form of nightmares, even psychotic behavior. Perhaps, it is what contributes to the well-recognized Post-Traumatic Stress Disorder. Do we have a God-encoded sense that exacts a self-imposed penalty for our misdeeds and drives us to value a principled, good conduct behavior? I believe we do. I also believe that man possesses a faculty, perhaps an instinctive attribute, that can be tapped when challenged to survive a harrowing and life-threatening experience. Sometimes, the result may be a tale of desperation and ultimate submission with ruinous consequences.

Other times, the ordeal can end in a life-changing triumph. Ours was the latter.

On hindsight, my family and I, as if wading through marshes full of threatening alligators yet striving to reach and reaching a desirable destination on land, did feel the same sense of survival. Regrettably, my mother's demise had made us less whole, yet I was unable to weep. Perhaps I was drained by then of emotion. The tragic, premature loss of my mother had surely been, even if to an unknown degree, attributable to her heart-wrenching, tension-filled experiences during the war. The traumas she suffered on top of the stress over her loving concerns for her children and husband must have been unfathomable. We would all grow to maturity devoid of the counsels, the nurture, the love and care that only a mother can bestow. As survivors of the incredible terror, the consequences to us—my father, now a widower and us youngsters, now motherless—are personal hurdles yet to unfold. Overall, we overcame those days of War by being guile and suppliant, by finding strength in our family union and, by prayer. They were experiences that have left a lasting memory. Personally, I would aim to deport in the coming years of adolescence more inured to acquire confidence in my growing abilities, and develop a realistic measure of my capabilities to cope. For now, my family and I prepared for the future, to live our lives with newfound will. We were grateful to be alive.

Of the protagonists I cited as having had significant roles in the battle that was fought in the jungles, the seas, the skies, and the communities of Perla del Mar de Oriente, now hallowed by the many lives that had come in harm's way, there was General Tomoyuki Yamashita. He was accused and found guilty for having unlawfully disregarded and failed to discharge his duty as commander to control the operations of the members of his command, permitting them to commit brutal atrocities and other high crimes against people of the United States and its allies and dependencies, particularly the Philippines. It was a decision by a

U.S. Military Tribunal. The Supreme Courts of the Philippines and that of the United States refused to hear appeals; their refusal implied concurrence with the decision. Dissenting opinions the decades thereafter would involve constitutional and war crimes experts; their studies will hopefully provide fruitful lessons for concerned humanists. The General was sentenced to die by hanging on 23rd February 1946; he was fifty-eight years old.

General Douglas MacArthur had personal reasons, if not an obsession, not to bypass the Philippines in the march of his combined forces toward the occupation of Japan. His strategy was contrary to that espoused by Admiral Chester Nimetz of the U.S. Navy before a high-level conference with President Roosevelt on 26th July 1944. MacArthur's view prevailed. His forces fought doggedly and valiantly. In Manila their superior firepower effectively trapped the enemy forces; feeling no recourse but a suicidal defense, the Japanese engaged in unbounded destruction and wanton carnage. The victory parade in Manila that the General had envisioned as a symbol of his promised return did not happen. Instead the city, indeed, the country, its treasures, and countless Filipinos had been severely victimized in the battle. Would history view the price that MacArthur's persistence exacted justifiable? Nonetheless, his place among revered heroes and patriots of America is secure in the annals of the ages. MacArthur died 5th April 1964 in Washington, D.C. at eighty-four years of age.

President Manuel Quezon's efforts to achieve neutrality and avert the danger he feared for his countrymen was for naught. He did not live to witness the full extent of destruction which his beloved country suffered; he died from complication of a longstanding tuberculosis on 1st August 1944, 65 years old. He will be long honored for his guiding leadership of a country approaching a tipping point in its quest for autonomy and sovereignty.

The atom bomb that dropped on Hiroshima and Nagasaki would have ramifications beyond its dreadful power to destroy lives and property. It would usher a period of profound changes in socio-political thinking and policies of multiple nations. Predictably, it would influence the course of technology development, and fuel a dangerous arms race. The events of the coming decades would be revealing.

Unquestionably, the many advantages that the United States provided its Philippine colony not withstanding, the sacrifices that Filipinos gave throughout the War were incalculable and deserve its rightful recognition. The loss of lives—combatants and non-combatants; the massive destruction of property; the unraveling of economic well-being; the irreplaceable loss of treasure; and, the retrograding affront on its culture and mores, in my view, are the lamentable aftermath that the Perla del Mar de Oriente experienced for becoming a battlefield of the War. Unavoidable? Would the country, when its quest for self rule ultimately comes to fruition, resolve "never again"?

POST-WAR ADOLESCENCE

A boy's will is the wind's will... And the thoughts of youth are long, long flights of thought.

—Henry Wadsworth Longfellow
(Author... b1807–1882)

You are as young as your faith, as old as your doubt; as young as your self-confidence, as old as your fear; as young as your hope, as old as your despair. So long as your heart receives messages of beauty, hope, cheer and courage, so long you are young.

—General Douglas MacArthur
(Soldier... b1880–1964)

God grant me the serenity to accept the things I cannot change; Courage to change the things I can; and wisdom to know the difference.

—Reinhold Niebuhr
(Theologian... b1892–1971)

Before retracing our way back to Ormoc, we left Manila by boat for Cebu and stayed with my grandparents for several months. Inter-island travel by sea was re-established in stages, the priority being between important cities, Manila and Cebu among them. The only vessel available to Ormoc from Cebu was an underpowered motorized outrigger boat. It took over twelve hours for us to navigate the sixty nautical mile distance.

THE BATTLE OF ORMOC

As the town came into better focus from sea that first early morning of my return, I could hardly believe what I saw. The pier had been bombed into fragments. Its remains appeared precariously unstable and useless. The lighthouse by the foot of the pier, standing tall yet unusable, had been cracked from its top to the base. Luckily, the Seaside Hotel and our house beside it were still standing, their window panes shattered with several sections of the walls splintered by exploding shells, shrapnel and bullets.

Ormoc devastation razed homes and buildings leaving only their charred remains that had blurred street demarcations. The destruction was compounded by the continuing back and forth battle of American and Japanese forces, 1944--45. Note lighthouse and the Seaside Hotel beside it.

the right time, and vise versa. I wondered what unfortunate fate befell that Japanese soldier I had befriended in Cebu who was an involuntary participant of the War. Shortly, Dading tempted me to smoke a cigarette. I tried. Inhaling the cigarette smoke left me coughing and very dizzy. It was my second attempt at smoking. When I was ten, Dading had rolled a dried up papaya leaf in the shape a cigar. We were seated on a wall whose open window was of Papa's clinic office. On lighting the cigar, it flamed and smoked sufficiently as to waft its aroma directly to Papá's nostrils. Instantly, he confronted and dismissed us out of the premises, after exacting my promise never to smoke until after graduation from High School. The second experience promptly dissuaded me from the habit.

SEEKING NORMALCY

Until Papá was discharged from the army, we remained in Cebu with my grandparents. From my limited view of the city, it appeared to have been spared the extensive destructiveness of war, a welcome contrast to the havoc that had fated Ormoc. In reality, the entire province had been a hotbed of guerilla activity, keeping the 14,500 Japanese troop garrison in near constant engagement. On 26th March 1945, a naval bombardment of the port facilities was followed by the landing of American troops. The Japanese resistance required offshore battleships and on-land tank battery fire support to force their retreat from the city to the mountainsides. Fortuitously, it prevented additional damages to the city and loss of lives. Japanese resistance, however, would not end until 5,750 Japanese had been killed. American and Filipino guerillas cited 417 of their comrades were killed and 1,700 wounded.

As the educational system gradually recovered and school after school reopened, I enrolled at the San Carlos High School. It was the private Catholic school my father had once attended.

The curriculum turned out to be ill-defined because the faculty was a hodgepodge version of its past quality. The students took several weeks and months of reorientation before becoming well-focused, manifesting the aftermath of a long-disrupted schedule of learning. Toward the end of the school year, in March 1946, I became acquainted with a schoolmate whose personal experiences would imprint indelibly on my mind and in a few years help direct my own life path. Vince was a couple years older. Earlier the year before, he met and befriended an American soldier who enabled him to visit America on a student visa. When I met Vince, he had just returned after spending three months during late autumn in the USA. Although homesickness abbreviated his visit, compelling an early return, he raved about the beautiful city with friendly and hospitable inhabitants. Vince unwittingly had helped fertilize a germinating plan of my own to materialize my longing to see America. The plans, however, would take the backseat to my more current challenges. The place he visited was Duluth, Minnesota.

I had been suffering recurrent bouts of tonsillitis. One day, in April of 1946, I had my tonsils removed. Tio Nené, Mamá's eldest brother, was the surgeon. With the health facilities of Cebu City still in disarray, the operation was performed under makeshift conditions. It happened one day when I sat on the edge of a cot in a room of my grandparents' home. Opposite me, my surgeon sat on a stool. I opened my mouth to receive the local anesthetic injections. I have no recall of the length or size of the needle; my eyes were shut tight. I do recall, however, hearing and feeling the associated manipulations in my throat to remove both tonsils. Lola Empíng was a very attentive nurse, and she was a steadfast comfort throughout the surgery and my convalescence. I now recall the experience awed by my stoic deportment and become better able to empathize and sympathize with children who in war-ravaged or starvation conditions, despite being sadly depicted in an environment fraught with danger and want, appear to be seemingly impervious to the insults to their being, numb and unperturbed. Like them, on that day of my tonsillectomy, the war years must have robbed me the luxury of choice and doubt; instead, I was left without a sensible measure of peril to my person.

The Cebu interlude ended when Papá received his army discharge by December. We returned to Ormoc. Papá resumed his medical practice. In the immediate post-War months, even years, public conveyance in town was limited to the tartanilla since most privately owned cars had earlier been surrendered to the Japanese for their use and were now likely destroyed. As a consequence, patients sought his care by presenting themselves unannounced at the clinic, walking from great distances. For the non-ambulant, he went on house calls.

Penicillin, then, was regarded as a miracle drug. When indicated, the antibiotic was given in periodic increments by injection—parenterally, usually every four hours around the clock. Once, for the treatment of an infection on a bedridden patient, I accompanied him on his house visits arriving by tartanilla, testing my mettle. I joined him until the midnight dose but desisted getting out of bed for the four a.m. visit. I became even more impressed by Papá's dedication and less so of my own persistence.

We children enrolled at St. Peter's Academy except for baby Tonio and Linda, whose brain tumor symptoms of facial and limb paralysis; slurred speech; and unpredictable, worrisome blackout episodes pointed to a steady downhill course. While her problem might have been correctable in less constraining circumstances, in Ormoc the brain operation was not feasible. Even the medical centers of Cebu or Manila had yet to be fully restored. I am certain that Papá agonized while we prayed for a miracle.

One Thursday morning, I was left with Linda while everyone was at church. In my presence, she frothed at the mouth, convulsed, and lost consciousness. Helpless, I ran to church to fetch Papá, who came running back with me, very sadly, only to pronounce her demise. It was 20th June 1946. Although her loss had seemed inevitable, the death was particularly painful as I had witnessed the process first hand. For Linda, I am comforted that a Divine hand had given her the eternal rest from suffering for which I and my family are forever prayerfully grateful. Following tradition, there were days of prayer after the burial and a year-long black dress wear for women and a black sleeve-wrap for the males as an overt sign of mourning. Linda rests in the Yrastorza mausoleum at the Ormoc cemetery.

INDEPENDENCE—THE AMERICAN REQUITED PROMISE

On 4th July 1946, the United States of America granted the Philippines its independence. For a third time, the Philippines would declare itself an independent republic, a unique record in the annals of the nations of the world. The first Philippine Republic of 1898 resulted from the revolutionary quest to unshackle Spanish colonial rule. It coincidentally occurred when Spain had lost a war with the United States. At that time, the Spanish Crown ceded sovereignty of the Philippines to the United States and the colonial governance of the Philippines was effectively transferred from Spain to the United States. It was followed by the Philippine-American War—The Forgotten War—that were years of turbulent relations the Filipinos had with the Americans. To the Filipino advantage, the U.S., during its half century of colonial control, introduced western models of education and health-care systems. The governance, however, reinforced a system of land holding that favored an oligarchy. Tenancy and elitism that mixed with the Spanish feudal patron-client relationship was not reformed. They remain touchy, divisive issues of the land.

The second declaration of independence was made by duress of the Japanese interloper while the country, by de facto, remained under martial subjugation. It became null and void with the American and Allies' victory over Japan in 1945.

The third time the Philippines proclaimed itself a republic, its independence was granted by the United States of America. It was a fulfillment of the promise given in 1935. The momentous occasion was celebrated in Manila, attended by a bevy of Filipino and American officialdom before a massive witness of onlookers, complete with a parade of military and civilian marchers. It was a realization of the dreams and struggles of the Filipinos. As the first President of the Republic, Manuel Roxas pointed out the country was wantonly degraded, ingloriously sacrificed as a battlefield of the conflict between imperialist Japan and an alliance of American-Allied powers. The socio-economic infrastructure was nearly inoperative. The losses of life, property, and treasure were devastating, beyond measure. It had eroded the people's mores with the pervasive disrespect for law and order. The President pleaded for the citizens to unite in the herculean task of reconstructing the incalculable morass of destruction before them. He sought hope and succor by awakening the Filipino determination to achieve a country of plenty. Will Filipinos rise to the challenge?

The grant of independence occurred only a few months after VJ Day. Nonetheless, I wondered if there had been a determined effort to delay the grant of independence? Might an extended American sovereignty have better compelled and ensured the just reparation for damages resulting from the wraths of War? Would postponement have provided a more suitable climate for self-government? The author Theodore Friend's "Between Two Empire" examined the circumstances and deliberations that Filipino political leaders, with their divergent views, discussed with representatives of the Truman administration and MacArthur's personal overpowering influence. Suffice to state that the harangue over concern for the welfare of the Philippines reeked with intrigue and self-interest; I highly recommend Friend's reportage for eye-opening clarity on the seminal decision. Ultimately, the questions not withstanding, the nation would feel coerced to begin its formative years in a dire state, cast off American largesse. On analysis, many Filipinos would come to regard the American bequest as one of mixed blessings. Onerous!

An independent Philippines was, in fact, immediately challenged by an American wish to obtain concessions favorable to its own interests. On 2nd July 1946, the U.S. Congress passed the Bell Trade Act. On approval by the independent Philippines, it prohibited the Philippines from manufacturing or selling products that might "come into substantial competition with U.S.-made goods." It further required that the Philippine Constitution be revised to grant U.S. citizens and corporations parity access to Philippine minerals, forests, and other natural resources. Philippine Commonwealth President Sergio Osmeña was moved to label the act a "curtailment of Philippine sovereignty...virtual nullification of Philippine independence." In hearings before the U.S. Senate Committee on Finance, Assistant Secretary of State for Economic Affairs William L. Clayton described the act as "clearly inconsistent with the basic foreign economic policy of this country...clearly inconsistent with our promise to grant the Philippines genuine independence." Nonetheless, the U.S. proposed the ratification of the Bell Trade Act. To ensure Philippine consent, the U.S. Congress threatened to withhold post-World War II reconstruction funds. The Commonwealth of the Philippines Legislature obliged on 2nd July 1946. In so doing, two days later the newly formed Republic was promised the aid. Albeit, with a telling caveat. The U.S. Army, Navy and Air Forces would establish bases in the country while exempting their troops from prosecution by the local judicial system for transgression of national laws. The agreement would also effectively provide the United States opportunity to infringe on local affairs and control Philippine political and economic concerns. In 1955, nine years after passage of the Bell Trade Act, it was abrogated as a duplicitous gift by a departing colonial overseer. It was replaced by the accord that abolished U.S. authority over the exchange rate of the Philippine peso currency and, in deference to the influential oligarchs, extended the favorable quota for the export of Philippine sugar to America. However, it provided Americans parity privileges in land ownership and investment in the development of the economy. Also, it applied tariffs on goods exported to the United States. Arguably, a seemingly hollow triumph for the Filipinos.

Domestically, the country's challenges were legion. Perhaps most destabilizing to its peace and security was the insurgent conflict brought on by Hukbalahap, the group bent on Marxist revolution; how to settle peaceably? Then the Moros and their fermenting disaffection with perceived discriminatory policies on Muslims, represented a major problem that unresolved would impede harmony. Another grave concern was the state of the traditional mores and ethics: how well would the Filipinos overcome the tolerance for graft, corruption, deceit, and fraudulence, behaviors that were ascribed as compelled by the war years? Could Filipinos nurture a sense of citizenship and stewardship to bloom with pride? Will the people take ownership of their nation? The answers would unfold in time.

ATENEO DE CAGAYAN

In antebellum Philippines, the school year traditionally started in July and ended in March. It was not until the late 1946 academic year that most schools had regained stability in the aftermath of the destructive consequences of the War. St. Peter's Academy was no exception. I completed my junior year there in 1947; later that year, I enrolled as a senior at the Ateneo de Cagayan High School as a boarder. The school had early regained and augmented its high standing by having collected a staff of Jesuits newly arrived from America. The institution was located in the City of Cagayan, province of Misamis Oriental, island of Mindanao. I was joined by the same Ormoc group of friends that together had undergone the circumcision that Papá had performed years before. In the interim months, the school days at St. Peter's Academy were comprised of makeshift provisions and deficiencies, yet to be corrected by the on-going post-War reconstruction programs. Of interest was an unplanned barter that my teacher of the national language—Tagalog—would offer me. Taking me aside, he admitted that his knowledge of the language was limited and had planned to teach the daily course by simply learning it the evening before. He had been aware that I had spent time in Manila, where Tagalog is the dialect of choice and assumed I had expertise, which I myself believed was questionable. He proposed to give me an "A" grade in exchange for promising to avoid participating in class discussions and keeping me in the rear seat of the class. He did not wish to risk revealing his limitation. I've long since forgotten his name. My ill-gotten "A" would soon short-change me when I enrolled at the Ateneo de Cagayan High School.

Meanwhile, in 1946, I would witness an unbelievable event. Putting what I saw in perspective, there is the need to recognize that in preparation for the American invasion of Japan, tentatively set for November 1945, the Philippines had become an important staging base for the troops. It also served as a depot for countless—even infinitesimal—numbers and varieties of armamentaria, materiel, and supplies. There were depots at various locations in the country, including one in Leyte. Fortuitously, the Japanese surrendered. The invasion now aborted, a salutary event but posed the disposal of the mountains of supplies problematic. One day in the month of June, before my very eyes were dozens of U.S. Army amphibious landing crafts—those vehicles that carried soldiers to landing sites in attack of enemy positions—floating to the middle of Ormoc Bay. Each was loaded to capacity with equipment, the kind not discernable without binoculars.

They were motoring to the deepest part of the sea. Shortly, the boats began sinking, joining the cemetery of destroyed Japanese and American battle ships. Undoubtedly on purpose. The process continued for days until counting the numbers was no longer of interest. I surmised that the undertaking was probably repeated elsewhere in the country. I theorized that sinking the surplus, rather than returning them to America as additions to its marketplace must have been preferable, perhaps to avoid an undesirable disruption of the nation's economic equilibrium. Months later the Philippine government, from its national to its smallest community units together with the military, had added assets which were distinctly of U.S. military origin. The country-wide assumption held that the largesse had come from the residual surplus, over and above the intentionally sunken mass of materiel. For the Filipino, the bounty was of mixed blessings. In the short term, it aided the restorative process of the infrastructure. However, although the quid pro quo details were unclear to me, it shortly became apparent that segments of the surplus had been consigned to the Philippine government as war-damage compensation. Another portion had been offered for public bidding. However, only a select number of citizens, primarily public officials, got to participate in the bidding that aroused grumblings of graft and bribery. Jeeps were the attractive surplus; their sale to the public enriched the fortunate bidders by having a monopoly on the sales. Papá was among those who purchased a surplus jeep to replenish the coupe, which, unfortunately, failed to survive the Battle of Ormoc.

The Ateneo de Cagayan school building and its campus were contained in a large plot of land ringed by a high wall. Many of the students were boarders hailing from varied parts of the Visayas and Mindanao. As a captive group, the priests were able to exercise discipline that prominently included structured study times at the library, daily Mass, and special passes to leave the campus. Unconsciously, I felt an attraction to the school's library;

it's copious stock was a delight that nearly matched the fun of being in a candy store. It had books not only for academic references, but a variety of others that, subliminally and in time, would pique my own evolving intellectual curiosity.

There were many added consequences of my Ateneo stay, besides learning to cope with a rigorous curriculum of study. Through courses on religion, I was acquiring a more reasoned belief from inquiry about my Catholic faith. Singing as a tenor with the Glee Club, well conducted by Fr. Cuna, was another activity I enjoyed; we were often a popular feature at musical events of town. Reading and interpreting Shakespeare's classics were a chore, difficult and uninteresting; I don't recall getting a noteworthy grade in the course study.

The Tagalog teacher, Fr. Antonio Cuna took only two weeks to uncover my novice status and promptly reassigned me away from the advanced to the beginner's section. I actually felt relieved. Another Filipino on the faculty was a lay teacher of physics; unlike Fr. Cuna, he seemed to me more interested in showing off his knowledge than sharing his expertise. The rest of the faculty were Americans. All were Jesuits, reputed to be excellent teachers. The rector, Fr. Edward Haggarty, was a famous participant in the guerilla movement for which he received the U.S. Bronze Star; he was in one of Mindanao's mountain lairs throughout the Japanese occupation. For a few years after my graduation and until his demise, we remained in mail contact; he even offered his name as a reference when I began applying for my profession level University studies.

The student body was drawn from varied socio-economic backgrounds and personal ambitions which added to my own broadening world view. There were those similarly interested in the health field. Together, we familiarized ourselves with requisite studies for medicine and dentistry, almost always with an American priest as facilitator. Of particular interest to me, those priests would provide more familiarity and appreciation of

Americans and their mores which was of particular interest to me as I hoped to pursue college studies in America. Finally, I felt myself gradually weaning away from a priesthood calling, in part gaining comfort in my religiosity outside of the vocation. I graduated with all those memories in 1948.

At home after High School graduation, Romy and I renewed our connection through the mail; he and his family still had not returned to Ormoc. Romy was by then a seminarian. He was destined to be a committed priest; in time, he served a large parish in the city of Bacolod, Negros Occidental. His congregants were devoted to him until he retired sometime in the early 21st Century. I continued to accompany Papá on house calls while researching the possibilities of enrolling in an American college. This gave us the opportunity to talk about our visions. He, to speak of his own views on the practice of medicine and his family values; I, to speak of my future. We agreed about commonly held Filipino constraints that influenced ones choice of a career. Of paramount importance to the equation were the parents. Autocratically, but in good faith, they tended to have an over-riding influence in their children's future, decisions more often in consideration of family needs rather than personal ambitions. Moreover, the limited in-country educational opportunities tended to shorten the list of choices. Those able to afford a college education tended to focus on the grand professions, such as healthcare, law, engineering, architecture or business administration. My own goal had long been molded by parental direction. I wished to be physician or, as an alternative a dentist, to Papá's delight. He did expound on the personal rewards to be derived from extending care to the needy, the destitute; he certainly lived by that credo. I, in turn, made known my wish for an American education. The belief I harbored was that, perhaps, attending an American college would give me liberty to change career goals, should I become attracted to a different field.

For a foreign student applying for admission to an American college at that time was a process filled with hurdles. For one, exchanging mail between Ormoc and places in the United States took weeks, if not months. Meanwhile, I enrolled at the University of the Philippines in Manila for an academic year, beginning the second semester 1948. I took liberal arts courses: philosophy, sociology, German, more English literature and physical education. Shortly, the campus would relocate to a northern outskirt of the metropolitan zone, away from its original locale since its inception in 1908.

MANILA REVISIT

I was alone at seventeen in Manila. When I left the city with my family to return to Ormoc three years earlier, the city was in its throes of re-building and rehabilitation activities. At this stay, detritus from damaged, destroyed homes and buildings were as yet being collected, the reconstruction far from its completed phase. People still seemed in a slow-motion reaction to the aftereffects of the war and the resolve to continue living. Would the Perla del Mar del Oriente regain its brilliance now undressed of it treasure and priceless relics?

I found a boarding house where a dozen students were staying. It was within walking distance to the university and provided meals. The university studies were a departure from High School. Homework and use of the library were essential to augment lectures. The extramural activities were abundant. I joined the Newman Club for Catholic students; the ROTC; the Foreign Students Club, being from the province of Leyte I qualified after some convincing discussions; and the non-varsity swimming team. Although swimming was primarily an enjoyable past-time, I participated in at least one competitive meet. I would retell the event by claiming I took third place in free-style, invariably omitting that only three of us competed. The Newman Club was a consoling place to meet fellow-Catholics; the membership was encouraged by priests as an aid for naïve provincianos to ward off temptations at a secular environment. ROTC was compulsory; however, in my view, it offered no personal future in lieu of my yearning to go overseas. The Foreign Students Club would prove a very pleasant experience, helpful to my plans to study abroad. Shortly, I found myself in comradeship with a group of American students, some High School-aged—all dependents of the U.S. Embassy staff. I was included when, on occasions, we went to movies and dances at a nearby Cavite Naval Station, reached by U.S. Navy launch across Manila Bay. At other times, we would gather at their expansive residential compound for parties and sometimes Protestant services.

I recall one impressive occasion. A teenage girl, with whom I was sometimes paired at social events, invited me to dine at her home in the company of her parents. The table was set formally with Philippine-made individual placemats; the setting included chinaware properly positioned, and the meal was preceded with a prayer that was customized to the occasion as opposed to the standard Catholic version. The food, in my mind, was decidedly not Filipino and was eaten with a fork, not a spoon. The conversation was cordial, and I felt comfortable, as did everyone. I observed that the parents were engaged and not differential with their daughter or me. That evening, they commiserated with my hope to study in the U.S. by providing me up-close visions of their everyday life. I remained in contact with the girl and the group until my departure for America. The entire experience contrasted with the Filipino custom I learned while in Cebu. I once had a date with a beautiful girl to take in a movie. To my surprise, we were accompanied by her aunt, as a chaperon who wanted to sit between us. She was unsuccessful.

Around Fall of 1949, my persistent search and applications for admission to an American college resulted in the following options: enroll at the San Mateo Junior College in California;

become an alternate candidate at Louisiana State University in Baton Rouge; and, matriculate at the University of Minnesota Duluth as a freshman for the Winter Trimester, beginning the second week of January 1950. How to choose?

Although Papá had surely shared the excitement that accompanied my unceasing search for openings in an American school and now the letters of acceptance, we both also harbored a mixture of anxiety and insecurity over a life-changing foreign adventure. He, now a widower, must have been saddened, if not regretful at the prospect of seeing his oldest offspring venture away from the homeland, perhaps not able to share with him the many lifetime experiences that would unfold in the future. I would be convinced that Mamá, if only being motivated by motherly love, might have viewed my wishes tepidly.

Again and again, I would spend time in self-examination on the many concerns of the venture I was eager to undergo. How knowledgeable and well prepared was I about America and Americans? Would I cope with the unforeseeable? The "what ifs?" How well could I actually succeed, as I had self-assuredly proffered, in finding opportunity to help earn my keep? Will my determination and self-assurance overcome homesickness as to avoid a premature homecoming? When would I return home?

ON REFLECTION

My family and I, just as did many other ordinary compatriots, lived in a time and place filled with contrasting experiences. They spanned a pre-war stage of carefree halcyon days, a war-filled interlude of destruction and tragic loss, followed by a post-war era of rebirth and renaissance. I point to our faith as the dependable source of succor and guide for our ready acquiescence to overcome adversity. I valued my post-war adolescent years for the times I got to better know Papá, as an individual with life views that were guiding his private mores; as a practicing professional who doled care and charity in congruence with his moderate lifestyle; as a contributing member of our community in the various civic and societal affairs; and, as the widowed father whose directed influence was helping define the hopes and aspirations of his children, in particular, me. I regarded him a fitting role model but with a caveat. I wished my own sprouting life-views, guided yet unrestrained by traditional values, would blossom and prevail in anticipation of the adventurous path before me.

The Philippines gained her independence shortly after the end of World War II, as did other countries in Africa, the Middle East, and Asia. Unlike those who won their freedom by force from European colonial rulers, America had fulfilled a promise made in 1935. It was, however, given at a most inopportune time and circumstance. The Republic began the years of self-government with gargantuan obstacles. Some problems had pre-dated the War days, but others were its aftermath. They involved broad socio-economic concerns. All were equally compelling and pressing for solutions. The circumstances beg one to ask questions. Had the nation's leadership considered opposing the grant or advocating delay of independence, as some influential American policymakers had suggested—see page 122? Had the nation's leaders of 1946 represented the best interests of the nation? Furthermore, many Filipinos would be conflicted by the seeming lack of a reciprocal relationship by the United States. The reaction stems from the concept of *utang na loob*, that embedded behavior, which in practice manifests as a sense of one's obligatory fealty and gratitude in exchange for favor gained or, for belonging to a kindred group. In the matter of the Philippine-United States relationship, the hurt feelings of Filipinos would be harbored in such questions as: didn't Filipinos die with Americans fighting against the Japanese? Did their sacrifice in lives, property, and treasure receive a commensurate regard? Was the post-war American largess and the Japanese reparations settlement that the American government exacted from a common enemy a sufficient demonstration of gratitude?

As if to add further insult to injury, on 9th May 1962 Filipinos received yet another utang na loob affront when the US House of Representatives rejected the $73 million additional war payment bill. The indignation it ratcheted was reflected in an incalculable erosion of Filipino-American good will. Subsequently, on 4th August 1964, Philippine President Diosdado Macapagal signed Republic Act No. 4166 statutorily prescribing 12th June as Philippine Independence Day. The historic decision had recognized the proclamation of independence from foreign rule that President Emilio Aguinaldo had announced to the world on that June day in 1898. Fourth of July would thereafter be recognized as Republic Day.

The excitement I had over my impending departure for America would mount as each step of the preparations came to completion. I obtained a U.S. student visa; it carried compliance regulations. I needed a carrier to transport me to a western port of America and beyond, taking into account the least expensive and the most suitable travel modes, and it had to comply with the enrollment timetable of the school of my choice. I arranged the transport. Papá agreed to subsidize certain of my expenses while I, confidently believing in the ability to find employment, would help ease his financial burden as much as possible. We were mutually comfortable with the agreement. On occasions when alone with my pensive moments, I wondered how my past personal experiences, particularly those of danger and insecurity, might serve me. Sensibly, they were questions of concern. Instead, I felt emboldened in believing that when thrust into the big world I was going toward, the experiences I had undergone would empower a personal initiative to face life's challenges with confidence and humility, even with a handy bit of cynicism to buffer my youthful vulnerable proclivities. At the Ateneo de Cagayan, we had once discussed a poem by William Henley from a Book of Verses published in 1875: "Life and Death." Its message, titled "Invictus" has always been inspiring:

> Out of the night that covers me,
> Black as the pit from pole to pole,
> I thank whatever gods may be
> for my unconquerable soul.
>
> In the fell clutch of circumstance
> I have not winced nor cried aloud.
>
> Under the bludgeoning of chance
> My head is bloody, but unbowed.
>
> Beyond this place of wrath and tears
> Looms but the Horror of the shade
> And yet the menace of the years
> Finds and shall find me unafraid.
>
> It matters not how strait the gate,
> How charged with punishments the scroll,
> I am the master of my fate:
> I am the captain of my soul.

ONWARD TO AMERICA

You can kiss your family and friends good-bye and put miles between you, but at the same time you carry them with you in your heart, your mind, your stomach, because you do not just live in a world but a world lives in you.

—*Frederick Buechner (Theologian... b1926).*

Look not mournfully into the past. It comes not back again. Wisely improve the present. It is thine. Go forth to meet the shadowy future, without fear, and with a manly heart.

—*Henry Wadsworth Longfellow*
(Writer... b1807-1882).

Let your vision be a guide to that boundless horizon... then Unfurl your wings... and fly like an eagle."

—*Patricia Anne Laverty Yrastorza*
(Nurse, Wife, Mother, Grandmother).

My choice was the University of Minnesota Duluth-UMD. San Mateo Junior College, located in the metropolis of San Francisco, which was ringed by its many satellite cities, was not appealing. Besides, the area was reputed as having several large Filipino communities; I felt, I could be going from one Manila to another Manila. And I had firmly intended to optimize my American immersion. Louisiana was but a distant possibility with no place in the priority scale. UMD had been established anew, less than a decade old. It had a 1,500 student population, a modest size that I felt could be more suitable and facile for my wishes to integrate into the community. The city itself had 90,000 inhabitants. Although well-meaning people, the Jesuits and Sr. Editha included, had tried to describe how intricate and hazardous living in a freezing climate could be as that of Duluth, my mind was unable to properly conceptualize the foreign ambient conditions. Instead, it was recalling what my acquaintance—Vince of San Carlos High School of Cebu—had given: a favorable account of the city and its people. That view became my more persuasive and attractive perception of Duluth.

In late 1949, the most available, practical, if not the cheapest, mode of transport to America was by sea, either as a passenger in a freighter or on a steamer. A popular steamship company of the time had a number of ships known as the President Lines. S.S. President Wilson, advertised as a luxury cruise ship, was one of them.

My father and I standing on the wharf before S.S. President Wilson, the cruise ship that would take me across the Pacific Ocean to San Francisco, California.

It was over five hundred feet in length and could carry up to five hundred passengers, nearly one-third in first class accommodations; the remainder spaces were for the steerage class. It was scheduled to depart Manila on 13th December 1949 and dock in San Francisco, after stopovers in intervening ports, on 3rd January 1950. Twenty-one days of travel by sea. My preparations to depart had begun nearly six weeks earlier. It happened that Tio Dinoy had assumed the captaincy of a passenger ship larger than the type that had taken the Cebu-Ormoc route before the War. His would cruise southerly with stops at a number of ports in northern and southern Mindanao. It took ten days for the round trip. I was invited, ensconced in the captain's quarters, dining privately, taking in the sights and relishing the special relationship with an uncle who was gregarious, affable and a doting relative. It was a special farewell gift. In Ormoc, there were the good-byes and well-wishes. They came from a circle of relatives and family friends, replete with hugs, kisses, and prayers. The bon voyages—*despedidas*—would continue in Cebu and Manila where, included in the farewells, were those friends from the American Embassy. My siblings and I would not fully imagine the aftermath of our separation nor how it might nudge their own urges to broaden their worldview; only time would tell.

The rounds of good-byes would have an intriguing moment. It happened onboard ship. Papá, with a group of relatives who had come to bid me *adios*, was proudly guiding the party on a tour of the cruise ship. I remained by myself, seated in the main saloon. The only other person was a woman who proceeded to inform me that her husband was below deck, meeting with leaders of the ship's crew, strategizing ways to enlist more members of their co-workers to unionize. Before long, the husband appeared and continued to elaborate on the purpose of his visit. Before they both got off the ship, I was given the names of the crew leaders, urging me to seek them out with assurances that their acquaintance would provide me more food and untold benefits during the voyage. To my surprise, the husband was a well-known leader of the Philippine Communist Party who had led the Huks during the guerilla resistance to Japanese occupation: Luis Taruk. Wow, I thought, a live meeting with a dreaded communist. What an utterly remarkable way to begin my journey.

From the loud speakers came a general request for visitors to get off the vessel, the hooting horns underscoring the preparations for departure, set at ten o'clock that evening. Anchors aweigh!

After the excitement of the farewells, heartwarming wishes for a pleasant trip and abundant luck with my collegiate studies, I saw the hawsers unhitch and recoil as the ship inched off the pier while leaning on the railing of the open aft deck. I was waving along with the other passengers but with mixed emotions: heavyhearted, valorous, audacious, apprehensive, excited! I stayed on that railing watching Papá and company slowly blur and recede from view. Only the night lights of Manila remained visible although they too would be but twinkling little dots in the horizon, gradually enveloped by the darkness of the night. As the ship neared the outer, western mouth of the bay, the famous Corregidor Island came into view. It had historic role in defense of Manila and the country itself: in the attack by Chinese marauders in the tenth century; in the Spanish colonial war in the fourteenth century; in the British invasion and temporary occupation of Manila in the eighteenth century; in the Spanish-American war at the beginning of the nineteenth century; and in the Japanese invasion and the American re-conquest during World War II. When the ship had turned northward, clearly coursing away from Manila and the Perla del Mar de Oriente, I descended a lower level to reach the Steerage Class section, at the aft of the ship for passengers traveling economically. My fare was around $200. In my attire: short-sleeved shirt and a well-worn Levi jeans, the warmth of the area did contrast rather comfortably to the outside air.

The sleeping quarters were primarily a large dormitory, the beds lined in rows with an adjustable partition to separate males from females. It was nearly empty. The low passenger census would be augmented when taking passengers at stopovers in Hong Kong, Kobe, Yokohama, and Honolulu. A limited number of cabins with two bunk-beds, one on top of the other had its own lavatory, supplied with towels and toiletries. Shower stalls and toilets were for common usage elsewhere. Luckily, I was assigned to one of the cabins. Until my roommate was scheduled to board in Hong Kong, our first stopover after a full day of cruising, I would be by myself. I chose the lower bed. I marveled at the luxury, even in steerage class!

The bed would turn out to be among my early challenges as a traveler. It was confounding! The mattress, not overlaid with the familiar palm mat, was instead fitted with a cotton cloth sheet, which was itself covered with yet another cotton sheet that was itself overlaid by a woolen blanket. Every piece was tightly tucked in. At which of the multiple layers would I lie? Should I force myself inside one of the cotton sheets? Or between the cotton sheet and the woolen cover? With no one to ask that late evening, I slept without undressing laying topside, uncovered, that first night. Comfortably, I recall. I awoke in time for breakfast, quickly washing my face and brushing my teeth. The repast was served in tables that could seat six per side; I ate what was served without questions, including at lunch and supper. The edges of the tables had a strip of wood, raised slightly to contain whatever was on top should they sway to the seesaw motion of the boat. That first day I spent mostly on the open deck enjoying the sea as some passengers were retching. Seasickness, the advisory suggested, could be avoided by being outdoors. I did want to avoid it. I did so throughout the voyage, successfully.

The slow approach to the Hong Kong harbor was in early morning, after breakfast. From the open deck, the panoramic view of the city, although it did seem more developed and busier than that of Manila was actually less interesting than what was happening around the ship. It was approached by flat-bottomed boats large enough to accommodate a family of numbers and steered by oars, called *sampans*. Many aligned the sides of the ship and thrust upward to the height of the deck, a bamboo pole at its end of which was fashioned a basket. Each of those baskets had a live baby, a girl. The intent, we would be told, was to offer them for the taking. The commonly held regard of the Chinese, at that time, was their disdain for adding a girl to their already destitute family. Revolting! Fascinating! I did not see any takers.

I got off the ship for a short walk, enough to purchase a tan woolen jacket that I wore faithfully thereafter since the weather would remain cooler than that of Manila. On my return, I met my roommate. He was a very pleasant, friendly Chinese lad of my age. He was headed for a Christian college in Missouri. He not only articulated well in English, he had been imbued with American know-how from being in an American missionary school. I don't recall his name, so I'll refer to him as Sam. Sam promptly clarified the confounding bedding setup. Importantly, thanks to Sam, I learned to enjoy for the first time ever a warm-water shower by manipulating the two faucets with "C" and "H" engraved on them. He and I would remain on friendly terms throughout the days at sea. The next stops were in Japan. Passengers were not allowed to disembark at either the Kobe or Yokohama ports. Security concerns? Watching the Japanese workers by the wharf was disturbing to me, feeling as I did then they were the enemy. The unconscionably depraved actions of their soldiers in the Philippines was yet fresh in my memory. I had no interest in going ashore. I retired, instead, to the lower level of the ship, content to exchange stories with Sam in the lounge. We both looked forward to the days at sea as we coursed toward Honolulu. On the open deck, the fresh air was successfully combating seasickness, even when the ship responded to the varying degrees of troughs and swells. There were times to get better acquainted with the fellow-students. Among them were two Japanese girls destined to a Junior College in Venice, California where they apparently had Japanese relatives as sponsors. I had a chance to inform them of the showers since their homes also had no hot water system; they took tub baths filled with boiling and cold water carried in buckets. Getting to interact with them gave me time to categorize and better define my enmity of the Japanese. Were the ladies complicit or supportive of the barbaric behavior of their warriors? What moral qualities and ethical behavior did they espouse? I was pleased to have befriended them as upstanding individuals who, like me, were looking forward to the opportunity to savor America without reservations. A highlight of the voyage was a birthday party on the twenty-third arranged by the ship's officers, which was complete with balloons and confetti, surprisingly for me.

Among the number of passengers that came aboard in Yokohama was a Catholic priest, an Italian. I am unclear how I came to meet him, but I did. The priest spoke to me in Italian, and I spoke in Spanish, each of us understanding sufficiently to communicate, albeit rudimentarily. He said daily mass, and I was the acolyte. The chapel was in the first-class compartment, and that is how I came to climb the three levels to get a look-see at that portion of the ship.

QUID PRO QUO

On the morning the ship was slowly moving toward the Honolulu wharf, the sea was calm; the sunshine was warm, not hot; and the sky azure blue. The city and its verdant arboreal façade and colorful flowers showed off the cityscape to a wondrous advantage. The scenery was an awesome contrast to that of Manila, Hong Kong, Kobe, or Yokohama. Awaiting Sam to disembark were his relatives, prepared to take him on a tour of the city and its surroundings. A memorable tour was planned. By fortuitous luck, Sam had invited me to join him. As a result, I had an unexpected, pleasurable Hawaiian stopover, viewing Diamond Head, which overlooked the famous Waikiki Beach among other vistas, particularly the cursory tour of Pearl Harbor Naval facility and the expansive Military Cemetery. I was particularly impressed that by wharf-side, the Dole Pineapple Company had instilled a drinking fountain from which pineapple juice could be had, at no cost and in unlimited quantity. Unbelievable abundance! At our departure that early evening, we all got flowers to throw to the sea, the common belief being that on their wash to shore, the thrower was assured a return to Hawaii. I threw mine, hoping it would come to shore. I did wish for a chance to return.

In the remaining three days before reaching San Francisco, finding a way to return Sam the favor of including me in the Honolulu tour preyed on my mind. On the last day at sea, I piqued Sam's interest and curiosity when I mentioned the communist Taruk's invitation to seek out the allegedly powerful crew members whose influence could net us untold favors. And so, we descended another level from Steerage Class and found the crew members huddled with others of their mates, asking us to "wait a while." Sensing the sinister nature of the ongoing discussion, I whispered to Sam for us to abort the wait and return to our cabin. Sam remained. Shortly, he did return, looking disturbed and dismayed. He not only had determined the crew members were "communists" strategizing to unionize the crew, he had disclosed our plans to check-in at the YMCA hotel near the San Francisco Embarcadero and take the train to our respective destination: he to Missouri and I to Minnesota. Meanwhile, at the chapel I met a teenage girl from Idaho who was returning from a Hawaii vacation with her grandfather. As she had boarded in First Class, she was able to invite me to view the docking at San Francisco from the foredeck and to arrange to meet her at the hotel they were staying just off famous Union Square. Standing outdoor, I was struck at the weather by the Bay; it felt cold and for the first time, my breath smoked with each exhalation. It did get me to wonder how different the winter might be in Duluth. Together, we watched the ship ply under the world-famous Golden Gate Bridge. It was built and completed in 1937 to be the longest suspension bridge to span the city of San Francisco to Marin County to the north. It had become regarded as among the beautiful wonders of the world. To me, it was the gateway to America, a dreamed-for entry to a country that I was eager to avail of its limitless opportunities.

SAN FRANCISCO

On that morning of 3rd January 1950, I disembarked down the gangplank and firmly planted both feet on the ground in San Francisco, California. In America! I carried with me my entire treasure: $980; a near-empty valise because I was wearing most of my wardrobe—a prized U.S. Army-issue woolen pants; and the newly purchased woolen jacket I had paid $20 for in Hong Kong worn over a G.I.-issue khaki long-sleeved cotton shirt. I was feeling comfortable and self-assured. Triumphant! Courageous!

The sensation I felt being in the city and among Americans was not as a foreigner. I did not feel overwhelmed. Rather, I felt smugly at ease and even tickled for having accomplished a long-held craving, alive in America. Sam and I walked out of the YMCA hotel by dawn the next day to roam the neighborhood for a few hours. We had decided, fearfully, not to be present when the crew members of the ship were to meet us that early morning, as Sam had innocently arranged. They intended to pursue their connection with us, even willing to provide assistance with train ticket purchases. They had also wished to supply names of organizations to join at our destination. Communist-leaning? The thought of beginning my life in America by having the faintest connection with un-American organizations was abhorrent, beyond the pale.

Walking around the blocks of streets of downtown San Francisco, I was notably impressed at how the youngsters were dressed in short-sleeved shirts, impervious to the cold morning air. I felt we were walking in a canyon of tall buildings that had sprouted in orderly fashion. Sam and I ultimately settled on a café for breakfast. Until that moment, the food I ate, whether at my home or at my relatives, in restaurants, in boarding houses, even on the ship, was set before me, courtesy of others who did not always seek my personal preference. That morning, I was prepared to order my choice which I had practiced and committed to memory: ham and eggs. The opportunity came as the bouncy waitress elicited our order.

The exchange with the waitress:

Me: ham and eggs
She: how to you want your eggs?
Me: uhhh…what? (I get a choice?)
She: sunny side up or over?
Me: up…? (confounded and uncertain of the difference)
She: Okay…bacon and sausage?
Me: uhhh… ham?
She: Canadian or regular?
Me: … regular (now bemused but losing confidence)
She: Wheat or rye toast?
Me: … white (will this cease?)
She: want coffee?
Me: yes
She: there's milk on the table
Me: (whew!!! this is incredible! unbelievable…)

I proceeded to enjoy breakfast. The experience opened my eyes early to the prodigious assortment and abundance of choices for Americans. It would draw attention to my meager know-how and goad me to become increasingly more informed, more engaged. Although not clear at the time, it would be the beginning of a lifelong education in being familiar with the food I would thereafter be consuming, even cooking. My next lesson would not wait long.

That afternoon, I met my Idaho friend for soft drinks at her hotel's coffee shop. She accompanied me to Macy's Department Store, where I purchased an outer-coat, sufficiently able to ward the San Francisco cool weather, for $40. The following day, Sam and I bid adieu, and I boarded the train for Duluth. We were both pleased not to have seen or needed the crew members and thankful to face our futures unburdened by thoughts of communists. We were eager to employ our best efforts to embark on an unbounded future in America. While Sam and I continued to write letters to each other, the coming years would leave our brief friendship but a memory. The same fate occurred with my Idaho friend and those offspring of the U.S. Embassy staff in Manila. The two-night YMCA lodging cost each of us $5.

THE EMERSION

From San Francisco, California, to Duluth, Minnesota, is approximately two thousand miles, nearly a two-day travel by train with two connecting transfers. The train first stopped near midnight in Salt Lake City, Utah. I got off to await another train connection to Minneapolis, Minnesota. Outside the railway station, I first felt the cold of winter of which others had forewarned me. I was exposed only briefly enough to find a mound of snow with which I excitedly made my first snow ball.

Earlier that evening at the dining table, on scanning the menu, I chose the cheapest item: chicken pot pie. Seated across from me was a young soldier who, like me, seemed shy and hesitant to engage in conversation. He ordered similarly. Both of us were served the dish at the same time. I looked at the pie, which was contained in a bowl topped by a freshly baked crust, enticingly pleasant to the smell. And, I thought: another challenge! How to eat the chicken which I assumed was hidden underneath the crust? I sneaked a glance at the soldier and noted he was equally puzzled and, I surmised, waiting to see what I would do. He made me less insecure! Puncturing the pie crust with my spoon, I resolved the quandary. I ate my first chicken pot pie, the pieces of chicken bathed in a delicious creamy mix of vegetables I couldn't identify. It was satisfying. The soldier followed suit.

In Minneapolis the following morning was another train switch to get to Duluth. The countryside was covered with snow. The changed vista from that of San Francisco suggested an even colder weather waiting for me. As if to convince me, I got off the train in Duluth, and on my short walk to the station in a matter of a few minutes, I feared my ears would snap off from being frosted. My brand-new overcoat, on top of my wardrobe, did little to warm me up. It was Saturday 7th January; from someone I was informed of the outside temperature. It meant nothing to me. It was, however, the first time I learned the meaning of the expression "brrrrrrr!"

Awaiting to welcome me was a three-student group accompanied by the Dean of Students Dr. E. R. Wood. Noting me shivering, they promptly whisked me to the warmth of the YMCA hotel and settled me in my room for the evening with promises by the students to return the following day to keep me company. In the solitude of my room, the reality of my adventure, the unnerving feeling of the irreversibility of my solitary venture away from home, and now away from things familiar was dawning on me. As I sat by the tableside with the few family photographs facing me, I took forlorn, pensive inventory of what I had left behind. There was the Seaside Hotel, now reconstructed and resuming its business undertaking; Ormoc itself was getting re-energized with visions of a progressive future; and, Papá's medical practice was regaining its activity, as was his societal participation in the community. Of my siblings, Fenny would soon complete high school at St. Theresa's College for women in Cebu as a boarder with plans to pursue collegiate studies at the Philippine Women's

University in Manila; Indáy and Jun, bonding together like two peas in a pod by their single year's difference in ages, were growing in adolescence seemingly undaunted by being without Mamá's love and protection, as was little Tonio.

I felt as if those earlier years, together with the preparations and excitement of the trip, were memories now vividly etched in my mind. They would become a phase of my life that seemed to be separated by a curtain. And there, in Duluth, alone in a bedroom of the YMCA, that curtain had opened to expose my new, uncharted life. Realizing that my chances of returning home prematurely would be beyond consideration, I resolved that evening to direct my drive and undertakings focused on a life in America, returning to the Philippines only by choice with success among my credentials. I willed my future to be an odyssey from Perla del Mar del Oriente. It would be full of challenges! Boundless opportunity! All in a land where hard work and singleness of purpose, I believed, would reap commensurate rewards. Still, I felt alone and youthfully vulnerable. For the first time since my departure, I sobbed myself to sleep.

DULUTH...THE UNIVERSITY

Vince—my acquaintance from the San Carlos High School days—was right! Duluth did strike me that winter as awesomely attractive, coated as the city was with the pristine look of the newly fallen snow. Snow, I would learn, sometimes falls to accumulate up to a few feet. Snowfall would visit and revisit the remaining months into springtime. Then, during the time I lived in Duluth, predictably, the cold of winter would yield to the gentler, if rainier weather of spring. The season would usher in, as if re-awakening from dormancy, an eruption of blooming flowers with names strange to me, in colors of yellow, purple, white, blue, violet; and, the trees, sprouting youthful leaves the color of pale green and magenta, were maple, elm, oak, and the evergreens.

Summertime would follow, the Duluthians light-heartedly joke as lasting but a few days: before and after the 4th of July. The warmth of the sun, unlike that of Ormoc, would be comfortable and less humid even as the temperature did rise to equal heights; at sunset, the ambient conditions cooled down. Autumn would follow, a season at which the city and the State would be a technicolor of nature as the foliage changed colors before shedding; a telltale sign of the return of winter. Minnesota, a land of ten thousand lakes, I discovered and enjoyed, would have a year of four distinct seasons.

The city was plotted on a hill, gradually elevating from the shores of the western end of Lake Superior. The lake is the largest of five contiguous, navigable body of fresh water that ultimately empty into the Atlantic Ocean about two thousand miles to the east. Through its port, mined ore from northern areas of the State got transported by container ships to far-away destinations. I found the residents friendly and solicitous. Many were of Scandinavian stock with surnames that ended with "–son," a suffix to identify their ancestral relationships, as for example, a son whose father's last name was "Peter" would adopt the name "Peterson." In turn, to my new acquaintances pronouncing my surname was perplexing and difficult; some of my professors would conveniently resign to calling me "mister Y." Most Duthulians were openly inquisitive about a land whose people had rarely visited their place. So, within a few weeks, most likely out of curiosity, I was a guest speaker before such organizations as the Daughters of the Revolution and the B'Nai B'rth, enjoying the after-talk questions about the Philippines and Filipinos. Their curiosity allowed me to articulate my wish to avail of a good education, to imbibe the American way, and describe a goal on my return to the Philippines. I hoped to partake in what I envisioned would be an era of profound reconstruction with its citizens the yeast of a country-wide effort to wrest itself from the

War-induced morass. Filipinos, I believed, would become equal to the challenges of rebuilding their war-torn nation, triumphantly.

Before the end of my first week, the Dean of Students and his wife had me for dinner at their home. As curious as they were about the Philippines I was, likewise, entranced and engrossed. It was by a toy their four-year old son brought out to show me, named Tinker Toy—a collection of wooden spools and sticks that allow and inspire children to apply them in a variety of ways, using their imagination. Before long, I found myself sprawled on the carpeted floor with the son, constructing with him structures designed by our imagination. I once glanced up and found the parents amused at my child-like fascination and enjoyment. At dinner, we all—if sheepishly—got better acquainted with each other and, for me in particular, with the contrasting upbringing of American and Filipino children. I was praising their hospitality in my letters to Papá who, in turn, had thanked the Wood family for their willingness to watch for my welfare.

Within days after the start of the winter trimester, I went shopping to be better dressed for winter. Soon I owned a funny-looking furry cap with turn-down flaps to cover the ears against frostbite, a woolen neck scarf, a hefty woolen sweater, a full-body woolen underwear, woolen socks and rubber over-shoe boots that kept the shoes dry when trudging through snow and puddles. An effective get-up, albeit, radically different from the Ormoc attire of cotton short sleeve shirt and pants. They kept me comfortable, suffice to ward off the freezing elements. I checked out of the YMCA soon after the Dean of Students helped find me a private home that accepted a boarder and provide breakfast and supper. It was a walking distance from the university classrooms. The host couple was warmly hospitable, making me feel a comfortable member of their family. I would reside there until the summer. Thereafter until graduation, I stayed at a house, the rooming arrangements managed by a faculty member and his family who let boarders occupy the third floor. My roommate Ken came from a town in western Minnesota. He was a son of a dentist and had a Scandinavian surname that I have since forgotten. We became good friends throughout my Duluth stay. Fortuitously, a Catholic church was in walking distance. I was easily recruited to join the choir and had the opportunity to meet people of my Faith, especially students from the all-girl St. Scholastica High School.

The university student body of thirteen hundred was parochial. But for a small minority hailing from adjacent States of Wisconsin, North and South Dakotas, the rest were Minnesotans. There were four foreign students: two from nearby Canada, one from Latvia, and me. My pre-medical curriculum had the standard requisite courses. Among them were comparative anatomy, the various levels of chemistry, physiology, zoology, and, the liberal arts: English, Spanish, physical education plus a bevy of psychology courses sufficient to receive a Bachelor of Arts degree in June 1953 with a major in the science. I did feel thankful to have had that year at the University of the Philippines, aware that a comparable U.S. high school graduate would have had twelve years to my eleven scrambled years, preparatory to college. I also felt comfortable with the English language, except on those occasions when I would hear such colloquial expressions as "ya betcha your life"…"raining cats and dogs"…"here's two bits"… There were, of course, extra-curricular activities: joining the tennis team; being a member of Mu Delta Pi, a fraternity of pre-medical and pre-dental students who were studious and motivated—in time most, if not all, did join the health professions; and, being a cast member of a Silas Marner and Christmas Tale productions of the Art and Drama Club. The Christmas Story production before the holiday break, a traditional play surrounding the birth of Jesus, featured a scene where the three wise men, guided by a star paid a homage bringing gifts. I participated, dressed as Melchor. I now regard my thespian experience limited.

At the beginning of the 1950-51 school year, I got the foreign students to form the nucleus of a Non-Residents' Club to which those coming from outside Minnesota joined. The well-rounded activities included sponsoring a homecoming queen candidate, dances, and get-acquainted meetings. The club attracted so much interest that the By-Laws were shortly changed to allow Minnesotans to join. I was its first president.

I looked forward to the athletic programs. On an autumn day of 1952, Ken and I marched across the football field to join the gathered candidates working out and scrimmaging to qualify for the football team. Walking toward us with his arm in a sling was a burly member of the previous year's varsity team. He informed us that he had just broken his wrist in the trials and was going to the infirmary for definitive care. Ken and I looked at each other as the burly athlete walked past us and, without a word, we turned around, bidding good-bye to our dreams of becoming football players. That day, prudence had trumped indiscretion

As I had anticipated being a tradition among American Universities, we always had an annual homecoming weekend celebration in early autumn. It was fêted with a parade that included floats and a football game, usually against a team, suspected beatable. To complete the affair, there invariably was an evening bonfire and coronation of the homecoming queen. One year, Mu Delta Pi had a float atop which Jack Dahl and I were dressed in football uniforms, mocking a surgical operation in jest. So I at least got to don a football uniform. My penchant for athletics remained, if yet to be fulfilled. At one edge of town was a ski slope, equipped with a rope tow to facilitate ascent to the top. I was equipped with war surplus skis and boots that a famed US Army brigade of mountaineers used in the European theater of World War II. A friend, eager to teach me the sport, was my companion. I succeeded to reach and get off the rope tow at the top. From the peak of the hill, I looked down and was frighteningly surprised. The people below had shrunken to the size of midgets. I stood there unmoved by fright. The weather, however, was uncooperatively making me feel increasingly colder. I forced a win over my terror. Keeping in mind the basic rule to "edge the skis on descent," I sloped down. The trip was plain scary, but exhilarating and enjoyable. I took a few more downhill turns before calling it quits. I was hooked on skiing. Duluth, it seemed to me did not lack for sources of entertainment. Uniquely, it had a movie theater at which, for $0.25 or "two-bits," one could spend hours watching movies of yesteryears, projected one after another. There, I did while away a few Saturday afternoons in air-conditioned comfort, getting acquainted with flicks that were not available in war-torn Philippines.

To supplement the $50 Papá remitted as my monthly subsidy, I took a number of part-time jobs, the openings posted at the school's library. Within my first weeks, I was shoveling snow off driveways that winter, paid generously for the first time ever for my labor. Then, at one time or another, I was hired as a general helper at a florist shop on weekends that included trimming thorns off roses and delivering flower arrangements to customers by van. At the train station, I worked as a janitor—the graffiti inside both men and women's toilets were copious and shockingly candid reading. At all the jobs that I had, I frequently pinched myself in thanksgiving for my good fortune at being able to perform my assigned tasks, receiving commendations and providing me income. The tasks were made easy and efficient by using innovations I had never used or did not know existed such as the vacuum cleaner, the squeegee, the mop, and, of course, the use of a vehicle. I would recall how our helpers at home would tire themselves scrubbing floors, sweeping dust, and swatting flies; each chore done manually.

Now, in Minnesota, I savored the rewards that came from honest labor rendered with courtesy and concern to those I served; I improved my driving skills and familiarity of the city; and, I would affirm my belief in America as a land of opportunity. There were other tasks I considered extraordinary. During the summer of 1950, I worked as a construction laborer, pushing a wheelbarrow filled with wet cement from the mixer to a foundation for a radar station. Together with me was a seasoned outdoorsman, classmate Mark Magney. It was a remote site of northern Minnesota. We lived in a tent pitched by a river, the water of near-Arctic temperature, that served as our bath tub. We prepared our own meals. The undertaking, building a sizeable structure for a radar station, seemed to me ambitious, particularly with its completion targeted for late autumn just weeks away. While I was astounded at the relatively few workers for the undertaking, I soon appreciated how intensely a variety of machineries were utilized to optimize the manpower. It would, of course, contrast with projects where the lack of technical appliances needed to be compensated with large number of laborers, yet unable to have comparable results in time and finished products. I would recall witnessing the contrast at a number of reconstruction projects while in Manila. There, despite the large number of laborers, their results did not seem to compare in time and finished products; and, I imagined how much agricultural production in agrarian Philippines could profit from mechanical contrivances. Here, I was well-paid but for heavy physical labor. I soon realized I was ill prepared, even worrying I would develop a hernia. I lasted only a couple weeks. The physically demanding manual labor was an eye-opener. The experience tightened my determination to be a collegian aiming for a profession.

Later that late summer, I drove for a kindly, indulgent elderly couple on their month-long sight-seeing vacation. By prior arrangements, we took guided tours of historical importance at the particular stopover. We spent time in Detroit, Michigan; the Canadian cities of Ontario, Montreal, and Quebec; and drove through New England. We stopped in Boston, Massachusetts, and Philadelphia, Pennsylvania, before returning to Duluth. I stayed at well-known hotels, dined at selective restaurants and was paid $100 for the vacation experience. Indeed, in that short period, I was given an enviable acquaintance of the country far more than I imagined. The car I drove was a brand-new Buick. Unbeknownst to the couple, both of whom were napping, at one point of the travel, I nudged the speedometer gauge to one hundred miles per hour for an instant somewhere in Michigan. Thereafter, I maintained a sane and safe cruising speed. Recalling that nano-moment of foolhardiness still gives me the shivers, and I am thankful for having been given a divine pass.

During my first year's winter break, all my house-mates returned to their homes for Christmas. I was left alone. The Catholic church and my choir helped to while away the holidays; we sang at midnight Mass. That Christmas day, my landlord family invited me to dinner. I came downstairs. Their place was decorated for the holiday: a Christmas tree, its branches weighted by a variety of colorful trinkets which, I was told, had especial meaning to the family; on its base were toys that had been opened that morning; and the radio softly playing records of familiar tunes. The lady of the house announced the dinner menu with dishes that seemed like that which the school cafeteria had served the Thanksgiving weekend of November. The couple had prepared a program that featured a recital by their pre-kindergarten-aged child. I was overjoyed. More so when their son who said he was "nearly four years old" recited a poem that was so new to me, I was determined to commit it to memory and brag about it to my siblings in Ormoc. Proudly, the admirable youngster begun: "T'was the night before Christmas, when all through the house …not a creature was stirring, not even a mouse. The stockings were hung by the chimney with care, in hopes that St. Nicholas soon would be there." The recitation ended wishing a "Happy Christmas to all, and to all a good-night."

The poem, The Night Before Christmas, was written by Henry Livingston in 1822. My young friend had recited it flawlessly. I was amazed beyond words and very moved to have spent a precious day with them. That evening was yet another look-see at the interactions of an American family and the upbringing of their child whose deportment and knowledge struck me as impressively precocious. And, it had contrasted with my own upbringing. Sadly, I have long since forgotten his or the parents' names. I still wonder, however, if the boy wasn't really several years older than a pre-kindergartener! That entire evening, I thought, was Americana.

Sometime before the summer vacation of 1951, I landed a job to which I would return whenever possible as it paid me well plus tips and provided the uniforms. My primary task was to conduct guests to their rooms carrying luggage, sometimes multiple pieces in both arms. I was a bell-hop at the premier Hotel Duluth. The experience gave me another insight into the equitable manner in which workers and servers were regarded by employers and customers. I was struck by the easy climate of mutual respect; if there was the societal pecking order that was notable in Ormoc, it escaped my notice. Importantly, it honed my formative knack to relate with people easily. I resumed the position whenever I could till my last days in Duluth.

It was there I would form a lasting friendship with a classmate, a Mu Delta Pi fraternity brother and a local Duluthian, Jack Dahl. We were fellow bell-hops that summer of 1951. That early autumn Jack and I took two weeks off to visit Chicago by Greyhound bus, nearly 500 miles distant. To me, as it likely was to Jack, coming as we did from Duluth, Chicago seemed a gigantic metropolis. The trip felt a fitting similarity to my wide-eyed intrigue when coming from rural Ormoc as a *provinciano,* I would visit Cebu awed by it urbanity. Of course, Cebu was no comparison. The Chicago scene was full of high rises, sky-scrapers. Busy. The city transports featured a rail system that coursed through subterranean and elevated tracts from one end to the other; we availed of them. People were aplenty, more racially mixed. To continue on our spartan, lean-budget strategy, we stayed at a YMCA for $5 a night, two in a room. We took in the tourist attractions that included getting ushered out of honky-tonk bars for being

underage, but only after getting a quickie glance at strippers wiggling on bar-tops. As previously arranged by Jack's mom, we took
in radio shows of national popularity. It included being a contestant at the Welcome Traveler Radio Show where we received
a number of high-priced gifts; we thereafter gave to Jack's mom.
More later on about the intertwining relations our futures would
take to create a lifelong friendship.

*In Chicago, MC Tommy Bartlett of Welcome
Travelers radio show pose between Jack Dahl and
I as guests of the popular program, 1951.*

The Catholic Church choir I belonged to was often invited
to performance events at Catholic High Schools, particularly
that at St. Scholastica, a school exclusively for women. Among
the students was an attractive, friendly senior, Mary Sue Peacha.
I was her escort at her Senior Prom, the late autumn of 1951.
She lived in nearby Cloquet where, quite by serendipity, a friend
Terry Swenson also resided. He was a precocious musician who
played the piano, drum, and guitar adeptly; he also managed a
music store in town. For a few days of the Christmas break, Terry

invited me to stay at his home. It was as much for our friendship as it was for me to broadcast at Cloquet's radio station an advertising message about the music store that he had composed and I translated into Spanish. He was convinced the message, with me delivering in a foreign language, would resonate approvingly to the listeners. I don't know how the Cloquet audience responded. Nor do I recall being asked to record a sequel message. On one evening of my visit, I had a date to take Mary Sue to a movie, not far from her house. We had many other dates during the school year in Duluth. Terry lent me his car. I drove by an icy patch and promptly lost control, sliding the car to a shallow embankment. That night-out ended by walking Mary Sue back to her house, requesting her Dad to pull the car off the bank and driving back to Terry's home, repentant and learning how challenging winter driving can be, particularly on icy roadways. To my good fortune, Terry would remain a friend, and we would go on double dates at other future occasions in his car. The car was undamaged.

During my last Minnesota summer, 1952, I took a full-time night-shift work at a paper mill in Cloquet. It was a rewarding job. I learned that paper is formed from wood pulp. At the plant, workers were involved in the process of reducing the pulp to fibers and combine the product with cotton and linen fibers. With the mechanization of the production, workers were assigned to a specific portion of the many steps contributing to the making of sheets of the finished product. The quality of modernly produced paper is a remarkable difference from the earliest paper—papyrus—which was made from reeds in ancient Egypt. My earnings that summer allowed me to acquire a used 1944 Buick coupe. Owning a car was liberating. Where in the past I either relied on friends or hitch-hiked to get to places, I now was able to travel at will. Yet, the fun and adventure of hitch-hiking remains in my store of pleasant memories. Once, two elderly ladies stopped to pick me up for my twenty-mile destination. The driver offered me the front seat as her companion took the back seat. In the course of the drive and cordial chit-chat, the backseat companion announced she had a knife and was prepared to harm me if I misbehaved. They unloaded me at my destination with all of us comfortable and pleased to have had the brief acquaintance; I was amused at their candor.

While working at the paper mill, I rented a room with board in Cloquet. I was able to keep my relationship with Mary Sue intact but also with that of her parents and her younger brother who was born with Down's syndrome—an impairment which limits cognitive ability and physical growth. Jimmy received the unbounded support of his family, and was very friendly. On the Christmas break that winter, I spent days with the Peacha family. In town, there was a portly gentleman with a full beard and moustache, bleached white for the occasion; he had a kindly face and a spirited voice. On Christmas Day, he would dress in a Santa Claus outfit and visit homes that had engaged his services. There, gathering toys and gifts that parents left in the alcove and placing them in his sack, he rung the doorbell and announced his presence. He then handed out the gifts to delighted children ho, ho, ho-ing all the while, and then departed wishing everybody a "Merry Christmas." It was a marvelous, unforgettable custom for the families in Cloquet. It was for the Peacha family, Jimmy was particularly ecstatic. The whole Christmastime experience, for me, was wonderfully memorable.

1953

I was about to graduate in early summer, at age twenty-two. While Papá and I had religiously maintained contact by airmail, it was primarily to give each other personal accounts of notable happenings. My siblings, also sensitive to the happenings about Papá, our relatives, the community, and the country would provide their perspective of occurrences during the nearly four years since I left home.

The family had adjusted well to my absence. Each of my siblings was excelling at school and having a satisfying cadence to their daily lives. Inday was becoming an adept pianist from having lessons by Sr. Adalrica and Jun was engaged with violin lessons by Sr. Carmen, each at the St. Peter's Academy; they had both begun their lessons while in 6th grade. Inday wrote of the thrill of her solo recital. Jun was increasingly attracted to the priesthood and seriously considering entering the seminary. Fenny completed her pre-collegiate years as a boarder of St. Theresa's High School in Cebu in 1950; her infrequent off-campus passes were to visit Lolo Otic and Lola Emping. From the occasional letters we exchanged while she was preparing to graduate as a pharmacist at the Philippine Women's University in 1954, she expressed a hope to pursue her studies in Hospital Pharmacy in Michigan where I had described the snow and freezing weather of winter. Tonio ensconced in the primary grades of SPA, simply growing up. Ormoc, meanwhile, acquired daylong electricity, surely enjoying the many advantages it provided.

Papá had sought a partner shortly after I had departed to manage the modest sugar cane plantation he owned. He chose Mr. Kierulf, Tio Paeng's brother-in law. It was a partnership aimed to unburden him of a planter's chores, limiting his business oversight to the Seaside Hotel and his medical practice. Ultimately, by 1953, Papá divested himself of the plantation, the sugar cane enterprise having been short of the success he had anticipated. Instead, he joined in a venture with a close family friend, George Tan to open a movie house where once our home was located. At that time, he and my siblings were residing in a separate private portion of the Seaside Hotel.

On 25th June 1950, North Korea invaded the Republic of South Korea. The United Nations Security Council responded by unanimously condemning the aggression. In less than a decade after World War II, America would re-arm and send its armies to battle, as the principal component of the United Nations Police

Force. As the Supreme Commander of the UN Forces, General Douglas MacArthur had the North Koreans initially retreating to regions close to the Chinese border. Arrogantly championing defeat of the enemy by the strategic use of atomic bombs, his advocacy came in defiance of dictates by his Washington superiors. Fearing the potential of Chinese and Russian armed intervention in support of the North Koreans and incurring massive loss of civilian lives, President Harry Truman relieved the general of command in the spring of 1951. The general's actions had been judged as subterfuge and insubordination of civilian authority. On the general's return to America he addressed the Joint Assembly of the U.S. Congress, a fallen hero but to popular acclaim and respect. The American involvement would increasingly become controversial and poorly supported by the public. The dissent spilled into college campuses, including those of Duluth. At the university I recall participating in discussions about the dangers of a spreading monolithic communist world and the peril that a U.N. defeat in Korea would foretell to the nations of South-East Asia, including the Philippines. While I argued in support of the intervention, what most impressed me was how American citizens freely posited divergent views, without fear of recrimination. It was another insight into Americanism. Before the Korean conflict was resolved by an armistice agreement on 27th July 1953, the Philippines was persuaded to participate as one of the multi-national combatant force. On the 31st October 1950, Filipino soldiers would battle on foreign soil. Of the 7,420 soldier complement, 112 were killed. The American casualties of the conflict had 128,650 killed in action and 92,134 were injured, as tabulated by the American Battle Monuments Commission (ABMC) of the U.S. government.

The Filipinos, in the 1953 national election, denied the re-election of their incumbent President Elpidio R. Quirino and staked the nation's future on Ramon F. Magsaysay. The former was accused of corruption, incompetence, and without an effective program to aid a majority of the citizenry that, as yet, remained in abject penury; the latter was renowned for the courage of his convictions, persuasive in his ability to resurrect the damaged integrity of the government, purge the entrenching culture of dishonesty and indolence, and elevate the dignity of every Filipino. From my distant perspective, it seemed that the Quirino years of self-serving policies had been rooting a harmful association with the long-held Filipino custom, utang na loob. In this instance, the patron-client behavior was likely employed nefariously to mask commitment of illicit acts or, by cronyism, escape discovery and prosecution. Had the Filipino wellbeing been marginalized by misuse and abuse of misguided politicians? Might the well-intentioned reform programs of Magsaysay succeed in reversing the acquiescent tolerance of graft and corruption?

STEPPING ONWARD

At the spring trimester 1953, I had a wake-up incident. I was chosen to greet at the train station a guest speaker for our annual convocation at which people of note and prominence were the invited. In this instance, she was the daughter of Sergio Osmeña, ex-president of the Commonwealth of the Philippines who, like me, was raised able to speak Binisayá. After our customary greetings and being informed of our common dialect, she soon switched languages. It had been the first time since my arrival to America, nearly three years past, that I had heard or thought of speaking the dialect. I was tongue-tied for an embarrassing lapse of time. My lesson dawned shortly: a language know-how can rust from disuse and that, apart from the Osmeña lady, I had remained out of face-to-face contact with my countrymen, there being few if any where I lived. I had, of course, needed to submerge my longing to become acquainted with fellow Filipinos—*kababayan*—while in Duluth and repress desires for a return visit to the Philippines; both circumstances had seemed to me beyond the possibilities.

With the forthcoming graduation, the pervasive topic of conversation among students was of the immediate future. Many were to graduate as school teachers or librarians, their appointments at the various school systems of the State affirmed, and others with diplomas in business were in search for opportunities in the commercial world. They all were looking forward to being productive members of society. There were a few of us in the pre-medical and pre-dental programs who, instead, were looking to additional years of study. I was very pleased for a chance to pursue a profession in the health field.

In June 1953, I graduated from the University of Minnesota Duluth with a Bachelor of Arts degree in Psychology and Zoology. Together with the Peacha family, we all partook in a dinner at their home, in celebration. Sadly, yet unavoidably, I had to settle with the consolation that my family in Ormoc shared my accomplishment, in spirit.

ON REFLECTION

It is with ease and gratitude that I reflect at how fortunate and blessed I was to have acquired the many friends and acquaintances since my arrival in San Francisco. My journey was filled with a variety of memorable goings-on: the self-improving opportunities and returns that part-time work had rewarded; the lessons gained from misadventures that mixed with those pleasurable adventures; and, the benefits that came from scholarship. All those experiences became a collage of the viewpoints I gained and regarded about America as a land of boundless prospects for success. I felt I had thoroughly integrated and accustomed myself to this once foreign land. The eagerness to return to the Philippines that I had once expressed before the Daughters of America and B'Nai B'rth in early 1950 was wavering. My growing comfort with the country would continue. Nonetheless, I found that the more I became acquainted with America and the Americans, the more I had to learn.

My relationship with Mary Sue, I remember, as a happy and satisfying experience at being in love; the subsequent breakup was my first heartache. The kindness and love that I received from the Peacha family were endearing, caring and unselfish gifts—to my good fortune. They had given me their amity with compassion. It was a nurturing gift that would help cultivate and define my sense of family. Equally comforting was the knowledge that my own family was living and adapting favorably to the evolving events of the Philippines. They would contrast to the pervasive corruption and rampant poverty, surely retardant hurdles to the country's progress and prosperity. Would the administration of newly elected President Magsaysay serve as a beacon of hope, a harbinger of needed improvements?

At the University of Minnesota Duluth the learning process differed from the methodology of the University of the Philippines. The faculty, in the main, was open to, if not actually encouraging an engaged student participation, aiming to develop critical thinking. While I had not been comfortable partaking in the liberal environment throughout the collegiate years, the system allowed students to challenge conventional teachings and allowed independent problem solving. Perhaps, now about to tackle post-graduate studies at the Washington University School of Dental Medicine in St. Louis, I would become more emboldened.

In the pursuit of a dental profession, I envisioned having to overcome many hurdles. The didactic studies and the practicum with its demand on manual dexterity that dental procedures require—they would be intensive and comprehensive, with a demanding learning curve. They are the essential groundwork for the competent practice of the profession. To surmount challenges—whether they be in the mind or in the physical being—I

have learned to value positive affirmations. They are well-advo-
cated avowals to help suppress negative thoughts and instead
fuel an empowering positive mind-set. Mine is: *"I think I can, I
know I can, I will."* I felt prepared and willing to face the challenges ahead.

PURSUIT OF A
PROFESSION

We all have dreams. But in order to make dreams come into reality, it takes an awful lot of determination, dedication, self-discipline, and effort.

—Jesse Owen (World-class Athlete... b1913–1960)

Education should consist of a series of enchantments, each raising the individual to a higher level of awareness, understanding, and kinship with all living things.

*—Thomas Stearns "T.S." Elliot
(Philosopher... b1888–1965).*

Training for the professional qualifications involve technical, specialized and skilled study, and continuing education. Professions enjoy high esteem arising primarily from the function of their work, regarded as vital to society for its special and valuable nature.

—P. C. S. Lian & A. W. Laing (Educators).

By early autumn 1953, I had spent the months following graduation in June working as a bellhop, optimizing my coffers. Bidding good-bye to many friends, a few of whom were pursuing their careers in medicine and dentistry away from Duluth was joyful yet poignant. There was the unspoken knowledge that the parting would loosen the ties of friendship, particularly as my world would re-anchor in distant St. Louis. Leaving Mary Sue and her family was a sentimental, heartwarming moment; I felt very fortunate that her family, by extending me surrogate care, had profusely given of their love and concern. Mary Sue and I parted with my deep regret, certain that we were destined to take divergent paths. While we remained connected by letters, with passing time and distance we became more estranged. She was my first-time love, my first heartache.

I applied to both medical and dental schools for admission as my preparatory courses conformed to their respective requisites. The number of applications was limited by my funds and anticipated tuition costs. I was accepted to enroll in the 1953 freshman class of the School of Dental Medicine of Washington University in St. Louis, Missouri.

ADIOS, DULUTH... HELLO, ST. LOUIS

In the company of my Buick coupe and a valise fuller than that which I carried when coming down the gangplank of S.S. President Wilson in San Francisco, I drove southward, about five hundred miles. Parenthetically, the years in Duluth had fattened me from the skinny 150-pounder to twenty pounds heftier, thanks to the fresh milk I drank in abundance and the Midwestern appetite I developed for meats, gravy, and sundaes.

Passing through the undulating highways of Iowa before entering Missouri, the countryside was filled with endless fields of growing corn, their tall stalks waving with the breeze. It was a beautiful, soothing and impressive sight that spoke to me about the abundance and wealth of the country's agricultural foundation. The farm homes dotting the roadside added to the bucolic panorama. During the American Civil War of the 1860s, Missouri was among a few Border States that served as a demarcation between the rebellious southern States and the northern Union States. The allegiance of those Border States was divided such that pockets within them favored retention of slavery while the rest of the citizenry espoused emancipation. St. Louis, even in the 1950s, had covert, if not overt signs of racial prejudice; demographically, there was a higher density of African-Americans than in Duluth. The August weather in St. Louis, unlike that of Duluth, felt extremely hot, humid and offered no relief during the night; it was reminiscent of the warmth in Ormoc. The city itself, founded in 1764, is among the oldest west of the Mississippi River that borders its eastern flank. In its earlier years, it was a focal point of European immigrants, many of whom marched westward to help inhabit the many western States. Thus, it is nicknamed the Gateway to the West. The city is richly endowed culturally: museums, symphony orchestra, and a zoo among them. Today, the city is the fifteenth largest in the nation.

Washington University's main campus offered programs leading to bachelor's, master's, and doctoral degrees in a broad spectrum of traditional and interdisciplinary fields, including Law and Engineering. The Health Sciences complex consisting of Barnes Hospital, the Schools of Medicine, Dentistry, Nursing, Physical Therapy, and Occupational Therapy was located east of the expansive Forest Park. We had access to all athletic and cultural programs at the main campus but because of the nature of our class schedules I, in particular, attended but a few of the offerings. I did avail myself of the indoor swimming pool.

The School of Dentistry was founded in 1866 and permanently closed in 1991 shortly after it had changed its name to the School of Dental Medicine in the 1970s. The city is also the site of St. Louis University, which had a School of Medicine and a School of Dentistry.

Getting settled on arrival in St. Louis, I found a room that included breakfast, selected from a list of rooming ads posted at the library. The home was within blocks of the school and did have another boarder, a classmate from Arkansas named Jim Buck Hays. Together with a number of other upperclass schoolmates, I got introduced to a new dish: pizza pie. What I thought was a dessert turned out to be a delicious Italian entre. My naiveté served as the ice breaker with fellow students' collegiality, which I willingly sought for advice and direction.

That first Monday, Les Long was just ahead of me in the registration queue. After introducing each other, he asked where I was aiming to setup my practice. He was from Illinois and had already mentally staked out the locale for his dental office. Since my concern was focused only on signing up to begin the freshman year, Les's forward vision, I would view, was foretelling of classmates with a singleness of purpose, anxious to apply themselves to the needed studies. Nearly half of the class were returning veterans of the Korean War. They had served as assistants in the Dental Service and gained experiences which attuned their motor skills and manual dexterity to the exacting demands of the laboratory practicum, a decided advantage. They were married; the rest of us were single. Fewer than a tenth were from Missouri. The rest hailed from Arizona, Arkansas, California, Idaho, Illinois, Hawaii, Kansas, New York, Oklahoma, Oregon, Wyoming, and, of course, the Philippines. Our rigorous courses during the first two years were geared to prepare us for clinical experience with patients. The basic sciences included human anatomy, physiology, bacteriology, pathology, and pharmacology; they were coupled with pre-clinical laboratory practicum courses which were exercises that instilled attention to exacting detail and honed the necessary manual dexterity. My own resolve was to tackle the courses with purposeful study as they were scheduled, believing that achieving competence during the first two years would prepare me well for the final two years.

Anatomy is an important core subject of dentistry and medicine. Taking the course in the freshman year signified to me as unmistakable evidence that I was finally in a privileged preparatory track to care for patients. The lecturer was the respected dean Dr. Leroy Boling. We sat in an amphitheatre for his daily lectures at one o'clock in the afternoon. It was just minutes after lunch when everyone had to fight post-prandial somnolence and attention to his monotonous recital. A few of my classmates did doze off, snoring, only to be jarred awake by the silence in the room from everyone's focused attention to the culprit; it always was welcome comic relief. On alternate days of the week, we went to lunch after hours of anatomic dissection of cadavers preserved in formaldehyde; feeding one's self with hands still faintly malodorous was a challenge to overcome. Other science courses also had their occasional humorous moments to break the monotony. One welcome break of the day came from one of my classmates. He was often the center of attention because he had TV at home, rare in the fifties. He would recount the programs that most of us knew only by hearsay. Regrettably, he failed promotion to the sophomore year and discontinued the studies.

Common to most, if not to all of us was a desire to seek part-time employment. I was clear that whatever position I was to consider needed to allow optimal time for studies, as a priority. Within the first weeks, I was hired as a part-time admissions clerk for a nearby Jewish Hospital, paid by the hour plus dinner at the cafeteria. At the post, I was scheduled to work from six until ten o'clock five days a week. At orientation, my instructions were brief and clear: patients were admitted to the hospital only if having a reservation; and, walk-ins seeking medical care were to be directed to Barnes Hospital, the major training hospital of the School of Medicine of Washington University, a few blocks away. On my first evening, seated comfortably and undisturbed in my study, I was congratulating myself for having found a suitable, cushy job. Just about the time I was preparing to depart, a harried gentleman, very nervous and speaking in a rush, came in. He announced that his pregnant wife, in the car he had just parked at the driveway, was having birthing contractions and wanted me to escort her to the Obstetrics Floor. Calmly, I first asked for her name so as to check the reservation list. While thumbing through the file index, he persisted to urge me to get a wheelchair to fetch his wife. Frustrated at not locating the surname and worried I would be deporting inappropriately, I was persuaded to bring the wheelchair to his waiting wife, at a fast pace. The husband opened the car door, and the wife spread her right leg preparing to alight. Promptly, she yelled to me: "my water broke." There I was, a freshman dental student who was as unfamiliar and flustered about pregnancy as the husband. Calmly, I shelved my panicky self, helped the lady to the wheelchair, turned around to push the chair toward the elevators located at the opposite end of the building and assured all three of us: "It's okay; it happens all the time." Frankly, I had not actually known what "my water broke" implied. The crisis, however, would not end. Halfway down the long corridor, I turned to the husband, informing him that the evening was my first day of work and I didn't know where the Obstetrics Floor was located. Urging me on with his prior knowledge, we three made it to the third floor. Shortly after returning to the admission office and before I could recover from the shocking experience, the obstetrician phoned to inquire of his patient's admission. Within minutes, the doctor was beside his patient. Soon, a new baby was born. At supper the next day, I was seated at a table with nurses to whom I recounted my obstetrical adventure. Their suggestion—surely, they were pulling my leg!— was to have a handy hemostatic clamp to be better prepared in the event I found myself needing to assist in the delivery, the parturition. I never did have such an opportunity.

At the start of the second semester, I became a babysitter as well. In exchange, I lived with a young couple and their three-year-old boy. It saved the expense of a boarding house. I was to monitor the youngster while asleep, three nights a week when the parents were out. On off nights, I could continue to work at the hospital on weekends and still dine at the cafeteria. The dual arrangements continued to be suitable for my purposes, even more so when during the summer vacation months, I had added hours at the hospital as a courier for the billing department. I would come to patients in their room as they prepared for discharge, handed their outstanding billing account and wish them continued good health. I often wondered how welcome a visitor I was. I kept both jobs until the Christmas holiday vacation of 1954. Two nursing students from the Jewish Hospital were Denverites who were prone to brag about the Rocky Mountains and ski facilities. They persuaded me to spend time in Colorado and take advantage of skiing at nearby Berthoud Pass. I took a Greyhound bus to Denver, checked in at the YMCA, and resumed my fascination with the sport. I skied and socialized with newly formed friends. Amusingly, the father of one of the nursing students had suggested that I consider changing my surname to a more easily pronounced and remembered name, a decision he had done to mask his ethnicity. Of course, I would not consider the thought. I returned to St. Louis eager to resume studies but had mentally earmarked the State of Colorado as an attractive destination. For vacation? For living?

In January 1955, I landed an even more suitable and agreeable job. It was as a part-time clinical laboratory technician at the St. Louis City Hospital, another of the training institutions of the medical schools of St. Louis University and Washington University. The part-time work force consisted of medical and dental students; we were tasked to complete analysis of urine and blood samples of patents for the staff physicians who were either interns or residents in training in a number of specialties. We roomed in a section of the hospital that once was a patient ward; most of us were bedded in a large open space. We had access to all three meals and after-dinner light supper. Within a few months, I was assigned the head coordinator & supervisor of the part-time staff; in exchange, I had a large private room and relinquished the laboratory work. I retained the position until I left St.Louis in June 1957.

The hospital had a well-regarded psychiatric ward staffed by faculty members of both Schools of Medicine. By prior agreements, students of nursing schools were arranged a rotation of three months' duration in the ward to gain the required psychiatric nursing care experience. Their schools were located in parts of Missouri, Illinois, Mississippi, and Iowa. All the students were housed in a dormitory adjacent to the hospital and had their board in the cafeteria with others of the staff, employees and us, the part-time workers. In effect, every three months fresh faces of nursing students would grace the hospital.

One day in early September, I came to the St. Louis airport to meet Fenny. She had graduated from Philippine Women's University in Manila with a Bachelor of Science degree in pharmacy that same year. Now, she was on her way to Ann Arbor, Michigan, to begin an advanced study in hospital pharmacy at the University of Michigan. I was eager to see her after not having had personal contact for six years; it was also an opportunity to get an update on goings-on at home, the rest of my siblings, family relations and friends, and Papá. Although my father and I religiously exchanged airmail letters over the years, there would be no substitute for the face-to-face chance. She had to be at Ann Arbor in time to register for the fall semester; also, locate and settle in at a pre-arranged housing facility.

The days together were to give us time to drive the distance through Illinois and Michigan in ease as sightseers. I was to begin classes immediately after the time-space the travel allotted. Her airplane arrived on schedule. After all the passengers had deplaned, there was no sign of Fenny. Concerned that she had missed the flight for unknown reasons, I requested a review of the passenger roster. It confirmed that she had boarded the airplane as scheduled; on further query, the airline uncovered that she had fallen asleep while the airplane continued on its secondary destination in Memphis, Tennessee. The very extended travel from Manila across the Pacific, then the connecting segment from San Francisco to St. Louis had been obviously overwhelming and tiring, if not worrisome and tension-filled. Fenny was courteously placed on the next available flight from Memphis to St. Louis. She alighted nearly seven hours from the original St. Louis arrival, our planned travel time thinned to bare-bones limit. I was boorishly agitated when I should have been empathetically understanding. Instead of a happy, friendly welcome, I regret to recall with deep apologies that we drove to Ann Arbor speedily, with me selfishly concerned that I would compromise my own start with classes of the Fall semester. As it turned out, Fenny was graciously amicable despite driving all night instead of bedding in a motel along the way. She arrived in ample time to register for classes and settle in her housing facility, and we were still able to take a city orientation tour. I hurried back to St. Louis, also with adequate time for my own start of the junior year.

Fenny blended very well at Ann Arbor; she certainly possessed all the requisite preparations for the Master's degree in Hospital Pharmacy: intelligence, motivation and an attractive co-ed charm. The university had long hosted foreign students and competently expended all-out efforts to ensure their visitors welcome. In time, Fenny met an upstanding lad from a notable Manila family, taking graduate studies in engineering, and they fell in love.

The second half of the four-year study was overwhelmingly devoted to clinical practice on patients. I rotated to the various departments: treating patients needing the replacement of a missing tooth or all teeth; applying materials to restore parts of a tooth lost from trauma or caries; preserving a tooth by extirpating its devitalized pulp: nerves and blood vessels contained in the root canal; managing diseases affecting the surrounding structure complex of a tooth: bone, gum, connective tissues; applying preventive and treatment modalities of a child's dental problems; learning the non-surgical correction of mal-aligned teeth and jaws; and, learning oral and maxillofacial surgery (the contemporary name was referred in the past as Exodontia and Oral Surgery), a specialty which surgically manage a wide spectrum of diseases, injuries and defects in the head, neck, face, jaws and the hard and soft tissues of the oral and maxillofacial region—undergraduates like me were limited to extraction of teeth.

I was assigned my first patient at the start of the junior year. The lady had a small, pit-sized cavity in one of the groves of a lower molar. It needed a restorative procedure. She received the first local anesthetic injection I administered, successfully, as she reported having the symptoms I sought after. The objective of the cavity preparation was to have its walls drilled with adequate undercut to secure and stabilize the inserted amalgam filling material. I enlarged the cavity to four times the minimally adequate dimension; it was a novice over-drilling effort. I did benefit from my first clinical experience and continued to improve the rest of the summer with every patient thereafter. Throughout the four years in dental school, I was increasingly attracted to those studies that were in preparation for the specialty of oral & maxillofacial surgery: anatomy, bacteriology, physiology, pharmacology, pathology, physical diagnosis. By the beginning of the senior year, I took elective rotation assignments in the department of surgery where I received good reviews. I intensified the search for opportunities in a residency training program in the specialty. Others of my classmates, by that same time, were looking forward to opening offices for the practice of dentistry.

The summer before the start of the senior year, Carl Haiser, my close friend and workmate at the St. Louis City Hospital where we both resided, was interested in locating his dental practice in Florida. For a two-week period, he and I drove his trusty Ford sedan southward to Florida, determined to do so at minimum expense. The first night we pulled into a rest stop and slept seated inside the car, in Arkansas. The second night we pitched a two-man tent in a New Orleans, Louisiana park. Our sleep was rudely interrupted by police flashlights on our faces, the officer courteously advising us to uproot as sleeping in the park was unlawful. The carnival-like ambiance of the city, particularly the tourist section with the honky-tonk attractions, the oyster pubs and raucous tourists, were enjoyable. We managed to stay an extra day before heading to Biloxi, Mississippi where we spent the next two days as guests of nursing students who had rotated at St. Louis City Hospital. The State gave me the "old south" feel: toilets, water fountains, even cafes were segregated by "colored" and "whites only" signage; and, walking on sidewalks where, astonishingly, African-Americans would step aside as if compelled to do so.

We drove past Alabama and spent the next few days along the littoral beach communities of western Florida while headed for Miami and thereafter, on beaches of the eastern seaboard communities. Many evenings we managed to join an ongoing beach party and feasted on their food and company. Each night, we slept nearby in the open air on a blanket, to the gentle rhythmic swooshing sound of the ocean waves but awakening with sand-covered bodies and gritty hair. A dip in the sea and fresh water shower had us ready for breakfast and the travel. The Miami stopover was brief. The city was impressive for its tropical beauty. I was astonished to again see the racial segregation signage of Mississippi in drinking fountains and toilets. The coastal communities of eastern Florida had strikingly beautiful white sand beaches, the many tourists underscoring their attractiveness. At one of them, Daytona Beach one evening, Carl and I agreed to scout the streets by the beach separately and reunite minutes later to compare our luck at meeting college girls. I was standing in a corner, ogling passersby when by surprise, two suited men approached me flashing official-looking badges that identified them as officers of the Immigration Services.

Courteously explaining that they were in the hunt for Cubans who had illegally "jumped ship;" they were easily convinced I was a dental student innocently "checking out" girls while anxiously awaiting Carl Haiser to rejoin me. Shortly, Carl came into view to report no luck with his girl search; he thought my minutes with the officers more exciting. So did I. We returned to St. Louis by way of Atlanta, Georgia, and Memphis, Tennessee. We chose both cities for their Dental School venues; each had dental fraternities we were members of: Carl's is Xi Psi Phi—founded 1889, and mine is Delta Sigma Delta—founded 1882. If any had housing, we were certain to be welcomed to stay, free. Otherwise, the YMCA accommodations were always reasonable and adequate. The tour was very memorably enjoyable; as friends, we bonded ever closer. How much Carl gained in search for his dental practice locale was uncertain. I, however, was more convinced to pursue the specialty of oral and maxillofacial surgery. We still had an entire senior year of study before us. By that last academic year, the class had become even more comfortable with each other, and, despite the begrudging collegiality of some of the professors, there was a covert air of confidence in soon becoming dentists.

MEETING MY BETTER HALF

At the St. Louis City Hospital on the 19th November 1956, a fresh group of students from the Iowa Methodist Hospital School of Nursing of Des Moines, Iowa, had arrived for their three month psychiatric rotation. Among them was a fetching lady, bouncy and trim. At an initial get together in the cafeteria between her company of classmates and our part-timer group, I was able to single her out to become better acquainted. I learned more about her with each time we got together. We sometimes met at a nearby café the hospital staff frequented for inexpensive beer and dancing; more often, at the cafeteria; on dates to see movies, symphonies, and visits to the parks; and, as invitees to parties given by dental school classmates. She and I would become an increasingly predictable pair. She was a native Iowan, raised on a farm in the outskirts of Indianola, a small town thirty miles south of Des Moines, the capital of the State. Until reaching high school where she excelled academically and was one of the team of cheerleaders who rallied support for the football and basketball teams, she and her three classmates had attended together since the first to the eighth grade, taught by a single teacher, in a single room schoolhouse. Although accessible by foot, she came to school on the back of her pony named Bunny. Those schoolhouses were typically found in rural communities. Teachers of those schools were a special breed, well-qualified and had contributed importantly to the education of countless children in pastoral areas. They are now a piece of American history.

While enrolled as a scholarship-recipient freshman at Simpson College of Indianola, a coeducational institution founded by the Iowa United Methodist Church in 1860, she worked part-time as a receptionist for physician Dr. McGee, one of the two general practitioners in town. There she met the registered nurse who was compassionate and caring, qualities that attracted her to pursue a nursing career. On one of our dates, we talked of her long-standing interest and determined search for instructions leading to a conversion to the Catholic faith. While in St. Louis, she received the instructions from an Irish priest who was particularly encouraged when informed that she too was of Irish extraction. I wondered then if my dear departed mother and my Catholic ancestors had a twinkle in their eyes, speculating that this lady might find a future with me. Actually, she promptly set the record straight by declaring her conversion wish had long preceded coming to St. Louis and had nothing to do with my being a Catholic or my proselytizing attempts. Nonetheless, I recall well describing my own hopes and plans for the future, urging her to stick with me. I was enamored to a very attractive, kindly, and caring woman who struck me as principled and modest. That Christmas eve, we went to Midnight Mass; it was her first time. When greeting each other a Merry Christmas, I felt a very special feeling of togetherness. I hoped then that we would share visions of a future with a family of children and voice our willingness to offer mutual support and respect.

In past moments of reverie, I had thought of being married, believing the status to be yet another vocation to achieve responsibly and thoughtfully. While in the Philippines, I had meager occasions to mix with the opposite sex. Before my months at the University of the Philippines, while still in Ormoc, I was infatuated with a Chinese mestiza with whom my letter-writing efforts to kindle a romantic interest were doused after Papá's overly worrisome plea to desist had prevailed; then, there was the American mestiza whose family immigrated to town as the retirement destination of her U.S. Navy veteran father—I gallantly discontinued our relations knowing the youngest of the Varela brothers had wished to court and wed her; my departure for America was only months away. In Manila, of the many social occasions with college girls who hailed from the metropolis and the provinces, the female I recall being most comfortable with was the daughter of one of the U.S. Embassy staff. In Duluth, my dates with schoolmates ended as Mary Sue Peacha and I became a steady couple. The fetching, spunky nursing student, however, above all others, personified the character and person I would favor as my wife. A priority would be her religiosity as a Catholic. She was a green-eyed brunette beauty with Irish blood running in her veins. I came to know that in her family was the first Irish baby born in Warren County of Iowa; her pioneer great great-grandfather had been the initial surveyor of the county.

At a New Year's Eve party, 31st December 1956, held at my classmate Joe Mogab's apartment, near midnight at a back porch and both shivering in the cold, I proposed to this lovely charmer to marry me. Patricia Anne Laverty replied "yes!" We planned to wed on 19th June 1957.

1957

The first six months of the year were busy and stirring. At the clinics, there were patients I sought for their specific dental problems to be treated in order to satisfy the requirements for graduation: accomplishing a variety of dental procedures intended to round out a clinical experience in the basic scope of operative techniques. There were gold castings to construct for bridges to replace missing teeth; dentures to replace partially or totally edentulous mouths; teeth to extract; and so on. On occasion, graduating seniors would look to fellow-students as patient sources. Eloy Gutierrez, a senior from New Mexico placed a gold foil restoration in one of my lower incisors when I was a sophomore; it remains functional today. I had not needed to do so to complete my requirements.

Meanwhile, Patricia—"Trish" would be the endearing name I favored—and I continued to find optimum time to be together. Our togetherness while more often were at movies, visits to the cultural exhibits, and candlelight dinners at number of eateries, we also double dated with my colleagues. In effect, I felt we had a given each other a variety of circumstances and time to become enamored with each other. Her psychiatric nursing affiliation would end in February. Thereafter, the group was to return to Iowa.

During the days of the past Christmas season, Trish's parents, Jessie and Fay together with her sister Jeannine who is eleven years her junior drove from their home to visit, and met me. They were all kindly, gregarious, worldly, and, as I had imagined a farmer family might be, unassuming, principled, and well-grounded. I deported with my best behavior, even dressed in my favorite wool sweater, albeit with worn elbows. I remember we all were cordial and that they had not shown any reservations about their daughter dating a lad from distant Philippines. Jeannine was notable. Schooled under similar circumstances as Trish, she would complete High School with honors, become a member of the prestigious National Honor Society and receive full four-year scholarship to Middlebury College in Vermont.

At my school's spring break, I drove to Des Moines for a visit. Together, we went to her home in nearby Indianola. It was a modest, older abode with such accoutrements as a shed for machinery and farm implements, an underground storage for harvested fruits and home-canned vegetables. The farm was educational. In its 160 acres—around 300 hectares—the family raised cows, milked for home consumption as well as horses, pigs, and chickens; and, the land was cultivated and harvested for corn, grain and hay, using a tractor and other machineries she occasional manned to spell her dad. The house was edged with a vegetable and flower garden. Overall, the Laverty family had provided themselves a very comfortable living in a rural community of peers who were bonded by their religious, agrarian, and civic lifestyle. Trish's continuing bridal preparations included visits and agreeing to be married at the St. Ambrose Cathedral of Des Moines.

Patricia beside me in Des Moines, Iowa 1957 dressed in her starched white uniform and her coiffed hair to which was pinned the nurses' cap uniquely designed for the alma mater.

Shortly after returning from Iowa, I received an invitation to accept a Rotating Dental Internship at the Providence Hospital located in suburban Washington D.C. Although not yet a direct step toward the specialty training for oral and maxillofacial surgery, I was thrilled for the prospect and determined to take optimum advantage. Trish shared in the thrill of the opportunity.

Around two weeks prior to graduation, the school allowed access to the senior class by a variety of sales agents and recruiters with lists of job opportunities. Through those sources, we got informed about types of insurances, loan strategies, office equipment needs, and other temptations such as mortgages, loans, and

so on. To sway on our egos, there were sales pitches on the opportunity to obtain new vehicles on installment, as befits a "newly-
minted" dentist. I was persuaded to exchange my trusty Buick
coupe for a brand new Ford station wagon. We also received
an important advisory on licensure. All States of the Union are
mandated to provide oversight on the qualification and conduct
of healthcare professionals for the safeguard of its citizens. In
the 1950s and earlier, State regulatory agencies for dentistry conducted written tests and an evaluation on clinical competence
as performed on live patients as requisites for licensure. As none
of the States, by reciprocity, recognized the requirements of the
others, I had to undergo the process separately to be licensed in
Maryland, California, Colorado and Washington D.C. Today, a
liberal reciprocity agreement among all the States has eased the
licensure process for dentists.

In early June, of the fifty-four classmates of my freshman
year, forty-eight of us received our diploma as Doctor of Dental
Surgery (D.D.S.) or, electively Doctor of Dental Medicine (in
Latin: Doctoris Medicina Dentalis - D.M.D.). Gathered together
in our doctoral robes with my classmates at that graduation day,
15th June 1957, we all were exuding a variety of emotions and
hopes for our future. Our robe, typically black with the addition
of green velvet bands on the sleeves and velvet facing running
down the front of the gown was coupled by a tasseled head gear
in velvet. I was secretly awed at the symbolism that the graduation toga had meant to me: a personal triumphant achievement
of a purposeful study. Once more, sadly, neither Papá, my siblings, nor Trish were able to join in the ceremony. Nonetheless,
celebrate our class did as our faculty joined in wishing us all a
brilliant future. To top the celebration of the grand accomplishment, Carl Haiser and I shortly prepared for the drive to Des
Moines, where, before man and God, I was to marry Patricia
Anne Laverty.

ON REFLECTION

Since arriving in America eight years past, my immediate circle of colleagues had shrunken in response to the narrowing focus of my educational development. During those intervening times, the people I met and befriended had been diverse. They were laborers and trade workers with whom I served or had been served, as contributors to the traditional ideals of political democracy and standard of living; they were the families and leaders in civic affairs, education and religion who help mold the national fabric of the citizen; and, they were the youths and students that become the empowered guides of the future. They impressed me as a heterogeneous aggregation of people sharing an overwhelmingly harmonious vision, a societal culture in a melting pot where its denouement is the personification of an American. I willed to be a member.

The years of study to learn a dental profession were intensely demanding, yet they enabled a welcome interlude for relaxation and introspection. I was particularly grateful for the opportunities to engage in part-time employment to supplement Papá's largesse which he provided me willingly but at great sacrifice. Indeed, to have been able to roam the country with ease and become acquainted with a diversity of people, to have gained an appreciation for the rewards that come from honest labor and study, and, to experience the value of personal rights and live in a country of decent law and order—I felt fortunate and deeply at home. It was humbling to reflect, once more, that the more I felt I knew America and Americans, their history and grounded sense of exceptionalism, the more I longed to be better informed and partake in their communal undertakings.

I was eagerly looking forward to my forthcoming marriage and plans to be a breadwinner. My thoughts would, of course, turn to my own parents and their lives together. For Mamá to have died so young, the story of their union had ended prematurely. All of us survivors: Papá, my siblings, and I would be left with suppositions, projections, questions. Hopefully, I would carry with me in my marriage the good qualities and virtues my parents had inculcated to advantage. Trish, fortunately, was a supportive and confident ally, albeit like me, not thoroughly cognizant of the personal and inter-relationship challenges and hazards along the way. In the immediate future, we marched ahead buoyed by our naiveté and newfound love for each other. Like practicing Catholics, we had discussed family planning only in the context of religious tenets. The pre-marital counseling was conducted by the hospital chaplain. He underscored that among the obligations and rewards of marriage were the bountiful blessings that arise from a family of Catholic children.

A PARTNER...A CAREER

I love you, for putting your hand into my heart and passing over all the foolish, weak things that you cannot help dimly seeing there, and for drawing out into the light all the beautiful belongings that no one else had looked quite so far enough to find."

—Roy Croft
(Poet... b1905–1980)

The sum which two married people owe to one another defies calculation. It is an infinite debt which can only be discharged through eternity.

—Johann Wolfgang von Goethe
(Dramatist... b1749–1832)

Healthcare practitioners belong to a profession that blends science with art. Warmth, sympathy, and understanding can outweigh the drug prescribed or even the benefits from an incision with a scalpel.

Be willing to call in colleagues when their skills are needed for patient care. There is virtue, not shame, to say 'I do not know'.

—Gregorio Carillo Yrastorza, M.D.
(Physician, Caregiver... b1905–1986).

A week before my wedding day, I resigned from my City Hospital position and with my possessions half-filling the Ford's cargo space, drove to Des Moines. Carl Haiser showed up a day before he was to participate in the wedding ceremony as my best man and roomed with me. Fenny and cousin Raul Alonso also arrived that same day to witness our marriage; she traveled down from Michigan, and he had just arrived from the Philippines to begin an internship in medicine at a hospital in Chicago after graduating from the University of Santo Tomas School of Medicine that same year. Trish had chosen her bride's maid from among her nursing school friends. Partaking in the occasion, her parents and sister Jeannine, her aunts, uncles and a number of nursing school classmates, also arrived.

Wednesday 19th June 1957 was a beautiful, pleasantly sunny summer day in Des Moines. The Holy Mass, said for our express purpose in that cavernous, strikingly beautiful St. Ambrose Cathedral, had impressed on me, as we each slipped a wedding ring to our lover's left forefinger, the special meaning of the vows we made to each other. I would recall the ceremony with pride as being solemn, modest, and a tribute to Patricia's hardy efforts in preparing the important event; it would foretell of her organizational flair. The celebratory luncheon was as much to receive the well-wishes from everyone as it was to bid farewell since our plan was to take a road trip later that day. I was to report for duty as a Dental Intern of Providence Hospital eleven days later, Monday 1st July. The travel time to Washington D.C. was to be our honeymoon. Our first newlywed night was spent in a motel in outskirt Des Moines—actually a facility of no great consequence—where my romanticism was admittedly timid but sterling. The start of our togetherness and intimate relations, I then believed, would have a lot of room to develop promisingly in the future.

*On 19th June 1957, Trish and I married at St.
Ambrose Cathedral, Des Moines, Iowa prepared to
face, together, a hopeful future and raise a family.*

As scheduled, Trish and I took to the road, her trousseau and belongings together with my possessions had not quite filled the cargo space. We traveled through Iowa, Illinois, Kentucky, West Virginia, and Virginia before reaching the nation's capital a few days later. We lunched at a restaurant near the White House. While I don't remember the name of the restaurant, it was pretentious enough the *maētre d'* lent me a necktie and jacket to satisfy the dress code. During the next few days, we scouted a number of apartment rentals, visited tourist sights, and attended an orientation meeting at the hospital held the last days of June. The hospital was located at the northeast section of the city. Our one-bedroom apartment was at the second floor of a complex only a couple miles from the hospital in suburban Mt. Rainier, Maryland. It did not take long to empty the car of our possessions. The physical effort had me drenched in sweat, dripping from my forehead as I leaned on a window sill. Trish was surprised and aghast. She would learn that her husband perspires profusely.

Our immediate neighbors turned out to be remarkably friendly with whom we enjoyed many social gatherings and endless potluck dinners. One couple who was particularly gracious was the DeSimone from a New Jersey town. Sam was completing his law studies, and Eileen was employed as a nurse. Once a month, they would return to New Jersey and come back with a copious supply of food given them by his parents, who owned a grocery store. Eileen prepared Italian dishes; they ate well and were always ready for our company. Toward the end of a month's supply, the menu would become increasingly frugal, often beans or pasta. To this day, Trish follows the spaghetti recipe gifted by Eileen.

THE INTERNSHIP

At the hospital's orientation gathering, there were interns who had just graduated from American Schools of Medicine, including a couple from the St. Louis University and a half dozen South Americans; of the latter, I had opportunity to help translate their Spanish meaningfully. In addition, there were advanced trainees taking residencies in surgery, one of whom had come from the Philippines who was well-regarded for his exceptional surgical acumen and knowledge; with my limited Tagalog and his unfamiliarity with Binisaya, we found greater comfort talking in English.

My dental intern pair had graduated from Georgetown University School of Dentistry. The dental internship program, I soon determined was unstructured, leaving much of the learning opportunities to my liberty to uncover and configure to my interests. While my co-intern was dismayed, I was keyed up, determined to absorb as much medicine and surgery from the entire attending staff members who were welcoming, unselfish with their mentorship. Three of them had particularly enriched my surgical and patient care know-how. One was the Filipino surgeon, Dr. Montero; he had me assist at the operating table and accompany him on rounds, freely discussing principles of management and teaching surgical dexterity. Another was a nurse anesthetist of Chinese descent; when occasionally assisting her as she anesthetized patients, I benefited from her knack for explaining complex pharmacologic issues in their simplistic, more easily understood form. The third individual was one whom I sensed would be an unselfish mentor and friend. He was the elderly, kindly oral surgeon Doctor Victor Skinner. I assisted him at surgery for teeth extractions, extirpation of cysts and benign tumors, management of jaw fractures, and infections.

With encouragement of the medical-surgical staff and Trish's concurrence, I made known to the Emergency Room (ER) Service that I would be on their call, identifying for them an array of emergent problems I would be interested in managing. The ER staff did not wait long to respond. Later that evening, I received my first call. The patient had dislocated his jaw, a problem new to me. Quickly, I referred to the oft-relied book on oral surgery authored by the internationally recognized authority in the specialty, Dr. Kurt Thoma. Following verbatim the recommended management, I requested the nurse to inject the patient with the narcotic morphine, choosing the upper limit of the dosage range. I hastened to report to the ER, expecting to apply some force to manipulate the reduction of the dislocated jaw as Dr Thoma had forewarned. The staff greeting I received as they hovered over me, I surmised, was partly a curiosity at the new intern's conduct and know-how as I expounded on the mechanism of the jaw joint and its dislocation. I found the patient dozing in response to the narcotic, looking hapless with his mouth extraordinarily agape. His masticatory muscles felt sufficiently flaccid so that the jaw reduced without difficulty, without resistance. The ease with which the dislocation responded to my manipulation unduly impressed my observers; I, on the other hand, was flabbergasted by the unexpectedly unhampered reduction. The effortlessness, it turned out was aided by the narcotic, a drug I'd prescribed for the first time. I would learn to be judicious with the use of medications and aware of their import. Thereafter, the ER staff seemed eager to call me for patients I was seeking to manage, the rest of the year.

NEWBORN AND PARENTHOOD...BLESSINGS

By early August, Trish left for Iowa Methodist Hospital School of Nursing to complete her nursing education. She returned ten weeks later, a graduate, licensed Registered Nurse (RN), eager to practice her patient-care expertise and competence. Christmastime 1957, Trish was in her second trimester of pregnancy. We expected our first child in March the following year. For our first major extravagant spree to give our apartment a festive decoration and prepare for our newborn, we had loaded a shopping cart with items, feeling particularly privileged and special for my being a modestly paid dental intern. At checkout, we were amused and humbled as we lined up with customers whose carts overflowed with purchases; we felt ourselves beginners on a multi-stage, lifelong process of creating and comfortably affording a family, together. Our Christmas tree was modestly small, atop a side table. Following midnight mass on the twenty-fifth, we vowed the practice of going to midnight Mass a beginning of our family tradition.

The Christmas party for the hospital medical staff was very enjoyable. Trish got a big share of attention for being an expectant mother, a gracious wife, and contributor to the social milieu. A number of the surgical consultants and particularly Dr. Skinner had taken time to praise my conduct and performance; and, offered encouraging support of my search for training in oral and maxillofacial surgery.

Part of the excitement and thrill of our young marriage were the nine months of anticipation, sharing in pointing out the ever so slight tummy bulge; and hearing the first heart sounds within with the stethoscope. They were the undeniable evidence of a pregnant Trish who was thrilled by the prospect of being a mother. We spent months selecting a given name, trying out its resonance and its compatibility to the personality we envisioned and hoped the baby would be. Finally, we settled on a name, selected from as many as a dozen candidates. On 19th March 1958, Teresa Anne was born. She was healthy and beautiful. Trish delivered her at Providence Hospital; as a house intern, I joined her at the delivery room. In those days prospective fathers were not routinely allowed access during the parturition.

Having a newborn instantly added the role of parenting to that of being man and wife. Trish would breast feed, convinced of the health and bonding advantages; Terri Anne, we called her, responded well. The entire sequence was a routine we replicated for our subsequent newborns. Within days of her birth, the celebration of the traditional National Cherry Blossom Festival begun and lasted for three weeks. Then, Washington D.C.'s beautiful Jefferson Memorial Park was awash in and perfumed by the perfusion of cherry blossoms, peaking by the second week. The festival was first held in 1935 to commemorate a donation of thousands of cherry trees by the city of Tokyo, Japan, in an effort to enhance Japanese-American friendship. The U.S. government responded with a gift of flowering dogwood trees. Two-week old Terri Anne took a stroll in her daintily decorated carriage with her proud mom and dad, picnicking in the beauty of the surrounding. Thereafter, all three of us would take in as many of the attractions the nation's capital offered: visits to the museums, concerts, excursions to parks, parades and fireworks. Sadly, we never had the chance to climb the Washington monument. Meanwhile, the slats of Terri Anne's crib were filling up with surgical sutures tied in loops I had done by hand and instrument to be able to perform the procedure adeptly at such rare times when requested by Dr. Montero at surgery.

During the spring 1958, at last, I was having the opportunity to qualify for advanced training in a specialty of my choice.

The three of us took road trips to Wilmington, Delaware, and New Haven, Connecticut where each had a hospital I was invited to interview for a position as Resident-in-Training in Oral Surgery. The program, however, was of a single year's duration only. Fortuitously, I was also requested to meet with the program committee of the Georgetown University Hospital Affiliates; my interview was pleasant, and I felt assured of my chances. Today, I remain certain that, in large measure, Dr. Victor Skinner's supportive recommendation had been effectively persuasive in granting me the interview opportunity; for his confidence in me, I am forever grateful.

Meanwhile, on a sunshiny Michigan morning, the 14th June 1958, Trish, Terri Anne, and I arrived at Ann Arbor to witness and celebrate Fenny's wedding to Ernesto Manuel. I regretted that Papá couldn't join in the celebration; Mamá surely must have shed a happy heavenly teardrop on the occasion. Fenny, instead of completing her post-graduate studies, happily accompanied her husband to Ohio where they would reside while he was employed by Continental Can Company. Ernie would be among the select innovators of the easy-to-open metal can top. In the subsequent years, their union begot seven wholesome and intelligent children: Eric, Melissa, Michael, Rebecca, Allan, Gregory, and Sarah. We returned to Washington wishing the newlyweds a blessedly fortunate future.

In late 1959, a fifty-bed Ormoc General Hospital was created. It was a reward to the people of Ormoc that Papá had doggedly promoted to favor Ormoc with a government-funded health facility. For his untiring effort and perspicacity before legislative representatives, in particular Congressman Dominador Tan, I was proud of his vision and advocacy. Gregorio C. Yrastorza, M.D. was appointed its inaugural Chief and organizer of the staff and facility. Today it remains, renamed Ormoc District Hospital, as a 150-bed facility to care for a catchment populace of 200,000 Ormocanons.

TRAINING FOR THE SPECIALTY AND PARENTING

The primary objective of the Georgetown University Oral and Maxillofacial Surgery Training Program was to provide, during a three-year duration, a postdoctoral didactic and clinical experience of progressive responsibility. It was designed to meet the certification requirements of the American Board of Oral and Maxillofacial Surgery. Parenthetically, Diplomates of the Board are practitioners who, by successfully undergoing a rigorous qualifying examination by a committee of elite peers acknowledged for their outstanding knowledge and expertise, are considered to have matched their bona fides with the specialists of known competence and excellence.

I was chosen and excitedly accepted to receive training through the auspices of the Georgetown University Graduate Program. The course was organized as a combined post-graduate study through the medical and dental schools in physical diagnosis, internal medicine, anesthesia, general surgery, pathology and oral surgery; it led to a Master of Science degree in Oral Surgery. The well-respected authority of the specialty Dr. Gustav Kruger served as director. With me as first year residents beginning training on 1st July 1958 were Drs. Don Reynolds and Walt Edmunds. Our patients were treated at the University, Veteran's, and D.C. General Hospitals. I enjoyed our weekly seminars that allowed engrossing discussions on an eclectic range of topics. Overall, our study group profited from input by a pool of senior educator-mentor oral surgeons of the U.S. Naval Hospital and of the U.S. Army Walter Reed Hospital. Through the program, I adopted as my guiding principles to treat patients with compassion, respect, and acknowledgement of their inherent dignity; to possess high moral and ethical standards; to commit to life-long learning; and to maintain a technical competence in the full scope of the profession.

One of my close friend and colleague-Resident was a brilliant student with a deft surgical acumen and an entrepreneurial vent: Dr. Charles Infante. He, Dr. Phillip Boyne from the navy complement of affiliates and Dr. Jules Dubit joined the didactic portion of the program, having had earlier years of clinical training elsewhere. Toward the end of my first year, Charlie arranged with his dentist classmate to provide a dental office at which patients could be treated during the off-hours. He invited me to share the opportunity, each of us alternating the coverage to assure availability to our primary responsibilities as surgical residents at the hospital. To build the practice, we requested staffs of several area hospital ERs to refer patients to us for the care they sought. Our duo-practice was productive and remunerative. We eventually closed the office by my final year of training; Charlie had completed his enrollment by then and started a private practice in Plantation, Florida. Doctor Skinner, meanwhile, invited me to share his practice on weekends; the opportunity gave me on-site experience in the conduct of an oral surgery private-practice until I completed my training. Thankfully, the income from both practices substantially added to the stipend I was provided as a surgical resident and soon enabled Trish to be a full-time housewife and parent. We were able to move to a rental house with three bedrooms in nearby Arlington, Virginia. It was just across the Potomac River from Georgetown University.

Our family continued to multiply. On 9th April 1959, David Gregory was born. Where Terri Anne had the features of a sweet brunette nymphet, David had that of a strong-willed blond-haired Basque. On 6th August 1960 Timothy John followed. He had wavy dark hair and a charmingly bouncy gregarious disposition. All three children had first names of Saints and were delivered at Providence Hospital. Each were growing adorably sweet, healthy, and loving the ambiance that our house with its yard offered. It was a modest upgrade from our earlier apartment. Very often, we took advantage of the many attractions that

Washington and its surroundings offered. Our Christmas tree that year and every year thereafter while in Arlington rested on the floor, nearly touching the ceiling. It would be decorated with eager assistance of all the children, who were absolutely excited to open and enjoy the abundant gifts their parents gave and Santa Claus who, flying by a sleigh pulled by reindeers, alit in the dark of night to stuff their oversized stockings hanging by our mantle, with sweets and toys. As Terri Anne, David, and Tim sat enraptured by the copious Christmastime stories that Trish read before the rest of us those many days of the season, I thought of that youngster in Duluth reciting the Christmas poem years ago. Now, my children were soon going to be able to recite it equally well. Trish continued to excel in coordinating and managing the intricacies of attending to the demands of three youngsters, a household and me, a husband whose own obligations made joint parental moments disproportionate. What particularly moved me was how Trish abundantly read books and stories to the children, how frequently we all sang lullabies and how much caressing and cuddling were passed around among each of us on as many evenings as we could.

US CITIZENSHIP AND JFK RENDEZVOUS

The United States is a country peopled by immigrants and their kin. The majority of the population are native-born descendants and offspring of people who immigrated from distant lands generations ago. Fewer are those who have actually come before a U.S. judicial body to swear allegiance as naturalized citizens. In the summer of 1960, I joined the latter group. On our seats were an American flag, a copy of the Constitution, a booklet featuring the stories of prominent naturalized Americans, and a welcome letter from President Dwight Eisenhower. I felt honored to have qualified to citizenship, which, incidentally, I believe had derived from having married Trish.

My naturalization process was witnessed by Dr. Donald Reynolds and my family at an appropriate U.S. Court of Washington, D.C. Together in that roomful of the expectants, we stood to take the Oath of Allegiance. I took mine sincerely, willingly and proudly. We all then seated, as citizens of the nation. *E pluribus unum*—Out of many, one!

> An Oath of Allegiance: "I hereby declare, on oath, that I absolutely and entirely renounce and abjure all allegiance and fidelity to any foreign prince, potentate, State or sovereignty, of whom or which I have heretofore been a subject or citizen; that I will support and defend the Constitution and laws of the United States of America against all enemies, foreign and domestic; that I will bear true faith and allegiance to the same; that I will bear arms on behalf of the United States when required by the law; that I will perform noncombatant service in the armed forces of the United States when required by the law; that I will perform work of national importance under civilian direction when required by the law; and that I take this obligation freely without any mental reservation or purpose of evasion; so help me God."

My family and a host of friends celebrated the momentously significant occasion as the fruition of a longing dream. Meanwhile, on 25th November 1960, Jacqueline Kennedy delivered John Kennedy, Jr. at Georgetown University Hospital, where I, coincidentally, was assigned affiliation duties to the Anesthesia Service for a three-month rotation to learn and apply the rudiments of general anesthesia. That day, the hospital staff and personnel were excitedly jockeying to visit the obstetrics ward hoping to view a newborn of note, me included. I was hoping to run into Jacqueline in the hallways. The closest I got to see was one of Jacqueline's slippers. Her anesthesiologist had somehow failed to return the unpaired shoe to its rightful owner. Instead, he showed the souvenir to any of us in the Operating Room, swearing to its authenticity.

The following year in late Springtime, I opened a letter which had "The White House" as its return address. It was an invitation from the United States President and Mrs. John Fitzgerald Kennedy. Although I had cast my first ever vote as a U.S. citizen for Kennedy, I didn't believe the invitation had any reference to my franchisee right. Apparently, for unstated reasons on the card, the President and Mrs. Kennedy had invited for an informal reception at the south lawn foreign students enrolled in schools within the capital and some of the hospital staff members of Georgetown University Hospital. I was included. While anybody in the country can traditionally tour sections of the While House, it is usually guided and cursory. Rarely would the tour allow a meeting with the president. Only those who receive an official invitation from the White House, as I did, for a specified event at a designated section of the compound can have the look-see.

The reception I attended on 10th May 1961 was at the south lawn of the White House, entering the garden past a security-guarded gate. There, I found to my dismay that several of the invitees had taken the liberty of bringing relatives. While it was thrilling to join the queue to personally greet the special couple, I had not considered bringing my wife as I regarded the invitation literally. It was an unthinking, even gutless decision to go by myself. Trish has ever since not forgotten my decision albeit now hopefully forgiven me. There was music to entertain us with an eclectic selection of tunes—I like to recall now that the musicians may have been members of a U.S. Marine Corp Band. We were served a variety of tea cakes and soft drinks. President Kennedy and Jacqueline looked incredibly handsome, he impressively presidential. Both shook hands with me cordially. Although I outwardly looked calm, meeting them was the equal, if not surpassing the excitement of a face-to-face presence with a super movie star. The special experience struck me once again at the quality of America. Here was the president who had triumphed over an electioneering campaign at which the opposition party had geared the electorate to doubt his capacity to ensure the separation of issues of State from those tenets of his Catholic religion; as a freshly sworn U.S. citizen, I was impressed that the electorate had demonstrated themselves better informed. He became the first Catholic to hold the office of U.S. President. Overall, it was a very memorable event.

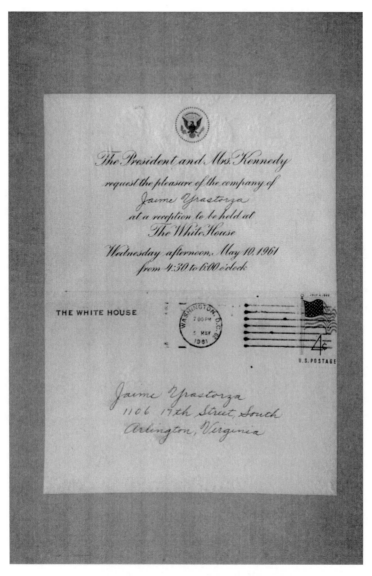

*My invitation for the reception at the White House
garden on 10th May 1961. I did shake hands
with President and Mrs. Jack Kennedy.*

AN EPIPHANY

Throughout my three and a half years of training, the patients in my care were varied in their personalities and deportment; I relished the patient-surgeon interactions and felt well-rewarded in extending care with respect and consideration. A number of patients did need management of concomitant problems; they required the cooperative consultation or care by colleagues of the dental, medical, and surgical disciplines. To be able to give relief from the agonizing pain, fever and dismay that arise from infections and tumors; to be able to repair a face distorted and robbed of function by a broken jawbone and lacerations by the judicious application of intricate surgical techniques; and, to extract teeth with minimal trauma and discomfort—they were a special privilege to value with humility and respect. On those occasions when I served as the surgical assistant, they underscored to me the contribution that every member of a team can bring to the surgical endeavor. During the last six months of the program, I received a grant from the National Institute of Health to conduct an experimental research on the use of a chemical adhesive in the repair of jaw fractures; it extended my training an additional six-months during which time I served as the chief resident of oral surgery, entrusted the managerial responsibility of the resident staff and undergraduate students while being the primary surgeon of the more complex surgical procedures. I would learn and share that on those critically challenging moments of a clinical decision when a surgeon ultimately weighs the risk of a procedure against its potential benefits, it is the surgeon's acumen and credibility that are being tested. It always helped to keep me conscious of the responsibility that patient care oblige.

Once during my last months as a chief resident, there was a tragic, unforgettable incident that had a curious, if serendipitous twist, recalling that the first patient I treated as an intern at Providence Hospital had a dislocated jaw. It was a Sunday. The intern on duty at D.C. General Hospital phoned me to seek advice for a problem. The patient, found a day earlier by police sprawled in a gutter, quasi-conscious, inebriated and incoherent, had been brought to jail. There, a medical student on duty, suspecting a dislocated jaw, urged transfer of the prisoner to the hospital for definitive care. At the ER, the intern's attempt to reduce the dislocation by a series of conservative approaches including use of a narcotic sedative, as I had once utilized, were unrewarded. Attributing the extended period of dislocation to have set the affected muscles in rigid spasm, I recommended that the patient be admitted, intending to manipulate the reduction of the dislocation under general anesthesia with me in attendance. I then drove to the hospital.

On entering the floor to examine the patient, I saw a ward nurse burst out of a room, yelling the code message that announced a patient in cardiac arrest. The intern by my side turned to me, aghast, recognizing the named patient as the one with the dislocated jaw. We rushed to his bedside. On examination, his pupils were non-reactive to light and there was no palpable pulse. I placed my stethoscope to auscultate over his left chest. Unbelievably, it reported utter silence. The heart was in standstill, in cardiac arrest. The intern repeated the examination. Following protocol, the senior general surgery resident was hastily summoned; he corroborated our findings and assumed the emergent care. With everyone recognizing the gravity of our challenge, the patient was rushed to the OR to begin the resuscitative operation. Although the process took mere minutes to commence, it seemed an eternity in slow motion. In the early sixties, the acceptable response to cardiac arrest was to apply direct, manual heart massage by opening the chest cavity under general anesthesia; I assisted the general surgeon. Today the contemporary protocol favor a non-invasive approach: cardiopulmonary resuscitation (CPR) by chest compressions and, when available defibrillation. It has resulted in significantly more rewarding results. Sadly, our patient did not survive. Correctly, the senior general surgeon deferred to me the task of informing the mother of the cascading circumstances that befell her son.

Until that moment, I had not considered in the slightest the possibility of having to explain circumstances of grave sorrow to parents or guardians. While I was wanting to empathize with my patient's mother, I was uncertain of the reaction I was about to encounter. With trepidation, I prepared to face and share the mother's deep anguish, face-to-face. To my relief, the mother was thoroughly understanding and conciliatory, even pointing to her son's incorrigible behavior and alcohol abuse as having foregone the fatal terminus. She was thankful for our efforts. To me, nonetheless, the circumstance underscored the weighty responsibility that patient care obligates the healthcare professionals, including the oral and maxillofacial surgeons; and importantly, as my father's guiding principle reminds, to "be willing to call in colleagues when their skills are needed for patient care." At a Mortality and Morbidity conference scrutiny, the cardiac arrest was ascribed to a vasovagally-induced reaction with such a foregone fatal outcome. (*Among the cranial nerves is the vagus; it courses to the heart and stomach with prior distributions to the throat area... among its many functions are the control of heart rate, peristalsis and the gag reflex... when the nerve is irritated, it can cause choking and heart malfunction; if prolonged, as had seemed in this instance, the risk is apnea induced by aspiration of sputum or foreign body. Worse yet, cardiac standstill*). The conference opined that we, the combined clinician team, had conducted and managed the crisis beyond reproach. Still, the loss of a life under my care, despite the best applicable efforts of the time, was a personally heart-wrenching experience.

On December 1961, I was awarded a Master of Science in Oral Surgery degree from the Georgetown University Graduate School, Washington, D.C. My dissertation, enabled by the National Institute of Health Grant #D-1059, was titled "Histological Investigation of the Use of Polyurethane Polymer in the Treatment of Experimentally Fractured Mandibles of Dogs." The experiment was insightful on the rigorous requisites of a scientific study, in particular the role and value of animal subjects. It was informative on the essentials for the publication of articles in peer-reviewed journals and presentation of educational matter before the healthcare community. My investigation proved that the polymer would serve only as "a precursor to other yet to be developed substances for the bonding of fractured bones."

By serendipity, Georgetown University is a Catholic institution run by the same Jesuit Society that administered the Ateneo de Cagayan High School were I graduated in 1948. This time, in attendance were my family: Trish, Terri Anne, David Gregory, and Timothy John. Once more, Papá regrettably was not present. He and I were both saddened not to have his personal witness to the culmination of three scholastic hurdles since we last were together. This time, the celebration carried with it the decision on how to proceed with my own family's future.

In my solitary moments, I took frequent stock of the bountiful blessings that had befallen me, the latest becoming a citizen of a wonderful country that I had come to regard as an unmatched proponent for human rights and personal liberty. Its people were diverse in race and religious belief but living with a historic quest to melt together in unity as one nation. Throughout the years, the people I met were welcoming and encouraging of my efforts to learn, work and assimilate. I was and am privileged to be an American citizen. Now, I was about to apply the learned competency in a surgical specialty of my choice with clinical experiences from association with Dr. Skinner, a practitioner who I felt added to my ability to manage and establish a private practice. I was determined to regard the welfare of patients under my care as a revered responsibility. Further, here I was just a few years since departing the Perla del Mar de Oriente, married to a fetching, wonderful lady whom I loved and who, to my good fortune, loved me and believed in our capacity to grow a family. I felt my life unbelievably dreamlike.

Our primary considerations, thereafter, would be two-fold: family welfare and professional opportunity. They were the immediate realities.

ON REFLECTION

The year 1961 was a watershed year. In attaining a dental profession, I had actually brought me a more enlightened realization on the value of, and my suitability for the study of Oral and Maxillofacial Surgery. I felt well prepared and eager to practice the profession.

To have become a United States citizen, particularly by the naturalization process, I considered, was a decision that underscored my love and patriotic regard for the country. The exciting opportunity that followed to personally greet the President and First Lady of the land was a rare moment to cherish and retell to my budding family.

The four and a half years that Trish and I spent in Washington, D.C. were a time filled with memories of our life together mixed with the joys and tribulations of child rearing. Having began our marriage with an abbreviated courtship, we needed to develop an extraordinary sense of accommodation with near-saintly patience and understanding. The surfacing challenges were those that emanated from differences in our backgrounds and personalities. Throughout the years, more so during those spent in America, I was unknowingly cultivating an alpha-male personality; succinctly, they were traits of a self-starter, self-confident, seemingly self-centered individual. I was certainly focused on accomplishing my goals successfully. While I willingly wished to adopt to social interaction behaviors I had observed and admired among my acquaintances, there were my own hardened upbringing influences to contend, to overcome, to merge in order to achieve compatibility. In turn, while I viewed Trish as a woman with traditional upbringing and values, she was pointedly contemporary. Her school years in modest environs had not barred from, even more realistically had goaded her toward excellent accomplishments in education, leadership, and nursing studies.

In our favor was and remains to be, our Christianity, our marriage having been ministered by a Catholic priest. We had vows to live chastely and wishes to respect our role in the procreation and rearing of a Catholic family. Of course, in the ensuing days, those obligations of a marriage partnership on every level—physical, social, financial, mental, and spiritual—would be among our challenges. While American wedded couples, as a whole, have had a high percentage of tragedy and failure to attain the standards for wedded bliss, I prayed that our marriage would endure. Nonetheless, we would have our hurdles. There was a disproportionate ratio of participation in our wife-husband-family responsibilities and chores, in part, because I gave generous effort and focus on my profession. I am grateful that Trish became the steadfast, loving wife and engrossed parent. Trish and I were looking forward to beginning a life together with our children, prepared to live in a community at which we planned to participate as engaged, responsible members of its society, belong to a church, find a suitable school for our children, and have the opportunity to earn a livelihood. Our choices would need to address all of those wishes.

REARING A FAMILY AND EARNING A LIVING

There is no difficulty that enough love will not conquer, no disease that enough love will not heal, no door that enough love will not bridge, no wall that enough love will not throw down, no sin that enough love will not redeem... It makes no difference how deeply seated may be the trouble, how hopeless the outlook, how muddled the tangle, how great the mistake. A sufficient realization of love will dissolve it all. If only you could love enough, you could be the happiest and most powerful being in the world.

—Emmet Fox (Theologist... b1886–1951).

It's not only children who grow. Parents do too. As much as we watch to see what our children do with their lives, they are watching us to see what we do with ours. I can't tell my children to reach for the sun. All I can do is reach for it, myself.

—Joyce Maynard (Novelist... b1953).

If a man love the labour of any trade apart from any question of success or fame, the gods have called him.

—Robert Louis Stevenson (Philosopher... b1850-1894).

During the last months at Georgetown, Trish and I mulled over the options available to me: seek a faculty position as a teacher of oral and maxillofacial surgery to dental students and trainees of the specialty; accept a commission as a captain in the U.S. Air Force; or, lunge into the private practice of the specialty, perhaps joining Dr. Skinner as his junior partner. Just weeks before gradu-ation, however, I was prevailed to accept a position in the Veteran Administration Hospital System. My responsibilities were to provide patients admitted to the Hospital facility the needed oral surgical care, head a Dental Internship Program, and, partake as a Clinical Instructor of the Oral and Maxillofacial Surgery Training Program of the University of Kansas City School of Dentistry, which was headed by the skilled and erudite Dr. Robert Allen. Importantly, the employment contract allowed me to terminate after two years, and it was to begin in late January 1962. The position gave me the opportunity to practice my neophyte skills worrying least about monetary compensation.

Fortuitously, the position encompassed options Trish and I had considered. Together with the prospect of providing care to military veterans while employed in the federal service of the U.S. Department of Veterans Affairs, the post was at the VA Hospital and Domiciliary in Leavenworth, Kansas. The 350-bed facility had the full complement of medical and surgical staff; its Dental Department had an internship program and hosted trainees of the Oral Surgery Program under the direction of Dr. Allen. I viewed the tenure to aid and boost self-confidence in my nascent expertise; and, be a tacit reward for the committed study of a pro-fession that would now enable me to serve as clinician, mentor, lecturer and contributor in peer-reviewed journals. As an added benefit, the employment allowed Trish and I substantial time to evaluate and decide the suitability of a venue for the anticipated private practice of the specialty, in consideration of the many family-related issues.

In town, we rented a commodious house for the duration of our stay and partook in the social activities of the hospital staff, neighbors and the community. Trish and I were pleased to have our growing children enjoy the rural ambiance, a contrast to D.C.'s cosmopolitan urbanity. They had fascinating fireflies to catch, tricycles to ride in open spaces without fear of danger, and, neighbors who exuded hospitality. Both Terri Anne and David were beginning to help Trish read children books as I, proudly and unbelievably marveled at how well the children were profiting from the parental care and interactive relations we were providing. Admittedly, my own contributions paled from Trish's important role. The capacity of well-nurtured children to absorb knowledge seemed inexhaustible; I was astounded and impressed.

On 15th May 1962, our fourth child was delivered at the city's Sisters of Charity–run St. John's Hospital. Laura Marie, like each of her siblings, was a happy, healthy baby with a tender disposition. She was a welcome addition to our family; a dark-haired beauty with a caring disposition. In due time, Trish and I reached the decision for the ultimate location of our home base.

ORMOC HOMECOMING

Wednesday tenth July 1963 would be Papa's sixtieth birthday; I wished to be able to personally greet him. My family gathered at the Kansas City International Airport to bid me von voyage for a momentous return journey to Ormoc late on the Fourth. Our boys were scurrying around in play and excitement. Just moments before boarding my mid-afternoon flight, nearly three-year-old Tim accidentally slipped and cut a corner of his left eyebrow. It needed sutures to coapt. It was a youthful "fooling around." He received the treatment at the airport's First Aid Center as I was boarding. Trish, on updating me while I was in San Francisco awaiting the trans-Pacific leg of my journey, reported that Tim had deported bravely to the surgical experience. He got congratulated by all of us.

It had been thirteen years and six months since my departure from Perla del Mar de Oriente. The airplane, after crossing the International Date Line, landed in Manila's International Air Terminal nearly thirty hours later, on Saturday the sixth. From the airplane's window, with the sun yet to rise, the meager scattered city lights appeared unable to illume Manila from its darkness. Still, I was consumed with excitement. My experience begun when, with the contrasting backdrop of the outside darkness, I saw pressed against the outside portion of the glassed windows of the arrival room dozens of paired eyes eager to identify the arrival of relations and friends, or just curious onlookers. They were an astonishing sight. Papá, Jun, and Tonio were there to greet me. Jun at that time was a medical student, Tonio a collegiate. Both brothers and my young-looking father were brimming with joy and full of energy. While in Manila, we toured nearby sights in a Jeepney—a surplus U.S. military jeep renovated flamboyantly as the ubiquitous passenger carrier that would find cultural permanence for decades hence. We stayed at the Manila Hotel, an erstwhile pride of the city and dined at its advertised gourmet Filipino cuisine restaurant. The food was savory, different from that I ate in Duluth. Thereafter Papá and I flew to Tacloban, the provincial capital located on the northeastern border for a three hour bus ride to Ormoc. The roadbed was unpaved and replete with potholes as well as wandering dogs and chickens who scattered to the oft-utilized horn-blowing as we traversed the sixty-mile distance. At some unmarked mid-point, the bus, fashioned in rows of benches and open sides to catch wind and dust, stopped without any forewarning. The alighting passengers scattered in haste to nearby bushes of the deserted countryside. To my open-mouthed amazement, some of the women in their billowy ankle-length dress sated their need while standing spread-legged and merely lifting the skirt forward. I stifled my urge to giggle and kept the surprise to myself. Perhaps, today such bus stops are scheduled at more commodious stations.

In Ormoc, the greetings included a party in my honor coupled with a celebratory birthday party for Papá that was held at the revived Seaside Hotel. Among the guests was Mary Sala. We conversed pleasantly while I pointedly informed her of my past infatuation; I believe she was amused and pleased. She was attractive as ever. I visited old familiar places, renewed acquaintances with cousins, uncles, aunts and friends. Inday as my constant companion successfully helped bridge the intervening years with updating information on everyone we ran into; of course, one and all had grown and changed with time. My sister, in fact, had matured and was being regarded an attractively charming and adroit lady to be courted. Two of her suitors were from well-respected families of Ormoc and Cebu. Interestingly, the one from Ormoc had availed of a tradition which involved a meeting of the minds of the respective fathers to persuade her betrothal. On 24th September 1961, at the St. Peter and Paul Church of Ormoc, she was married to Emeterio—Terry—Larrazabal. Terry belonged to a family reputedly among the sugar planter icons of the country; his grandfather was one of the immigrants from the Basque region of Spain. I dare suspect that Inday had, nonetheless, actually imposed her own free will. I predicted for her, learning of her consummate work ethos and broadminded viewpoints, a future as a contributing participant in her nation's welfare. As if in diligence to their Catholic beliefs and loving marital values, they gave birth to eight offspring: Maria Elena, Maria Modesta, Maria Aniceta, Maria Josefina, Maria Martina, and the youngest, Gregorio. Emeterio, the eldest, and Maria Angelina are deceased.

Papá exuded pride in my accomplishments, and I took every occasion to thank him for his support. Our tit-a-tit conversations were made more precious by the limited time together. My homeward bound flight had me saddened to once again bid *adios* to my family but thankful they were in good stead.

From my brief visit, I was struck by the day-to-day activities and concerns of the Ormocanos. Paradoxically, while I sensed a general feeling of contentment, I wondered if it represented a dissociation from the turmoil, dislocations and economic woes that seemed to be incessantly weighing down the country. Were Filipinos becoming inured to the admittedly pervasive graft and corruption? Were they resigned to a fate of want rather than motivated to partake in a communal effort to achieve the oft-promised fruition of a bright future? The homecoming turned out to be a blend of surprises, joys and unrequited expectations. I was eagerly looking forward to be reunited with my wife, children and career.

THE TRANSILIENT DECADES

During the 1960s and the following decades thereafter, future historians might well view America and the world with it to have experienced events that were foretelling of a paradigm shift. There were happenings that had people—including me—looking askance at themselves, at each other, and at traditional values and behavior. The cascading events may have begun on 22nd November 1963 when President John F. Kennedy was assassinated—an unbelievably disheartening event that I was informed, in real time, while in the midst of an operative procedure at the hospital. The loss of a beloved president was a national tragedy; Vice-President Lyndon B. Johnson then assumed the Helm of State. The following year, the fractious call for racial equality was epitomized by defiant sit-ins that were led by Rev. Martin Luther King and culminated in the Civil Rights Act of 1964. It was hoped to eradicate racial prejudice forever. However, both events—the death of a President in one instance and in another, a promise of civility—would leave tales of killings, rancor, uprisings, and suspicions of conspiracy. I wondered then how effectively the Ship of State would weather the upheavals and maintain its compass along its avowed programs.

Just seventeen years after VJ Day and a decade after the Korean conflict ended in an armistice, American troops began deploying to Vietnam. It was a commitment by President Johnson to prop the French forces who were in a losing conflict against Vietnamese anti-colonialists with American military combatants, most of whom were draftees. The U.S. participation was met with countrywide escalating protests. Before the conflict ended in victory of the North Vietnamese cause, American soldiery would be soiled by incidents of atrocities and massacre. The returning veterans were greeted with taunts, insults, and, sadly, many would suffer psychogenic symptoms associated with the dreaded Post-Traumatic Stress Disorder. The protests did morph into the hippie movement, a counterculture lifestyle that, among other behaviors, espoused "peace, not war." I wondered if the movement would persist and become the dominant identity of America and Americanism.

The Second Vatican Council—Vatican II—was convened by Pope John XXIII on 1st October 1962. From the pulpit on Sunday Masses we were informed that the Council was convened in response to erupting challenges in the political, social, economic, and technological changes that were occurring the world over. Indeed, the laity, who once may have been unquestioning of the seemingly distant and anachronistic Vatican, was now inquisitorial. I felt the long-range consequences would manifest in future church membership censuses and conversions to alternative religious practices. It befell on Pope VI, who reigned from June 1963 until his death in August 1978, to implement the mandates of Vatican II. As if to give evidence to the continuing strife within the Church, an assassination attempt was made on his successor John Paul II. The Pope survived and lived until March 2005; during his reign, he revealed the secrets of the Virgin Mary apparition in Fatima, Portugal in 1917. Pope Benedict XVI then succeeded on April 2005; he would resign on March 2013. His replacement Pope Frances, a Jesuit Cardinal from Argentina, would be heir to monumental confrontations that face Catholicism in an increasingly secular world. Hopefully, his religious and moral influence will extend worldwide so as to effect a tranquil planet. My own religiosity would undergo changes and lead me to espouse Presbyterianism.

The authors Abinales & Amoroso's "State and Society in the Philippines" noted that in the Philippines, a member of the House of Representatives in 1964, Jovito Salonga, offered a cautionary admonition, as follows:

> Democracy is on trial. It will face an even greater crisis in the coming years. The "revolution of rising expectations" will mount with ever-increasing intensity. Popular education, the accelerated tempo and volume of mass instruments of communication such as the radio, the newspaper, the movies and television, the sharpening appeal of mass advertising—all these tend to create wants and needs unknown to our forefathers...
>
> Those who see the tragedy of our condition are simply awed by the overwhelming problems that bear down on the nation—the problem of massive poverty, of the deteriorating morale in pubic service, the lack of social discipline... the increasing incidence of graft, the lack of respect for law and authority, and the revolution of rising frustrations...
>
> You ask me—what can be done, what is needed? We need strong leaders, dedicated leaders. Yes, but they must be leaders devoted to the ideals of a free society... for unless they are of democratic persuasion, strong leaders can easily become brutal, savage despots.

Despite Solonga's forewarning, on 21st September 1972 the Filipinos did come under martial law, imposed by the nation's tenth president, Ferdinand Marcos, who had been elected seven years earlier. The progress his administration had brought in agriculture, industry, and education came with rampant government corruption, widening economic inequalities between the poor majority living in shanty hovels and the affluent elite who appeared ensconced in gilded cages of high concrete walls topped by shards of broken glass. Parenthetically, U.S. economic aid and friendship with U.S. Presidents Johnson and Reagan had complicitly aided Marcos's rule. On 21st August 1983, Marcos's popular political foe, the émigré Benigno Aquino, his fate awaiting a return to Manila after expulsed to America, was assassinated as he alighted the airplane. It proved to be the tipping point for the country that had been aggravated by years of tyrannical conditions. The dictatorship effectively ended with a non-violent, grass-root revolution in 1986. Dubbed People Power, Filipinos felt uplifted with resolves of sweeping socio-economic reforms. Marcos was forced to flee into exile on 25th February of that year but not before his family and close associates had reportedly looted the Philippines' economy of billions of dollars through embezzlements and other corrupt practices. He died in ignominy 28th September 1989 at seventy-two years of age.

Conventional view attributed to the dictator not only a legacy of institutionalized corruption, but also crony capitalism and a moribund economy. His period of influence also began the continuing exodus of Filipinos in search of jobs elsewhere around the world. While the overseas workers have continued to help keep the economy afloat with remittances of billions of dollars to their homebound connections, the ramifications on social and human relations of the proverbially close-knit Filipino family are yet to be told. Presently, more than one-tenth of the workers are outside the country; it would—actually should—be a concern of importance to Filipino self-esteem and of the wellbeing of the societal fabric. Meanwhile, the diaspora is likely to continue.

In a nationalistic zeal to draw attention to its post-colonial autonomy and shed its ties to the U.S., President Diodado Macapagal designated 12th June the official Independence Day; it was the date in 1898 that the Acta de la Proclamación de Independencía del Pueblo Filipina—Act of the Declaration of Independence of the Filipino Nation—was promulgated. Further, in the aftermath of unremitting anti-American demonstrations, on 13th September 1991 the Philippine Senate refused to renew the 1947 Military Bases Agreement with the United States. It terminated the presence of U.S. military installations of the past forty-five years. The heightened sense of empowerment did spread beyond Philippine boundaries. In the U.S., the Filipino immigrant population and Filipino-Americans—who together now comprise a notable segment of the ethnic demography—have sprouted corps of advocates, scholars, leaders and activists. They have authored scholarly publications as well as participated in socio-political concerns at the local, State, and national levels. They have formed organizations, prominent among them being the National Federation of Filipino American Associations (NaFFAA), an umbrella organization that monitors legislation and public policy issues affecting Filipino Americans. Together with local affiliate organizations, they advocate for issues of common concern and aim to persuasively engage the innate character, virtues, and traditions of Filipinos to vent their beneficent forms so as to embrace a citizenship of principled purposes and constructive participation in civic affairs. In Colorado, the Philippine-American Society of Colorado and the Filipino-American Community of Colorado are among the multitude of like groups found in the fifty States that comport with the objectives.

GROWING ROOTS IN COLORADO...MY CAREER

As my family and I headed West that late summer of 1963, Trish and I felt adequately prepared and eager to face the future before us. After due diligence and serious study, I had assured my self that the private practice of my profession would be in Colorado. I had turned down a remunerative offer to associate with a distinguished oral and maxillofacial surgeon in Bellflower, California. While there, I could not envision my family residing in any section of the Greater Los Angeles metropolis. The tempo of living seemed unusually frenetic, and I worried it would be taxing to find a comfortable, homey community in the midst of the mass of people. Perhaps, my impressions were unfair since I only had a limited time for scrutiny. Au contraire, from my exploratory visit to Denver, Colorado, I received favorable feedback which I felt foretold of a suitable locale for the practice of my vocation and a favorable environment to raise a family. Of the former, the dentists, physicians, and specialists I met—most would become my core sources of patient referrals—were friendly, encouraging, and affable individuals. Dr. and Mrs. Manny Chavez hosted my stay at their home; the charismatic dentist would help the upstart of my practice. The couple became our enduring family friends. Metropolitan Denver impressed me as a community that evoked a comfortable sense of fellowship imbued in those Judeo-Christian principles. The area had well-tended parks, and its open spaces were yet to be subdivided into living units. Many of the homes had horses sharing their yards, a vivid display of the Westerners of legendary lore; indeed. The spectacular geography of the State was incomparable. Imagine! It had the Rocky Mountains, its peaks elevated to match the beauty and grandeur of alpine Europe; it had lakes and rivers, abundant and pristine; its fields of grain and ranches of livestock, pastoral and bucolic; and, its climate, bestowed with four distinct seasons. They were distinctions that made Colorado overwhelmingly appealing to Trish and me.

We inhabited a modest rental home in nearby suburban Arvada. A year later, we relocated to a house in Lakewood, closer to schools and a Catholic church as well as an easy commute to work and hospitals. It would be our home for the succeeding four decades to fill with memories of the many activities that come from a growing family and the social gatherings with our circle of friends and colleagues.

I now shake my head when reflecting at how audacious and forthright my modus operandi had to have been when choosing to take roots in Colorado for the sake of the family and my career. The many considerations to manage the move, such as the search for our domicile, establishing housekeeping details, having the children settled and connected with neighbors, church, the community and the day-to-day activities were predominantly undertaken by Trish. Her unwavering partnership and embracing parental qualities had made the activities seem facile; the children and I were immeasurably blessed by her yeoman efforts.

Establishing a solo practice in a specialty dependent on referral of patients by colleagues was a monumental and risky undertaking. Today, the majority, if not all healthcare providers belong to one or more medical-dental insurance organizations where, to obtain reimbursement, practitioners are compelled to refer patients in need of specialized care to specialists who themselves are members of the group. In the early 1960s, however, practitioners had no such insurance dictates. They referred patients to specialists selected for and persuaded by the referred-specialist's appeal and avowed expertise. As an oral and maxillofacial surgeon, I had to earn my worth.

My office was located in Wheat Ridge, a western suburb where it remained until my retirement in 1995. It was equipped for out-patient care in a building filled with dentists, pediatricians, gynecologists, dermatologist, infectious disease therapist and family practitioners. To each of them and their ilk of the Denver community, I offered my services, consistent with my bona fides. To be able to treat and perform complex surgical procedures in an inpatient environment, I obtained admission privileges at the city's Lutheran Hospital and the St. Anthony Hospital of Denver. And, as I had done in the past, I notified the Emergency Room staff of my willingness to care for patients.

I began seeing patients in September 1963. In the short days thereafter, the Lutheran Hospital ER called me, close to midnight, to attend to an adolescent lad who sustained multiple injuries from a car accident just minutes before. On examination, his face, blood-soaked from lacerations, was beginning to swell, aggravated by the traumatic blow against the dashboard. It was beginning to mask the facial bones and teeth which themselves appeared disjointed and fragmented; both his forearms, severely lacerated with embedded shards of broken glass, were bleeding profusely but the arm bones were unbroken. I teamed up with a very competent general surgeon, Dr. Frank Traylor, at the operating table. He proceeded to repair the lacerations and attend to the blood loss concerns while I began the reduction of the multiple fractured bones and teeth. It took Frank and me until seven o'clock the following morning to complete the repairs and stabilize the patient. Fortunately, the patient responded well and was discharged for out-patient follow-up days later. That patient and his outcome may have contributed to the collegial support and response to my request for patient referrals that I subsequently continued to receive.

My core of colleagues was enlarging, some with a practice located in outlying communities of Colorado, Wyoming, and Kansas. Their affirmation, I felt, reflected the accommodative, attentive, and caring competence that patients referred to me would receive; to be sure, they were the aims I had set for myself. During the ensuing years of practice, there were opportunities to elucidate practitioners of dentistry and medicine on the important role that my specialty contributes to healthcare. There were pioneering effort at both hospitals to accommodate a new section of oral and maxillofacial surgery. We obtained representation before the appropriate committees and our members were provided privileges to treat the broad scope of patient needs. I initiated the process and became the inaugural chief of the section of both hospitals. By attending lectures and presentations at the various local, State, national, and international dental, medical, and oral and maxillofacial surgery societies, my knowledge continued to broaden and improve. In early 1966, I took and passed the qualifying examination of the American Board of Oral and Maxillofacial Surgeons. I became a Diplomate.

In mid-June 1966, a seminal event that I attended occurred before a standing-room-only crowd that had gathered at the Walter Reed Army Medical Center in Washington D.C. For three days, the outstanding, internationally renowned oral and maxillofacial surgeon Dr. Hugo Obwegeser demonstrated an array of surgical procedures for the management of challenging deformities and deficiencies of the jaws, employing techniques that, until then, had escaped the perspective and application by American practitioners. *Time* magazine's 1st July 1966 issue, in covering the forum, reported: "Last week, 500 of the most eminent U.S. oral surgeons sat on edges of their chairs…as a respected Swiss practitioner described his radical jaw-splitting procedures… American oral surgeons have never been so impressed." Indeed, we specialists came to adopt such unfamiliar concepts as orthognathic osteoplasties, vestibuloplasties, skin-grafting, among others; the names were as intricate sounding as the procedures were to apply. Significantly, where once some of our surgical approaches where extra-orally accomplished, Dr. Obwegeser demonstrated them possible by intra-oral incisions, thereby minimizing operative morbidity and eliminating the telltale scars. The seminar was a pivotal event. In short time, impelled to conduct related clinical studies, research, and innovative improvements, our body specialty investigators enabled the clinician to apply bone-integrating titanium implants to improve the management of traumatic injuries, refine reconstructive surgery and tooth replacement procedures and utilize arthroscopy as an option in surgery of the jaw joint. The application of technological innovations did sophisticate the requisite clinical and imaging studies; the scope of oral and maxillofacial surgery would expand.

I was among the vanguard of surgeons prepared to apply the innovative procedures. In practice, I teamed with colleagues of the many disciplines of dentistry and medicine. Of the orthodontists, Dr. Harry Herman was the forerunner of my group of teammates. His congruent orthodontic interventions helped define and refine the functional and esthetic goals for the management of dento-facial deformities. The other exceptionally talented of his peers with whom I cooperated in patient treatment were Doctors Bruce Dinner, James Kerns, Jack Konegni and

Dick Rozehnal. Of the co-members of the Colorado Oral and Maxillofacial Surgery Society, one in particular was Dr. Larry Snider from whom I availed of his expertise and counsels as well as assistance on major surgical procedures. Overall, it was with these aforementioned healthcare professionals that we embarked in an exciting frontier of care with rewarding results.

Of the list of practitioners for whose patients I provided care, many became close personal and family friends. Among the many, was a Duluth friend whose whereabouts I had no earlier occasion to follow: Jack Dahl. He had become a well-received physician and surgeon and was among the singularly successful practitioners of the area. Serendipitously, both of our families resided in the same community where our children grew as friends. Jack would become my ally and an important asset in a nonprofit organization to which we later belonged. Others in our social circle were Stew and Jan Whitmarsh, Ron and Leah Ferrendelli as well as Frank and Marilyn Yantorno—they each took frequesnt trips with us to overseas destinations. Many who remain a vital part of our social milieu draw from activities at school, church, the Rotary Club, the hospital staffs, and the country club. The camaraderie and fond memories that Trish and I savor regarding each one of them are among the most rewarding and enriching gifts I cherish. During the ensuing decades, Trish was, and today remains my consummate mate. She was an accomplished partner in our efforts to socialize and entertain our many acquaintances. From them, it was comforting and encouraging to know that the concern for the well-being of their patients whom I treated was being sated. Importantly, to the extent that my career had taken time from my children, Trish was able to fill the void and yet configure quality moments together as a family unit; and, importantly, she helped attend to business concerns of my practice and assisted me in extending interactions with my loyal staff throughout the working years.

From 1989 to 1991, the United Nations Development Programme subsidized my consultancy to develop a three-year post-graduate residency training in my specialty for Filipino candidates at the St. Martin de Porres Charity Hospital of Manila. It was an ambitious undertaking, the success of which needed the volunteer participation of local and foreign specialists of my ilk. Supervening the number of obstacles, which included my own part-time commitment, was the unexpected implosions of the hospital governance and staff. While the program was compelled to terminate, the trainees, each one highly motivated, intelligent, and full of potential continued to develop through their own volition, diligence, and empowered acuity. Today, they are practitioners in the Philippines with focused interest in oral and maxillofacial surgery: Drs. Raddy Mabasa - who would become a steadfast friend, Xenia Velmonte, Glenda de Villa, Gerry Sunico, Henry Macalalad, Mon Hebron, Charo Musico-Lukban, and Ted Nicholoff, who served as facilitator. By the start of the twenty-first century, a full fledge training program in the specialty of oral and maxillofacial surgery in the Philippines was still unavailable. Hopefully, among the growing number of forward-looking youthful Filipinos with adequate training, expertise, and motivation, the specialty will surely find its deservedly enviable position among the ranks of healthcare expertise of the country.

GROWING ROOTS IN COLORADO...MY FAMILY

On 23rd March 1968, our youngest, perky, pretty, and precious Anne Marie was delivered at Denver's St. Anthony Hospital. We selected a combination of her two elder sister's names for the last of our children. She was a sprightly and playful charmer with her blond tresses and ease with people. She remains a joy to everyone.

Trish had championed our choice of living in Colorado. Thankfully, our children grew up to our satisfaction. Each one enrolled and completed their primary and high school education in a public school. The girls took ballet lessons and joined the Girl Scouts; the boys took their turn in football, band, and Cub Scouts. In the winters, we enjoyed gaining proficiency in skiing. Each one took horseback riding and piano lessons. In summers, there were tennis and swimming lessons; camping trips to marvel at and enjoy the grandeur of the Rocky Mountains; and, car outings to awesome destinations in surrounding States. Then, through membership in Ports of Call, a vacation travel club, we flew to many international destinations, often utilizing our scuba diving skills. We took trips to whet the children's curiosity about their mother's childhood home and community as well as the country of my birth. Of the former, the convivial visits with their grandparents gave insight to pastoral and rural living, residing as they were on an Iowa farm and, later, in a lakeside Minnesota retirement home. Importantly, the occasions gave the children pause to reflect on the labors that farmers contribute to the agricultural foundation of the country. Twice, we took excursions to the Philippines and the Orient. The first time, six week old Anne had to stay behind under the wonderful care of her godmother Vi, a friend and wife of my core referrer Dr. Ray Falasco; the second time was when she was five years older. On our visits with cousins, aunts, uncles, grandparents, and great-grandparents, the resolute kindred relationship of the Filipino family unit and the pariente/padrino custom were manifest, to the children's delight and awe. What made me particularly proud was how our youngsters comported themselves by being articulate, inquisitive, and assertive on their likes and dislikes while open to absorb the peculiarities and differences of other people, their customs and environs.

Each of our offspring pursued and earned a Bachelor's degree. Terri Anne proceeded to receive a Master of Arts degree in English literature and added studies on scholarship at Oxford University, England, and at the Université Paris-Sorbonne,

France. While in Paris, she met and shortly thereafter married an energetic, intelligent physician from Syria, Bassam Daghman. In pursuit of his specialty interest in interventional neuro-radiology, they lived peripatetically while giving birth to three lovely girls: Marie, Melissa, and Leah. Regrettably the marriage thereafter terminated. Today, the children—their pre-collegiate education in bilingual English and French—seem well prepared for a bright future; as their grandparents, Trish and I point with pride at how, by example, Terri Anne and Bassam show the reward that nurturing from committed parents can provide. After earlier years spent as a financial journalist for the Bloomberg investment firm, she is today a yoga professional with special expertise in the therapeutic modality for musculo-skeletal dysfunctions and imbalances. She resides in Berkeley, California.

David continued studies in medicine and the dermatology specialty at the University of Colorado. During the mid-years of Medical School, he married a bright, spirited lady who would become his invaluable partner and a caring mother, Wanda Tadych. They have enviably precocious children: Hannah, Luke, Cole, and Dylan who profit from a healthy mix of Christian values, active athletics, and musical influences. I see a bright future for them all. The family resides in Lakeland, Florida, where David successfully practices his specialty.

Timothy, following his collegiate years at the University of Colorado, enjoyed a responsible position with a water-purifying reverse-osmosis system organization for which he traveled to countries of the Orient, Europe as well as Australia with communities found wanting in potable water. Years later, he completed a rigorous study at Union College of Lincoln, Nebraska to become a Physician Assistant. Today, he is married to Arlin Miller, who has the charm and disposition of an archetypical wife and parent. Their children, Grace, Jaime, and John, are showered with parental affection; each is growing infused with far-sighted hopes for a rewarding future. Timothy practices his profession with an elite group of vascular surgeons in Lincoln, Nebraska.

Laura majored in microbiology from Vanderbilt University at Nashville, Tennessee, and years later completed a study of physical therapy at the University of California San Francisco, a profession she now practices with exceptional talent and acumen. She married a fellow physical therapist, Peter Emerson, with whom they gave birth to two lovely children: Gabriela and Jackson, both growing handsome, talented, and full of vim and vigor. Lamentably, the marriage did not last. However, by sharing in parental responsibilities, Pete assuredly will contribute to his children's well-being. Later, Laura married to a high school sweetheart, Kent Rieder. They are a loving and committed couple; both share their love of the outdoors and culinary adventures with their family. Kent is a head coach—with a winning record— at Boulder County, Colorado Monarch High School's Track and Field teams as well as the Cross Country teams for boys and girls, respectively.

Anne is the second of our five offspring to now reside in Colorado. After she graduated from Arizona State University in Tempe, Arizona, she married Jeffrey Brown, the prototypical athlete who received recognition and honors playing varsity football at the University of Southern California. Moving themselves, after years of living in southern California, to the alpine community of Vail, Colorado, feels, in Anne's words: "a realization of a lifelong dream!" They have two children: Elizabeth and William, who demonstrate early transfer of their father's athletic bent by garnishing recognition awards in swimming, soccer, baseball and skiing, in addition to attaining high marks at school. Jeff is senior vice-president of RBC Wealth Management. Anne, following in her mother's footsteps, is the majordomo of the family, which includes a menagerie of giant dogs and a cat.

Meanwhile, Trish and I, fortunately, were able to have Papá visit our family as well as Fenny and Ernie's brood in Chicago, even brought him to attend TerriAnne's wedding; and, he got his wish to tour the various religious shrines of Europe. During the later years of his widowhood, he sired three lovely girls: MaFeCaridad, Vanessa, MariTeresa. My half-sisters surely must have given Papá added comfort and rewarding joy. Sadly, on 20th October 1987, he did not survive the head injuries from an accidental fall. The tragic loss was heartbreaking. Our bereavement was shared by the Ormocanons, their expressions of gratitude and condolences piled before Inday and Jun who were the in-town residents. They were tributes to the acts of kindness and care that Papá had given of himself; he was eighty-four years old. We, of his family, all remember him as a man of many wonderful accomplishments who remained a kind-hearted, modest man, affectionate to his offspring and kinfolks.

Earlier, my brother Tonio had been undergoing therapy for Hodgkin's lymphoma, a cancerous malady. He succumbed on 14th January 1970, a youthful life abbreviated at twenty-six years of age. His demise and later that of my father caused me to pause and reflect on the mortality of man; and of the precious memories that come from life experiences and relationships with people. We all should value those moments; they are to be treasured.

Nearly four years before receiving the Doctor of Medicine degree from the Ramon Magsaysay Memorial School of Medicine, Jun wed Glenda Gines on 28th December 1963. They sequentially gave birth to Josephine, Erlinda, Gregorio, Isabel, Samuel and Jaime.

Inday served as governor of Leyte in 1989, receiving the grateful kudos of the Leyteños. She thereafter pursued post-graduate studies and received a Ph.D. in Hospital Administration. Presently, she serves as president of the San Lorenzo Ruiz College of Ormoc as well as board member in several private and quasi-government corporations.

On the 55th anniversary of my graduation, the Alumni Association of Washington University School of Dental Medicine

honored me with the 2012 Distinguished Alumni Award for "…
dedication and service to dentistry and mankind."

ON REFLECTION

The Philippines, in facing the new millennium, appears poised
to march onward with a promising outlook. On the culmination
of its own century of independence - if not on the 75th year
anniversary - as granted by America on 4th July 1946, hopefully,
Filipinos will come to relish the fruits of an energized, empowered stewardship over the fate of their country: a robust middle
class and a dwindling, disappearing population of the impoverished. Then, a celebration would be a triumphant fruition of the
dreams of their Founding Patriots.

During the years in Colorado and the lengthy period of tran-
silience, my family, my wife, and I functioned cognizant of the
dialectic challenges that traditional values, religious tenets and
family life were having to face. In effect, we were being moved to
coexist with the dynamic changes resulting from socio-economic
alterations and confrontations that the world was experiencing.
Within my personal reactions to the transilient era, I felt it valuable to recognize that a society is never utopian; it is more likely an
agglomeration of a rainbow of visions and viewpoints. However,
citizenship in a free society, as America is, obligates a responsibility to guard and participate in the democratic processes in order
to ensure the perpetuity of the freedoms and opportunities that
are its treasure.

I remained in practice until retirement in 1995. My thirty
five years of practice had exacted neuromuscular disabilities. The
professional hazard, in part, resulted from inattention to the
proper ergonomic posture of the neck and back when standing
long hours at surgery, using a headlight. In 1993, I underwent a
three-level fusion of my neck vertebrae to obtain pain relief and
regain tactile sensation of the fingers; and, in 2009, I had a surgical fusion of my lower back vertebrae to abate pain and regain

a normal gait. While the shooting pains have receded, I have residual atrophy of the muscles of my upper and lower extremities as well as loss of fine tactile sensation in my fingers, essential to the manipulative exercise of the hands at surgery. I walk with a cane to support my unstable legs. Of course, all-body arthritic changes are the known propensities of the aging, me included. Although now unable to exert the flexibility and mobility that playing tennis, skiing, biking, and running demand, I continue to swim regularly. Quite satisfying and revealing to me is my interest and aptitude in art, specifically painting in the different media. Regularly, as a budding artist, I join a collegial group with tutelage by an accomplished mentor whose exceptional talent and unselfish instructions are inspirational, Judy Patti. On the January 2013 New York Sunday Times, Matthew E. May took a snippet from the imminent educator Jim Collins' philosophy. Collins wrote: "A great piece of art is composed not just of what is in the final piece, but equally important, what is not. It is the discipline to discard what does not fit – to cut out what might have already cost days or even years of effort – that distinguishes the truly exceptional artist and marks the ideal piece of work, be it a symphony, a painting…or, most important of all, a life." Having sedulously favored my past actions to comport with the guiding mind-set, I now look forward to a future of private moments devoted to a hobby that gives me soothing rewards.

I am fortunate that each of our children weathered their early mature lives grounded in a good sense of personal decency and responsible social conduct. Trish, by having placed the welfare of the children and her husband at the forefront of her being, had to shorten a nursing career; to her credit, she has maintained her expertise to the benefit of many. She has transmitted to her children and me a love and compassion for nature and creatures. Importantly, I feel confident that her maternal love and influence will continue to fuel our children to seek a righteous life. But for a very few regrets, the path my life has taken is thankfully blessed. Of my career, I feel fulfilled.

THE CORNUCOPIA...
SHARED AND SAVORED

As we express our gratitude, we must never forget that the highest appreciation is not to utter words, but to live by them.

—John Fitzgerald Kennedy
(US President... b1917–1963).

Family faces are magic mirrors. Looking at people who belong to us, we see the past, present, and future.

—Gail Lumet Buckley (Author... b1937).

Charity isn't about pity, it is about love. Charity and love are the same—with charity you give love, so don't just give money but reach out your hand instead.

—Mother Teresa of Calcutta
(Missionary... b1910–1997).

Octogenarian! That's me. How time has gone by...

As I write, the horizon that presently faces me is forested, verdant and tranquil, a serenity that aids contemplation. I chose this province of Spain for a vacation with the special people of my life, so together we would once more reflect on the many blessings that we all have shared and enjoyed through the years. In my company are Trish, our five grown offspring and their spouses. Jeff, Anne's hubby, has remained home, unwilling to leave their children to a child-sitter, particularly as son Will risks life-threatening allergic reactions to certain foods. A supremely responsible fatherly love! At this get together, reluctantly we have excluded the grandchildren. Selfishly, it was my effort to optimize adult conversation and bonding. Before me is an expansive swimming pool and, just as my life is, it's azure blue water is blissfully shimmering in reflection of the sun now about to turn in for the day. I am comfortably prepared to muse over the happenings of my life.

OF COMPASSION WITHOUT BORDERS

We have responsibilities, one to another—we do not each face the world alone. And the greatest of all responsibilities, is that of the strong to protect the weak. The truest measure of any society is how it treats those who cannot defend or care for themselves—Paul Ryan (US Congressman... b1970).

In the decades that Trish and I resided in Colorado, we held membership in the Filipino-American Community of Colorado (FACC) and Philippine-American Society of Colorado (PASCO). And, I have already noted, both Denver-based non-profit groups are affiliate members of the National Federation of Filipino American Associations (NaFFAA) which subdivided the country into Regions. Encouragingly, the sum of organizations within the NaFFAA umbrella are attracting a younger generation among their members; the youth participation will surely help ensure a self-sustaining future as they become increasingly intertwined in the socio-economic fabric of America, as Americans. On 29th June 2003, after serving the previous year as Chair of Region V which encompasses Kansas, Nebraska, Wyoming, North and South Dakota, I was honored to receive the NaFFAA-Region V Lifetime Achievement Award.

Other organizations of Filipino-Americans in North America are also forming, bonded by their common regional birth places. Their contributions, aimed to preserve nativist customs and traditions, while employing newfound affluence and influence to sponsor projects of assistance to "back-home" neighbors in need, are notable. One such organization is Ormocanon Circle, U.S.A., founded and led by Californian Mario Y. Hermosilla. As an exemplary instance that attests to the important humanitarian relevance of such organizations was their ability to provide time-sensitive donations of food, potable water and medicines for the hungry, homeless and injured victims of the destructive Haiyan (Yolanda) typhoon of November 2013. The immediacy of their response may well have saved lives of the survivors.

Shortly after I retired from practicing surgery, I joined a group of highly motivated, civic-minded individuals whose binding motto: Service above Self underlie the humanitarian spirit of the members of the Rotary Club of Wheat Ridge. Actually, there are 1.2 million other Rotarians worldwide. Their fellowship is the continuing spark that has, and continues to engender meaning-ful community and international projects of help. Of assistance to the community, our club doles scholarship for deserving students aiming to pursue post-high school studies; participates in food banks for the homeless; and, contributes to parks and recreation projects. Among international projects, included are the construction of wells to enable communities in Africa and the Philippines to avail of potable water sources; and, being a sustaining supporter of a nonprofit organization that conducts mending care to children with facial deformity in the Philippines, Uplift Internationale. My Rotarian participation has been personally rewarding while providing me the pleasure of the company of an exceptional group of individuals, at home and abroad.

In the summer of 2012, I was honored to receive a recognition from the Colorado Asian Culture and Education Network, a nonprofit organization that promotes awareness and preservation of diverse Asian values, cultures, and heritage. I believe their advocacy will help facilitate the accommodation and integration of a segment of the U.S. population of Asian-Pacific extraction to the mainstream of America. I spoke of the value of benevolence that Americanism champions and thereby challenged the group to engage their altruism and compassion to extend charitable assistance to those of our fellowmen in need. The opportunity to partake in humanitarian projects, I predicted, could be among the most rewarding purpose we can add to our lives.

Indeed, we are all mindful of the plethora of disasters and mishaps that can befall mankind. Happily, peoples of the world share the humane virtue of empathy and compassion for our neighbors in need. How, when and where one channel's the charitable contribution of assistance, of course, is understandably dictated by the resources, talents and time at the disposal of the helper-volunteer.

OF UPLIFT INTERNATIONALE

The language of citizenship suggests that self-interests are always embedded in communities of action and that in serving neighbors one also serves oneself.—Benjamin R. Barber (Author... b1939).

In regard to the variety of health tribulations, communities ordinarily organize corps of supporters and caretakers who are tasked to provide for and sustain the health of the populace. In those instances when the available local resources are strained past their capability to cope, healthcare practitioners beyond their borders have a special opportunity to offer expertise to augment in-country capability. All those vital contributions, of course, ought always be appropriate and fit for the specific needs. For one week in March 1988, I joined a group of oral and maxillofacial surgeons to conduct a mission in a host hospital of Guayaquil, Ecuador. The sponsoring organization, Por Cristo was based in Boston, Massachusetts. The city and adjoining region of Ecuador were believed to have a populace with an endemic preponderance of a birth defect characterized by a unilateral malformation of the lower jawbone as well as deformity of the overlying soft tissues of the face and ear; the deformity complex is known as Hemi-facial Microsomia. The procedures for reconstruction of the facial deformities are complex. Suffice to say that I gained valuable lessons as a missioner aiming to extend surgical and medical care to patients in a foreign venue. Notably, the rewards that I derived from partaking in a mission of help was heart-warming. The immense appreciation that patients and their families conveyed had exceeded my expectations. Their heart-felt gratitude was movingly awesome, and at the same time, humbling. Another realization I gained was that while helping human beings, even just one at a time, may seem a modest goal, the reward to the giver is as it is to the receiver. It becomes an overwhelming humane experience. It is a precious and satisfying lifetime gift to be treasured.

In the autumn of 1989, buoyed by the experience of the mission in Ecuador, I led a five-member medical group to Ormoc, Philippines on the invitation of officers of Ormoc District Hospital and the city officialdom to assess the health needs of the population. We intended to determine how outsider assistance could benefit a targeted health need. Our findings, corroborated by those of national health studies, determined that Filipinos were subject to a litany of health problems such that their overburdened public healthcare system was compelled to prioritize in doling out its care. The conundrum ought to underscore to volunteer mission projects the advantages of focusing on a specific need, often times those problems deemed of low priority of need by the nation's health system. In this regard, we found that women were at high risk of delivering a baby with a facial deformity, primarily clefts of the lip and palate. Filipino women are estimated to risk delivering such a deformed newborn once for every 400 pregnancies, in contrast to the incident of one for every 1000 among Caucasians in developed countries. The babies, overwhelmingly, were being raised by impoverished families, in communities where their critical reparative care was either unavailable or unaffordable. Sadly, infant mortality rates among newborns with the deformity far exceed those of their normal counterparts; even more tragically, most of the survivors may likely die with their deformed faces untreated. While living, life of a child with a facial deformity that defies camouflage is burdened by taunts, ostracism from peers and a consuming sense of self-worthlessness; as a sub-group, they are more subject to speech impediments, hearing difficulties and malnutrition. Today, of the Philippines' population of one hundred million souls, the pool of children with the facial anomaly is estimated in the thousands. While the appropriate in-country expertise participate in the reparative care, the augmentative contribution by out-of-country surgical missions continues to be a welcome, if not a compelling need. With urging and support of the inaugural mission team: Doctors Ron Ferrendelli, Jim Hersey, Hideo Hirose, Kevin Whitaker, as well as by those many individuals of Ormoc, I responded by founding a nonprofit organization, Uplift Internationale (UI). Its project is named Operation Taghoy (a Filipino word for whistle, a function children with facial clefts can enjoy only after successful repair). The vision and objective: changing lives of children by mending their deformed faces, very soon attracted a core of healthcare practitioners whose superior expertise was topped only by their commitment and benevolence. Prominent among those early surgeon-volunteers who would become the propellant for the project's continuity were Drs. Fred Pratt, Etienne Piette, Larry Herman and Elliot Duboys.

The annual UI-Operation Taghoy mission provides the mending care of clefts of the lip and palate of impoverished children at no cost to the families and minimal burden to the host hospital. The project is hosted at an increasing number of public-funded facilities of the Visayas Region of the country, the visit rotated among them for one workweek. Teams of volunteer expertise— recruited from the many States of the U.S., Europe, Australia, Asia, and the Philippines—undertake the activities, pro bono. Significantly, the mission team includes an Outreach component that is composed of non-medical volunteers who provide essential supportive patient interaction and conduct the various operational concerns of the mission. The roster of mission volunteers now number in the hundreds.

Many children and adolescents have benefited since its inception. Tales abound of lives changed. Where once they faced days yearning to be like everyone else, the mending care has offered a more level playing field of life. They are triumphantly returning to school with confidence, having an easier time to commingle with peers. They are having an improved chance to participate in the workforce, even acquiring the guts to seek courtship and marriage. These are the life-changing treasures that the children receive as a keepsake of the helping hand that mission team members are privileged to extend. The encouraging results continue to resonate with donors and inspire the continuation of the charitable project. The support of individual philanthropists, as exemplified by the likes of Ken Allen, Buddy Baker, Rich and Judy Billings, Malcolm Collier, Tyler & Dianne Miller and Michael Heffernan, when added to those like-minded groups as are the exemplary Wheatridge Presbyterian Church congregants - led by Gay Cuthill, Betty O'Belmito and Nancy Rosi - as well as the Rotary Club of Wheat Ridge—they collectively represent a laudable resource for the organization's sustaining future. Importantly, I cannot cease to be awed and pleased at the outpouring of the human virtue of empathy and charity for these children. Thankfully, the broadening support by Rotary Clubs, in America and abroad, was ignited by the early visionary advocacy of one Rotarian, the Reverend Larry Angus.

Of note is the program Sharing Ownership that was conceived and implemented by the mid-1990s. It is aimed to encourage Filipinos to regard the goals of UI as that of their own. As such, the Operation Taghoy mission team intentionally began to include domestic volunteer applicants who, in turn, have become the nucleus of a community-based, self-sufficient Facial Cleft Clinic to provide the mending care of Filipino children, year-round. While the model Clinic in Ormoc—unselfishly led by surgeon Dr. Roland Tomaro—has rendered the mending care to no more than two dozen patients per year, the healthcare providers and philanthropic resources of the host community have embraced, participated and supported the program, in conjunction with the oversight and subsidy that UI has provided. The potential for the proliferation of Facial Cleft Clinics to other communities appears limitless. The fruition will be a tacit affirmation of my belief in a future when the care of Filipino children with facial deformities can be accomplished by Filipinos, the out-of-country assistance invited electively.

The managerial and stewardship responsibilities of the organization rests on highly motivated members of the Board of Directors who donate their talent and time pro-bono. Among the many who served with distinction and fealty to the cause over the past years, including serving on Mission Teams, were those with such surnames as Alexander, Angus, Bryan, Capoot, Carr, Charles, Dahl, Ferrendelli, Helldorfer, Hendershot, Hershberger, Kiernan, LaVigne, Matthews, Meyers, Moyer, Myers, Newman, Niquette, O'Day, Pasion, Postma, Remington, Santos, Savelle, Scott, Snelling, Steputis, Weber, and, my steadfast better-half Patricia Yrastorza. As a valuable executive coordinator for the Philippines, Megs Lunn together with executive director Beth Shepherd have unselfishly shared their talent and commitment to UI goals. Beginning the Fiscal Year 2013-14, Dr. Steve Krebs assumed the Presidency. Steve is a proven humanitarian; an accomplished Internist who is held in highest regard by his peers, the healthcare community and by his patients.

The Lutheran Medical Center Community Foundation, annually, recognizes a Physician on the Staff for outstanding community service. In presenting the Physician Community Service Award for 2011, CEO Dr. Kenneth W. Epperman pointed out that "Dr. Jaime A. Yrastorza was selected for his work with Uplift Internationale, an organization he founded in 1989 to provide oral and maxillofacial surgery to children in rural Philippines born with facial deformities" and, he added, "for making a difference in people's lives and enhancing the world we live in." The accompanying $1,000 cash award to the honoree, I donated to Uplift Internationale.

By 2014, the project Operation Taghoy will have conducted its 25th year of mission activities in the Philippines. In October 2013, at the celebration of UI's Silver Anniversary Gala event and before a sell-out group of supporters that included my family, I was honored to receive the organization's highest tribute: Lifetime Achievement Award. Meanwhile, in the Philippines, Drs. Raddy Mabasa - my commodious friend and ally, Joseph Macasiray, Primo Gonzalez and Marilyn Liung of the International College of Dentists, Philippine Section plus Ed Escaño, Joe Kuan and Megs Lunn of the Rotary Clubs of Makati and Forbes Park banded as a committee. Their avowed goal is: organize a celebratory Gala, set in Manila, in recognition of UI's humanitarian contribution to the well-being of Filipino children with facial deformity, planned for 2014-15. The fruition of their project would be an implicit recognition of UI's share in the improvement of health care of Filipinos. That the humanitarian UI contribution has endured amply reflect on the charitable, compassionate virtue of man. I share with the many supporters, partners, participants and well-wishers in taking pride in UI's successes and its binding motto: mending faces...one child at a time.

OF BLOODLINES

It is not the level of prosperity that makes for happiness but the kinship of heart to heart and the way we look at the world. Both attitudes are within our power.—Alexander Solzhenitsyn (Russian Author, Activist... b1918–2008)

Quite by serendipity, in early 1980s Papá was visited at his clinic by a stranger: Luis Irastorza of Pais Vasco (Basque surnames beginning in *"I" and "Y"* have long been used interchangeably), had come to visit Ormoc. He was in the country as a working engineer for a Spanish-Philippine cooperative project for development of a phosphoric acid processing plant in nearby Isabel, Leyte. On seeing Papá's signage, he immediately sought a meeting that soon became a joint assignment to crystallize the family connection. Shortly, Luis's bride-to-be Samira together with his parents, Antonio and Lucia, who are residents of Bilbao, Spain, came to Ormoc for a get-acquainted visit. From the filial occasions, a kinship thread knitted. Through visits to Spain, Trish and I thereafter extended our connections with Luis's siblings: Antonio, an international lawyer based in London and Luchi, a practicing physician in Bilbao, married to Alejandro Martinez. Trish and I have repeatedly savored their hospitality. Already, grownups from both sides of the world are making plans to develop a series of visit interchanges. It is noteworthy that although the family tree relationship is of unknown degrees of separation, the sanguinity attitude among the Basques appears to be a compadrazgo viewpoint, which is akin to the Filipino pariente-compradre custom. In this regard, the Aboitiz family of Cebu are also kin separated by several degrees. While they were not familiar to me in my youth, the easy travel and the ubiquitous Internet access of today have kindled our kinship relations, particularly through our shared interest in humanitarian causes.

One evening in February 2004, in Cebu City, Trish and I felt privileged to accept and take pleasure in an enchanting evening with another set of kindred relations, arranged by my charmer-*par excellence* cousin Ramon Moraza and graciously hosted by Montxu and Judy Aboitiz. At the gathering were members of the Aboitiz, Larrazabal, Mendezona, Moraza and Yrastorza families of the city, nearby Ormoc and distant Sydney, Australia. It was a memorable opportunity to renew old times, get acquainted with newly introduced kin, and exchange tales with *primos y parientes*—cousins and relatives. Quite surprisingly, if not providentially, I got re-acquainted with the *grande dame* of the family, Maria Lourdes Mendieta Aboitiz, more commonly known as *Lulu Aboitiz*. She had spent days, as both of our families and I had, at the Hospicio de San Jose convalescent home during those harrowing days of 1944 in Manila. We certainly had ample cause to celebrate our survival.

Concomittantly, the kinship relations that my family enjoys with those in the Philippines are enlarging in numbers through marriages and births; and, by virtue of the readily accessible social media avenues of the internet, we all remain in contact.

OF PARENTING

"I believe that what we become depends on what our fathers teach us at odd moments, when they aren't trying to teach us. We are formed by little scraps of wisdom."—Umberto Eco (Philosopher, writer.... January 1937)

Rehashing with our five children on their individual reminiscences about etched moments they had with their parents, in particular with me, was enlightening. The sessions were processes we delved into with grace, compassion, yet poignancy. At occasions over *café con leche* (blended coffee and milk), I found chances to point out that, as it was with my upbringing relationship with my parents, I had not felt a compelling need with any of them to discuss matters related to morals and good behavior pointedly. Instead, those issues would get discussed in the course of conversations or when in answer to specific questions. In turn, each one invariably mentioned recalling tidbits of wisdom that I had uttered, more often in the course of a casual chat. Those incidental bits of insight had become a part of their guiding principles At other times, the children recalled those bursts of pride and joy that came from me when each had excelled in a school assignment or triumphed in an athletic challenge, and, at few times receiving my ire and learning to accept responsibility for misdeeds, with the resolution to do better. And, there were disappointments, injuries, unrequited goals; and, in their adolescence, there were relationships with occasional heart-braking difficulties. Since I was not always present to share all the momentous experiences the children had with empathy, tears and tenderness, in real time, I was always gratefully comforted to have Trish available to attend as my teammate.

There is a popular song, Cat's in the Cradle that I feel is a thought-provoking reminder of my obligation as a parent. Harry Chapin, the song-writer frames the innocence of toddlers and their developing awe in their hero-parents when the child says: "I'm gonna be like you, Dad." As an ode to challenges of parenthood Chapin points out the risk of losing bonding opportunities. The lyric continues, it can result from parental inattention, even if unintended. The lamental consequence comes to roost when, in answer to the aged father's invitation to a get together, the grown son replies, "I'd love to, Dad, if I could find the time… I don't know when, but we'll get together then, Dad. You know we'll have a good time then."

Not everything of my experience as a parent was peaches and cream! Trish recalled an evening, standing in our bay window with pre-adolescent Terri Anne awaiting my return home to attend a father-daughter school event; I did not show in time. Despite Trish's compassionate explanatory efforts, my daughter, shedding tears, said: "Mama, my head understands, but my heart does not." Terri Anne's disappointment, once again, point to the sensitive and tenuous relations that children can present their parents. Having five children to extend parental care, sharing affection and providing the appurtenances as equitably as possible cannot always be successfully accomplished. Of course, I am amazed that siblings, more often than not, develop along unique, individual directions. Below are David's candid recollections:

> I often thought that you really didn't start investing yourself in your children until we were semi-adults, that is, college age. I thought the reason for this was that you didn't have much experience with children, were busy building your career, bank account, and generally getting established and enjoying the feeling of mastering your field... it's probably easier to talk to a college-aged person than being involved in the up and down swings of childhood... although I do have memories of you being with us as children. I remember you slanting your eyes as an oriental and making us laugh as you walked into walls 'cause you couldn't see... I remember you taking us shooting the .22 in the mountains, and then, when Anne (our youngest) came into the picture...she had a rapport with you different than the other children, seemingly. I can see her crawling up on your lap and dressing you in clothes she liked and you enjoying her familiarity.
>
> My thoughts and feelings about you as a father have changed as I have gotten older, lived through the experience of raising my own children, and experienced the role of provider throughout the years. I think you're a great grandpa. You have a genuine way about yourself that allows you to get close to the kids. I see it with my children as well as the others. I must say that this also makes me ambivalent. Part of me wants to say, 'why weren't you that way with me?' But it's fun to watch and I think it so valuable for my kids to have both you and Mom in their lives.

It is those heartbreaking disappointments and lost moments of bonding opportunities, however unintended the circumstances, that are painful and regretful to me as a parent. Surely, there have been a number of such failings during the past years. Thankfully, parents can have chances to reconcile and watch grown children become concerned and loving parents. Quite fortuitously, children on gaining maturity often reverse roles by providing counsel and kinship support to their parents. It is very heartwarming. Looking back, I believe being a parent, said simply, is a complicated, consuming life-time responsibility. The process is an intermingling of love, humor, patience, self-control and mutual self-respect. One strives to be a success; the reward comes best from the human being ones child has become. Indeed, children are a wonderful, divine gift!

OF MY FOURTEEN TWINS

Grandparents are a family's greatest treasure, the founders of a loving legacy, the greatest storytellers, the keepers of traditions that linger on in cherished memory. Grandparents are the family's strong foundation. Their very special love sets them apart. Through happiness and sorrow, through their special love and caring, grandparents keep a family close at heart.

—author unknown

Our grandchildren accept us for ourselves, without rebuke or effort to change us, as no one in our entire lives has ever done, not our parents, siblings, spouses, friends—and hardly ever our own grown children.

—Ruth Goode (Author, b1918–2010)

Despite the far-flung places that my own family now reside we have taken opportunities to be together through reunions. Sometimes, it is at the Lost Valley Ranch, set in the Pike National Forest by Deckers, Colorado. It always is a time for horseback riding through the splendor of the forest, a chance to watch for wildlife and breathe the fresh mountain air. Other times, we are together at Vail, Colorado, a town amidst alpine-like mountain peaks of nearby White River National Forest. The year-round destination is replete with attractions that include skiing, ice-skating, biking, hiking as well as a summer and winter schedule of cultural presentations. A sojourn to the Hawaiian Islands is another eagerly awaited get-together locale.

Trish and I travel to be with grandchildren, in addition to such times when their parents take work-related leave. Overall, at every occasion, family togetherness leaves us both renewed. And we continually marvel at how young bodies and minds develop so energetically, inquisitively, charmingly and, so wonderfully. Once, when Marie, my second eldest grand-daughter, was five years old, she sat on my lap, looked at me searchingly with her wide-eyed innocence, and asked: "Grandpa, how can my cousins and I be all your twins?" She seemed satisfied when I answered: "Because we are." Marie, however, was rightly bewildered and curious since I had swayed her and each of the grandchildren to regard their relations to me as well as to each other as being "twins." I aimed thereafter to convey to each of them that together we would be in a lifetime of commingling and transference of future experiences, hopes, and accomplishments. That they can become the guardians and preservers of the legacies of our family. And that, as different as we may look from each other, we are bound by the similarity of our inner selves.

It is on the repeated intimate moments and binding togetherness with my "twins" that I am reminded that there are guiding traits that Trish and I comport with as parents. We passed them on to our offspring, who now are imbuing their children with like values and customs. In the unfurling future, as my "twins" experience a lifetime of joys and sorrows that will arise from challenges they encounter, their reactions will, hopefully, draw from the steadfastness of the morals and standards that are at their core. Their responses will help to validate their parental influence.

To them all, Trish joins me—reminded as we are of a well-known Irish prayer, below—in sharing our hopes:

> "May the road rise up to meet you,
> may the wind be ever at your back.
> May the sun shine warm upon your face and
> the rain fall softly on your fields.
> And until we meet again,
> May God hold you in the hollow of His hand."

Front, L to R: John, Dylan, Will; Middle: Timothy, Arlin, Luke, Hannah, David, Wanda, Patricia, me, Laura, Gabriela, Kent, Ellie, Jeffrey; Back: Anne, Marie, Melissa, Cole, Teresa, Grace, Jackson, Leah, Jaime. The 2012 picture represents the legacy of the Yrastorza--Laverty union of 19th June 1957: our five offspring with their spouses and fourteen grandchildren.

ON REFLECTION

Another dawning!

This time it is that of the twenty-first century. Indeed, my life has been a continuum of daily beginnings. From the reminiscences that helped create this memoir, I feel fortunate to have grown in a family that valued perspicacity, kindness, respect, and ethical behavior. Thankfully, Trish, by sharing the same ethos has facilitated in passing those mores to our children. The moments of living that I experienced as a husband, a father, and a grandfather were—and are—lessons of personal benefit and joys to savor. From sorrows and disappointments, I continue to learn to rebound with renewed grit.

Uplift Internationale began as a vision fortified by single-minded willingness to bring to fruition a goal of humane purpose. Importantly, its development has become a triumphant tribute to the incredible capacity of the human spirit to extend charity and compassion to people in need. It is an affirmation of the remarkable humane resolve to contribute to the enduring aims of humanitarian programs.

The devastating Haiyan (Yolanda) typhoon of November 2013 was of epic magnitude. It affected the mid-portion of the 7,000 islands and 20 million of the inhabitants. Of the many cities and their neighboring towns and barangays, Tacloban and Ormoc bore the brunt of the loss in lives, property, and treasure. In response to the catastrophe, it is heartening to recognize the ready assistance provided by international government and non-government aid agencies. It is particularly inspiring to point out that like-minded Filipino organizations and individuals, from wherever in the world they have scattered in their diaspora---responded and raised an outstanding level of compassion, empathy, and humanitarian assistance for the survivors. Theirs was a tacit outpouring of the innate humane spirit of Filipinos.

Finally, the reminiscences and observations I have written are of my life that began in an idyllic milieu. It was followed by harrowing years of traumatic insecurity that led to an adventurous odyssey into adulthood. It has been a fulfilling life. My hope is that the reader can discern the rewards that arose from the fervor and perseverance of my actions and, relate to the enriching human quality of reciprocation and charity that I advocate. I wish that from the fullness of my experiences, others can gain useful pearls of wisdom.

YRASTORZA FAMILY
Coat of Arms

El escudo cuartelado: los 1º y 3º, en verdusco con un ciervo andante de oro y los 2º y 4º, en bloques de azur y oro. Las armas, pintado adjunto el heraldo como campos de helechos, partenecen el apellido de los moradores del caserio, desde tiempo immemorial en la villa de Zaldivia, partido judical de Tolosa, provincia de Guipúzcoa, Pais Vasco.

The escutcheon, in quarters: clockwise, the 1st and 3rd in forest green with a golden deer in gait and the 2nd and 4th in blocks of blue and gold. The arms adjacent to the heraldry, painted as fields of fern to represent the surname of the homesteaders who, since time immemorial, dwelt in the village of Zaldivia, jurisdiction of Tolosa, province of Guipuzcoa, Basque Country.

SUGGESTED READINGS

1. Abinales, P.N. & Amoroso, D.J.—"State and Society in the Philippines"—Rowman Littlefield Publ 2005

2. Aboitiz & Company—"The Men Behind It, The Story" 1960

3. Aguinaldo, Emilio—"True Version of the Philippine Revolution"—Public Domain Books, Dodo Press-2006

4. Aluit, A.—"By Sword and Fire...The Destruction of Manila in World War II"—Bookmark, Inc. 1995

5. Bain, D.H.—"Sitting in Darkness...Americans in the Philippines"—Houghton Mifflin Co 1984

6. Barber, Benjamin R.—"Jihad vs. McWorld"—Ballentine Books, N.Y.1995

7. Bergreen, Lawrence—"Over the Edge of the World"—Harper Collins 2003

8. Borja, Marciano—"Basques in the Philippines"—University of Nevada Press 2005

9. Bradley, J.—"The Imperial Cruise: a Secret History of Empire & War 2009"—Back Bay Books, 2010

10. Bradley, J—"Fly Boys: A True Story of Courage"—Back Bay Books, 2004

11. Colton, L.—"No Ordinary Joes: True Story of Four Submariners in War"—Crown Publishers, NY 2001

12. Connaughton, R., Pimlott, J., Anderson, D.—"Battle for Manila"—Presidio Press, 2002

13. Constantino, Renato—"Identity and Consciousness… The Philippine Experience"—Malaya Books, Inc. 1980

14. Costello, John—"The Pacific War 1941-1945"—Harper Collins 2009

15. Eisenhower, Dwight—"Mandate for Change"—Doubleday & Co. 1963

16. Francia, Luis—"A History of the Philippines"—The Overlook Press, New York, 2010

17. Friend, T.—"Between Two Empires The Ordeal of the Philippines"—Yale U Press, New Haven 1965

18. Gamboa, C.—"Cradle of Hope… Hospicio de San Jose"—Hospicio de San Jose Publication 2010

19. Graff, Henry—"American Imperialism and the Philippine Insurection"—Little, Brown and Co., Boston 1969

20. Ishida, Jintaro.—"The Remains of War, Apology & Forgiveness"—Globe Piquot Press 2002

21. Jeansonne, Glen—"A Time of Paradox"—Bowman & Littlefield Publishers, Inc 2007

22. Kamen, H.—"Empire…How Spain Became a World Power"—Penguin Books, 2003

23. Karnow, S.—"In Our Image America's Empire in the Philippines'—Random House, 1989

24. Kipling, Rudyard—"The White Man's Burden: The United States and The Philippine Islands."—Published February 1899 issue of McClure's Magazine

25. Kramer, Paul A.—"The Blood of Government"—Univ of North Carolina Press, 2006

26. Layton, Edwin—"And I Was There"—William Morrow & Co. 1985

27. MacIntosh, Robert—"Hugo Obwegeser Forty Years Later"—NY Society of Dentistry Journal, Nov 2005

28. McAllister Linn, Brian—"The Philippine War 1899-1902"—Univ Press of Kansas 2000

29. Manchester, W.—"American Caesar...Douglas MacArthur"—Little, Brown & Company, 1978

30. Miller, S. C.—"Benevolent Assimilation...American Conquest of the Philippines"—Yale University Press 1982

31. Moraza, Ramon—"With These Hands... an Autobiography"—Basic Graphics, Inc. Philippines 2007

32. Phelan, John L.—"The Hispanization of the Philippines"—The University of Wisconsin Press 1959

33. Sides, H.—"Ghost Soldiers", Doubleday 2001

34. Smith, Richard—"Triumph of Herbert Hoover"—Simon & Shuster 1987

35. Thoma, Kurt H.—"Oral Surgery"—Mosby 1956

36. Velasco Shaw, Angel and Francia, Luis—"Vestiges of War"—NY University Press 2002

37. Wall Street Journal—"Typhoon Haiyan—How a catastophe unfolded." November 20, 2013

38. Weller, George—"First into Nagasaki—the censored eye-witness..."—Random House, Inc 2002

39. Wolff, Leon—"Little Brown Brother"—Bookspan 2006

40. Wurfel, David—"Filipino Politics... Development and Decay"—Cornell University Press 1988

41. Yrastorza, Jaime A.—"Histological Investigation on the use of Polyurethane Polymer in the Treatment of Experimentally Fractured Mandibles of Dogs", (unpublished) Master's Dissertation, Graduate School Georgetown University, 1961

**My narrative has taken liberal reference to information
derived from the list of Suggested Readings,
as follows:**

The Dawning - # 1, 3, 5, 6, 7, 9, 13, 17, 18, 19, 21, 22, 24, 25, 28, 30, 32

Growing Up in Antebellum - # 2, 8, 13, 31, 32

Surviving the War - #4, 8, 10, 11, 12, 14, 15, 16, 18, 19, 20, 21, 22, 23, 26, 28, 29, 33, 34, 39

Post-War Adolescence - # 1, 13, 41

Onward to America - # 1, 13, 16

Pursuit of a Professions - #13, 35

A Partner...A Career - #36, 41

Rearing a Family and Earning a Living - # 1, 27, 41

The Cornucopia...Shared and Savored -

INDEX